GRUNT SLANG IN VIETNAM

GRUNT SLANG IN VIETNAM

Words of the War

GORDON L. ROTTMAN

CASEMATE

Philadelphia & Oxford

Published in the United States of America and Great Britain in 2020 by
CASEMATE PUBLISHERS
1950 Lawrence Road, Havertown, PA 19083, USA
and
The Old Music Hall, 106–108 Cowley Road, Oxford OX4 1JE, UK

Hardcover Edition: ISBN 978-1-61200-804-2
Digital Edition: ISBN 978-1-61200-805-9

A CIP record for this book is available from the British Library

Printed and bound in the United States of America

For a complete list of Casemate titles, please contact:

CASEMATE PUBLISHERS (US)
Telephone (610) 853-9131
Fax (610) 853-9146
Email: casemate@casematepublishers.com
www.casematepublishers.com

CASEMATE PUBLISHERS (UK)
Telephone (01865) 241249
Email: casemate-uk@casematepublishers.co.uk
www.casematepublishers.co.uk

Front page image: PFC Michael J. Mendoza (Piedmont, CA) uses his M16 rifle to recon by fire. (NARA 100310264)

Dedication

The book is dedicated to all Free World military forces serving in and supporting operations in Vietnam.

Officially, United States' involvement in the Vietnam War began on 5 August 1964. The first US advisors arrived in March 1955 and the first US casualty was on 8 July 1959. Official US military involvement with ground troops was 3 July 1965 through 23 August 1972.

Approximately 2.7 million American men and women served in Vietnam. A total of 58,318 US military personnel died including missing and deaths in captivity, and 153,303 were wounded. There were 766 prisoners of war of whom 114 died in captivity. The war officially ended on 7 May 1975.

Contents

Acknowledgments

Firstly the author gratefully thanks hundreds of veterans who provided bits of information and shared their knowledge and experience face-to-face and online. He is especially indebted to Steve Sherman (vvfh.org/burns), Brett Emblin (VietnamGear.com), Trey Moore (Moore Militia), and Michael Do (The Vietnamese American Community of the USA).

Introduction

Slang is a collection of informal words and phrases used by a specific group or within a particular environment. It is a vocabulary that defines people, establishes group identity and attitudes, excludes outsiders, or both. It can be humorous, self-deprecating, critical of other persons, groups, or institutions, and—in the context of war—can use as its subject anything that is a nuisance to soldiers and Marines, when conventional descriptions fail. At its most cynical, slang can be grime, dripping with dark humor and sarcasm. It is verbal shorthand to describe conditions, environments, and life in the user's particular situation. Slang is more common in speech than in writing, but some slang words and phrases can become accepted and actually enter the formal vocabulary.

The slang described as used in Vietnam focuses on the Army and Marine Corps, and particularly on the combat units and direct supporting units. The origins of this slang are complex, diverse, and often reach into the past. Much of it was, of course, a product of this strange tropical counterinsurgency battlefield. Slang was also carried over from World War II, the Korean War, and even pre-World War II service in China and the Philippines and earlier. Included in this study are various catchphrases and idioms borrowed from television shows, psychedelic pop culture, and the drug and antiwar cultures.

This disorganized vocabulary also picked up terms and phrases from the Vietnamese language and local customs. What is conveniently called Pidgin Vietnamese-English was never bestowed with a proper name by academia. It is basically composed of Americanized Vietnamese, sometimes a mix of Vietnamese and English words or phrases, and a lingering touch of French. "Pidgin Vietnamese-English" is discussed in Appendix B.

The Army and Marines were awash in abbreviations and acronyms and many Vietnam War slang dictionaries list these by the score. That is fine, but abbreviations and acronyms are not slang per se, although some slang terms are in fact acronyms and these have been included. Selected abbreviations and acronyms have been included owing to their relevance to the subject or to do exactly what abbreviations are supposed to do: save space and simplify text.

Both the Army and Marines possess their own slang vocabularies. But both services have borrowed terms from the other, sometimes with slightly different connotations. Both services also used some Air Force and Naval Aviation terms since they were supported by those air services and Marine Aviation had strong ties to its naval counterparts.

This book is not "politically correct," nor are there any "trigger warnings" or "literally safe zones." The term "PC" and its notions did not exist in the 1960s nor was there any real equivalent, other than common decency and minding your manners as you were taught. There were numerous words and phrases in normal use with their connotations viewed differently than they are today. Of course there were racist, sexist, and insulting terms, but common politeness and manners normally kept things civil. The image of the 1960s painted by many historians, editorialists, pundits, and media was that of an era of widespread turmoil characterized by riots, protests, and scandals. While much political unrest did exist, this did not define the times; in fact, the level of violence and unrest was probably moderate compared with that of more recent climates. The conflict and politics at home were just as much a part of the war as grunts busting brush.

The author makes no excuses for the language used in this book and for fully spelling out racially and sexually explicit words. To ignore such words and phrases or to "tone them down" would be a delusion. Such language should be faced head on in order to understand its use and the outlook of Vietnam-era servicemen. Dark, cynical humor abounded and may be difficult for the uninitiated to comprehend. For example: At West Point are plaques commemorating graduates who were KIA, MIA, and POWs in Vietnam. The cadets, knowing they were bound for Vietnam, cynically called it the "Memorial to Vietnamese Marksmanship." War is a nasty thing. That's why they call it war.

The author is no scholarly expert on the subject of slang, but a "user." I joined the Army in 1967 undertaking Infantry Advanced Individual Training, Jump School, and Special Forces Light and Heavy Weapons Training, then served in the 7th Special Forces Group at Ft Bragg, North Carolina. This was followed by 13 months in Vietnam in the 5th Special Forces Group, Detachments A-333 and A-332, Chi Linh and Minh Thanh Strike Force Camps, in the III Corps area. Besides living with Cambodian, Montagnard, and Vietnamese CIDG strikers, we occasionally worked with US 1st Cavalry and 1st Infantry Division troops as well as aviators. This provided a great deal of exposure to slang. I was impressed with the mechanics of slang and its origins and I developed a knack for remembering it. For another kind of slang I visited Saigon, Okinawa, and Sydney, Australia and listened to soldiers in those locales. After the war I joined the Texas National Guard's 36th Airborne Brigade and became a full-time battalion operations and training NCO. There were Vietnam veterans in the unit and I worked with Vietnam vets in the 82d Airborne Division and Marine Reservists, picking up their Vietnam slang. Later, I was the operations sergeant of Company G (LRRP), 143d Infantry, and had more opportunities to pick veterans' minds including NATO troops. They had nothing to do with Vietnam, but it broadened my comprehension of soldierly slang. I finished my 26 years in the Army Reserve's 75th Division (Exercise) in military intelligence positions and spoke to vets all over the country in our travels. An even broader opportunity to discuss slang with vets was during my 11 years as a civilian contractor Special Operations Forces scenario writer at the Joint Readiness Training Center, Ft Chaffee, Arkansas, and Ft Polk, Louisiana. Online informal discussion groups with Vietnam veteran soldiers and Marines have been extremely valuable. Another aid in compiling this work was two World War II slang dictionaries I wrote a few years ago, *FUBAR* and *SNAFU*. That research resulted in a better perception of the origins, double meanings, and uses of slang, not only in the American perspective, but British, Commonwealth—Australian in particular—German, Russian, and Japanese. Writing the "Slanguage" editorial for each issue of *Viet Nam Veterans for Factual History Magazine* was of benefit as well. Researching and writing over 130 military books on units, tactics, organization, uniforms, campaigns, soldiers' lives, weapons, and equipment helped immeasurably in collecting and understanding slang.

There are approximately 1,450 slang entries in this work. I aim to provide not only a simple definition for each term but also a comprehensive explanation of its meaning, use, background, and if necessary, its different contexts. Many terms were used by the Army and Marines, but those unique to the Marines are so noted.

Abbreviations

Abbreviations are kept to a minimum, but their use is necessary owing to the frequency of some terms and the length of others, as with, for example, "Military Assistance Command, Vietnam-Studies and Observation Group" (MACV-SOG). Single or limited use abbreviations are addressed in the narrative. Abbreviations for US rank titles are found in Appendix C. *Quod vide*, "q.v.," is used to cross-reference definitions mentioned elsewhere in the text. "Aka" is "also known as."

ACAV	armored cavalry assault vehicle
AN/	Army-Navy/ (designation system)
APC	armored personnel carrier
ARVN	Army of the Republic of Vietnam
ChiCom	Chinese Communist (People's Republic of China—PRC)
CIDG	Civilian Irregular Defense Group
CO	commanding officer
C-rats	C-rations (see MCI)
CS	ortho-chlorobenzalmalomonitrile ("tear gas")
CTZ	Corps Tactical Zone
CWO	chief warrant officer
DMZ	Demilitarized Zone
EM	enlisted men
FSB	fire support base
Ft	Fort
G.I.	Government Issue
HEAT	high-explosive antitank
HQ	headquarters
KIA	killed in action
KW	Korean War (1950–53)
LRRP/LRP	long-range reconnaissance patrol

LZ	landing zone
MACV	Military Assistance Command, Vietnam
MACV-SOG	MACV-Studies and Observation Group
MCI	Meal, Combat, Individual ("C-rats")
MEDEVAC	medical evacuation
MG	machine gun
MOS	Military Occupation Specialty
MP	Military Police
MPC	Military Payment Certificate
NCO	noncommissioned officer (corporals and sergeants)
NVA	North Vietnamese Army
OD	olive drab color
OG	olive green color
POW	prisoner of war
PX/BX	Post Exchange/Base Exchange System
R&R	rest and relaxation
RF/PF	Regional Force/Popular Force
RR	recoilless rifle
RTO	radio-telephone operator
RVN	Republic of Vietnam (South Vietnam)
SEAL	Sea-Air-Land
SMG	submachine gun
T/O&E	Table of Organization and Equipment
TOC	tactical operations center
USAF	United States Air Force
USMC	United States Marine Corps
USN	United States Navy
VC	Viet Cong
VNAF	Vietnamese Air Force
WIA	wounded in action
WWII	World War II (1939–45)
XO	executive officer

Phonetic Alphabets

Phonetic alphabets ensured that similar-sounding letters were clearly understood when spoken over the static of radio or telephone. They were habitually written in all uppercase. The International Code Alphabet traces its origin to the International Code of Signals adopted in 1897 as a means of communicating by flag, semaphore, and light. In typed message transcription the phonetic words were usually shown in upper case, e.g., VICTOR CHARLIE. The standard NATO phonetic alphabet adopted on 1 March 1956 was used by all Free World forces. South Vietnam or Republic of Vietnam (RVN) used its own phonetic alphabet unless conversing in English.

NATO phonetic alphabet

ALFA	JULIET	SIERRA
BRAVO	KILO	TANGO
CHARLIE	LIMA	UNIFORM
DELTA	MIKE	VICTOR
ECHO	NOVEMBER	WHISKEY
FOXTROT	OSCAR	X-RAY
GOLF	PAPA	YANKEE
HOTEL	QUEBEC	ZULU
INDIA	ROMEO	

There was a standard method to ensure the clarity of spoken numbers. Each number was spoken individually, not "fifty-six," but "five-six." "Two-hundred" could be spoken, but "two-one-zero" was necessary for "210."

0	zero (never "oh" or "ought")	**5**	fife
1	wun	**6**	six
2	too	**7**	sev-en
3	tree	**8**	ait
4	fow-er	**9**	nin-er

Vietnamese phonetic alphabet

Vietnamese is a tonal language and each letter can have up to five variations in pronunciation, which are defined by the proliferation of accent marks in the written language. Making it more difficult, there were also regional variations in pronunciation. When transmitting by radio and telephone, letters were spelled out using the phonetic alphabet, based on the English alphabet, and used three of the same words as the American phonetic alphabet ("foxtrot," "juliet," and "zulu"), for clarity through static or weak reception. There are 29 letters in the Vietnamese alphabet, which was initially created by Portuguese missionaries in the 1600s and finalized by the French after 1900, who forced a change from the original Chinese-based characters. Because of this the Vietnamese were eventually unable to read their own historical documents. The phonetic alphabet had no means of specifying accent marks, but the context the words were used in and their order generally clarified their meaning. (Diligent research found no NVA phonetic alphabet.)

A	anh-dung	**J**	juliet	**S**	son-tay
B	bac-binh	**K**	kinh-ky	**T**	tu-tuong
C	cai-cach	**L**	le-loi	**U**	ung-ho
D	dong-da	**M**	manh-me	**V**	ve-vang
E	e-de	**N**	non-nonc	**W**	wit-ki
F	foxtrot	**O**	oanh-liet	**X**	xung-phong
G	gay-go	**P**	phu-quoc	**Y**	yen-bai
H	hong-ha	**Q**	quang-trung	**Z**	zulu
I	im-lang	**R**	rach-gia		

Unit Designations

Unit designations are a broad and complex subject. Only the basic elements applicable to this book are discussed here. The depiction of numbers is important.

Unit designation numbers above 10 are not spelled out. It is the 82d Airborne Division, not "Eighty-Second." A unit's official designation is based on its Lineage and Honors Certificate and numeric designations are not spelled on those documents.

There is no comma in four-digit numeric designations; for example, 1002d Supply and Service Company.

Roman number-designated units are never appended by "nd," "rd," "st," or "th."

Officially the military used "2d" and "3d" in unit designations rather than "2nd" and "3rd" to include, for example, "842d Quartermaster Company."

"Regiment" was *not* included in the designation of Army infantry, artillery, armor, and cavalry units. These units were withdrawn from the Combat Arms Regimental System* in 1986 and reorganized under the United States Army Regimental System and then "Regiment" was included in their designations. For example, 2d Battalion, 18th Infantry became 2d Battalion, 18th Infantry Regiment.

Marine regiments do not include functional designations (infantry, artillery) or "regiment" in the designation. They are merely designated, e.g., 4th Marines. The 1st, 3d, 4th, 5th, 7th, 9th, 26th, and 27th Marines were infantry and the 11th, 12th, and 13th Marines were divisional artillery.

Letters identifying companies, batteries, and troops need not be within quotes; e.g., Company "A." Company B is correct. Companies/batteries/troops were identified by letters when organic to battalions/squadrons. There were also separate non-combat arms companies identified by numbers that were attached to larger units.

There was no Company, Battery, or Troop J. It is long rumored that an unspecified "Company J" in some unidentified conflict lost its guidon and no other Company J was ever raised again. That is a myth. "J" was not used in the 1800s, as the letters "I" and "J" were written the same and "J" was skipped to prevent confusion.

* The pre-1986 exception was armored cavalry squadrons assigned to armored cavalry regiments, the 11th ACR being the one example in Vietnam.

Words of the Vietnam War: Alpha To Zulu

A ALPHA

A-7A belt   12ft olive drab (OD) nylon web 1¾in cargo tie-down strap with slide buckle cut down to trousers belt length. It replaced the standard web belt and was considered a sign of a veteran. Aka "rigger belt."

A-, B-, and C- Teams   Special Forces Operational Detachments (SFOD)   The 12–14-man Detachment A (commanded by a CPT) was the basic operational element; 30-plus-man B Detachments (commanded by a MAJ or LTC) typically controlled four A-teams and included a small officer and NCO staff plus the NCOs of a normal A-team. B-teams also controlled a MIKE Force (q.v.) and various special reconnaissance projects. C Detachments were SF company headquarters with over 70 personnel controlling all SF units (through several B-teams) in a corps tactical zone. An SF "company" was a misleading term as it consisted of a staff and support elements commanded by an LTC with a total of over 60 officers and three times that many NCOs. There were also special project B-teams directly under the 5th SF Group (Airborne), which controlled all SF in Vietnam.

Abe   Little-used nickname for GEN Creighton W. Abrams, Jr. (1914–74), MACV Commanding General, June 1968–October 1972. Aka "Honest Abe." (The M1 Abrams tank, which entered service in 1980, was named after him.)

Above my pay grade   "It's not my responsibility or problem." "Isn't that above your pay grade?" That means none of your business; you don't need to concern yourself with this.

ACAV   M113A1 armored personnel carrier (APC) (see "one-one-three") mounting additional machine guns (MG) and retro-fitted gun shields. Used by Armored CAValry reconnaissance and some mechanized infantry units, making it more of a fighting vehicle than a "battle taxi." Pronounced "A-Cav."

accessory packet   Dark brown foil pouch in each Meal, Combat, Individual (MCI) (C-rats, q.v.) with a book of matches; small roll of toilet paper (TP); salt, sugar, instant coffee, and non-dairy creamer packets; two Chiclets (gum), and a pack of four cigarettes (removed 1972). The LRP ration (q.v.) accessory packet was similar but had two instant coffee packets, a soft wood toothpick, and lacked cigarettes. Individuals often kept a plastic bag of unused accessory packet items for when needed.

Ace of Spades Death Card   A small number of units left an Ace of Spades playing card on enemy dead. It was claimed to be a bad luck symbol to the Vietnamese according to a supposed folktale, but it had no such superstitious meaning. The practice was an American morale-builder. The US Playing Card Company (Bicycle brand) produced 25-card decks consisting entirely of Ace of Spades cards for private purchase. The Ace of Spades was occasionally seen on aircraft and gun trucks.

across the fence   MACV-SOG reconnaissance and strike missions across the RVN border into Laos and Cambodia to attack the Ho Chi Ming Trail.

Afro-American engineering   To be blunt, what was called "nigger-rigging," meaning temporarily, incompletely, or poorly rigged or repaired. A "baling wire and chewing gum" repair; "jury-rigged." While racially spiteful, anyone regardless of race could be accused of performing poor "half-assed" workmanship.

AFRTS   American Forces Radio and Television Service (AFRTS—pronounced "A-farts"). It initially operated Armed Forces Radio Saigon (AFRS) and became the American Forces Vietnam Network (AFVN) operating radio and TV stations. The last station was closed in 1973. Most programs were black-and-white. Color TVs were virtually unheard of. In the US color TV sales did not exceed black-and-white until 1972. US primetime programs went to over 50 percent color in late 1965.

A/G *or* marker panel   VS-17/GVX air/ground marker panel—17 x 72in reversible fluorescent orange and cerise (pink). Often cut into 12–17in squares for an individual marking panel. Reconnaissance team members sometimes lined a bonnie hat's crown with panel material for signaling.

Agent Orange   Mixture of two herbicides delivered as an aerial-sprayed defoliant from transports and helicopters during the 1962–71 Operation *Ranch Hand*. It caused serious environmental damage and traces of dioxin have caused major health issues for many exposed individuals, military and civilian. All veterans are eligible for an Agent Orange Registry health exam by the Veterans Administration. There were other defoliants employed—"Rainbow Herbicides" and the 55-gal drums marked by colored bands: Agents Blue, Green, Pink, Purple, and White plus the predominating Agents Orange I and II.

Air America   This dummy corporation airline service was owned and operated by the US Government supporting CIA operations in China (pre-Vietnam), Vietnam, Thailand, Burma, and Laos. It also supported US armed forces. Most of its missions were logistics delivery. It was operational from 1950 to 1976 with 80-plus aircraft at its height.

airborne-oriented AIT   In 1967 Camp Crockett was established at Ft Gordon, Georgia, to house an airborne-oriented infantry advanced individual training brigade. Remote from the main cantonment area, accommodations were spartan and the trainees housed in Quonset huts (q.v.). The 3d Training Brigade was one of the first to replace M14 rifles with M16s as they were standard for all airborne units even before Vietnam. The brigade concentrated on group runs and passing the airborne physical fitness test. One company a week was graduated and sent to Ft Benning for Jump School (q.v.). It was of little benefit as most airborne volunteers still came from the other AIT brigades and from throughout the Army. The brigade folded in 1972. See "Ft Garbage."

Aircat   The Hurricane Aircat 17ft, 42–65-knot armed airboat used by Special Forces and ARVN in the Mekong Delta. Aka "water jeep." (Swamp airboats as seen in Louisiana and Florida.)

air force gloves   A soldier was said to be wearing air force gloves if his hands were in his trousers pockets. A recruit who could not break the habit might have to fill his pockets with sand. The Marines called the infraction "army gloves."

AK-47   General term for the Soviet-made AK-47 and AKM (modernized) 7.62mm assault rifles or simply "AK." The most widely seen version was the ChiCom Type 56. More scarce variations were produced by different Warsaw Pact countries. Widely issued to the NVA replacing the SKS (q.v.) in 1967. Seldom referred to as the "Kalashnikov" (the inventor) in Vietnam, a name used in Africa and other parts of the world. AK = *Automat Kalashnikova* (automatic Kalashnikov).

alibi   Justifiable reason for not firing a shot during timed range firing for qualification, usually caused by a weapon's mechanical failure. When a firing session was completed the safety NCO shouted, "Are there any alibis?" If there were, the shooter would be permitted to fire the remaining rounds after correcting the malfunction.

All hands.   "All personnel, attention. Listen up. That means everyone!" "All hands on deck" means everyone assemble. "Every swinging dick"—a Marine term. The Army simply says "Fall in!" to assemble a unit.

All show and no go.   Looks good superficially, but won't cut it.

ALPHA boat   50ft assault support patrol boat (ASPB) was the problem-plagued "destroyer" of the riverine force. Hull numbers were prefixed by "A."

ALPHA-BRAVO   Radio code for an ambush. "Hawk" was used by some units.

ALPHA-CHARLIE   Air cover. Gunships and scout helicopters escorting line haul (q.v.) truck convoys.

ALPHA-MIKE-FOXTROT   "Adios Mother Fucker." An informal radio signoff or casual farewell. Never spoken as "A-M-F."

Ambush Alley   Ambush-prone section of National Route 19 between Pleiku and An Khe leading up to Mang Giang Pass (pronounced "Mang Yang") in II CTZ. There were other highway and road stretches called "Ambush Alley," one being National Route 8 south of the Demilitarized Zone (DMZ) running from Dong Ha west to Khe Sanh Combat Base and into Laos. National Route 1, running the entire length of RVN inland from the coast, was occasionally called "Ambush Alley."

Amerasian   American-Asian; principally refers to half-American, half-Vietnamese children irrespective of the American father's race. Amerasian children (now adults) are particularly discriminated against, with Vietnamese dismissively calling them *bụi đời* (bui doi—"dirt of life" or the less condescending "children of the dust"). It originally meant a "street-urchin." After the fall of RVN it was difficult for Amerasians to obtain ration cards and schooling. They were called "children of the enemy" (America). The awkward US Department of State tag was "Vietnam AmerAsians."

Americal Division   The better known title of the 23d Infantry Division. When first raised in 1942, "Americal" or "AMERICAL" was a contraction for "Americans on New Caledonia" where it was organized from separate units just as the 23d would be in Vietnam from separate units. Aka "AMCAL" (official abbreviation pronounced "Am-Cal") and "It's a Miracle Division."

ammo   Ammunition. Anything fired by small arms and crew-served weapons: cartridges, projectiles, rockets, and propellant charges. A "round" of ammunition was a single cartridge or projectile with propellant change. "Round" originates from when muskets fired a round lead ball and cannons a round iron ball.

ammo cans   There were several sizes of airtight steel ammunition cans that were airtight, waterproofed with rubber gaskets, and had a carrying handle on top. The hinged lid was removable. The M2A1 "big ammo can" held 5.56mm bandoleers and .50-cal belts while the M9A1 "small ammo can" held belted 7.62mm. Soldiers sometimes carried personal items in a can strapped to their rucksack.

ammo residue   Expended cartridge cases, MG gun links, loading clips, bandoliers, expended pyrotechnics, crates, boxes, tubes, and packing materials used on firing ranges. In Vietnam it was important to recover such residue for salvage and evacuate to prevent the enemy from making use of it.

amtrac   Amphibian tractors, the general term for Marine Landing Vehicles, Tracked (LVT). Pronounced "am-track." LVTs used in Vietnam included:

LVTC-5 (command) landing vehicle, tracked
LVTE-1 (engineer) landing vehicle, tracked
LVTH-6 (howitzer) landing vehicle, tracked
LVTP-5 (personnel) landing vehicle, tracked
LVTR-1 (recovery) landing vehicle, tracked

Note: There is confusion on designations. The improved LVTP-7-series were not fielded until 1972, but are sometimes credited to being in Vietnam. In 1984 the LVT-7A1-series was redesignated the AAV-7A1-series (Amphibious Assault Vehicle-7A1).

And there it is. That's the way it is (like it or not); it is what you got; so much for that. "Check it out." I agree with you.

angel track M113A1 APC used as a medical evacuation ambulance—ten sitting or four litter patients.

Angry-one-oh-nine AN/GRC-109 radio used by Special Forces for portable long-range AM Morse code transmission. Used since the 1950s, it was impractical in Vietnam owing to its weight, the need for a heavy G-43 hand-cranked power generator, and lengthy set up time—it could not be operated while moving. They were used for backup communications in remote camps. GRC = Ground-Radio-Communications.

Annapolis US Naval Academy, Annapolis, Maryland. "Annapolis" is a four-year naval college from which graduates received Regular Navy ensign commissions to serve six years' active duty. Graduates could be commissioned in other services. Midshipmen's four years in Annapolis did not count toward their naval time in service. (Future Marine officers could attend Annapolis [q.v.] or West Point, most the former.)

ANZAC Australian New Zealand Army Corps. Australian and New Zealand Army troops of the 1st Australian Task Force (1ATF). See "Aussies" and "Kiwis." Pronounced "an-zak."

APC truck 5-ton gun trucks mounting the stripped down hull of M113A1 APCs in the cargo bed rather than the usual crew-fabricated steel plate, plank, and sandbag "gun boxes." They were top heavy and perilous to operate.

APO or FPO SAN FRANCISCO Army Post Office or Fleet Post Office, San Francisco. Every Army and USAF unit and installation in the Pacific Ocean area and Asia had an APO San Francisco address followed by a five-digit code. Navy and Marine units, ships, and installations had an FPO San Francisco address.

Apricots off-limits Marine amtrac crews will not eat apricots owing to the myth originated in Vietnam that opening a C-rat apricots can draws enemy fire.

A-rats A-rations. Fresh and frozen rations consumed in garrisons supplemented by preserved, canned, or packaged foods (B-rations, q.v.). Many items required refrigeration or freezing and had to be cooked or baked. Aka "garrison rations" or "real or mess hall chow."

arches Arched bars indicating rank grades over the eagle US Coat of Arms on Army Specialist 5 through 7 insignia. SP5—one arch; SP6—two arches; SP7—three arches.

Arc Light Codename for a B-52 bomber strike. The use of strategic nuclear-capable bombers to attack insurgents hidden in the jungle was equated to "using a sledgehammer to kill gnats." The radio alert to units in the field of an impending Arc Light strike was a "heavy arty warning." Minimum distance from friendly troops was 3 kilometers. Also spelled "Arclight." See "BUF *or* BUFF."

Arc Light track The track (path) of a B-52 "cell" (three bombers). A "wave" was two or more cells assigned the same target—followed on the ground was an "Arc Light track" 1.2mi long and 0.6mi wide blasted through the jungle, creating a tangle of shattered limbs and trunks and uprooted stumps. It was extremely difficult to cross on foot, especially when new growth further entangled it.

ArCom *or* ARCOM Army Commendation Medal. Pronounced "are-comm." A lower-level decoration for valor, meritorious achievement, or meritorious service. For valor it rates below the Bronze Star. If awarded for valor a "V" device was attached. Each service has its own Commendation Medal of a different design and ribbon colors.

arm and hand signals Arm and hand signals are frequently seen in Vietnam movies, often based on modern military/SWAT hand signals, which are much more elaborate than those actually used in Vietnam. Arm and hand signals used in Vietnam were few and simplistic, as described in FM 21-75, *Combat Training of the Individual Soldier and Patrolling*. Some platoons and companies developed their own simple signals.

artillery raid A tactic employed by the artillery to rapidly helicopter-insert all or part of a 105mm howitzer battery (4–6 tubes) on a small LZ to fire a quick mission at suspected/identified enemy locations. The firing unit would immediately be extracted and delivered to another LZ. Several subunits would be undertaking such raids simultaneously.

arty Artillery, field artillery—105mm howitzers, 155mm howitzers, 175mm guns, and 8in (203mm) howitzers—"big guns." Pronounced "arr-tee."

arty party NVA short-term artillery attacks on US positions near the DMZ using Chinese/Soviet-built 85mm, 100mm, 122mm, 130mm, and 152mm pieces. Many of these pieces were longer ranged than their US counterparts.

ARV M88 armored recovery vehicle built on the M48A2 tank chassis to recover damaged, malfunctioned, or mired tanks using a dozer blade, A-frame hoist, and winches. (The M88A2 was not nicknamed the Hercules until 1997.) The Marines used the M51 heavy recovery vehicle on an M106 tank chassis.

ARVN camouflage Three-color (usually dark brown, medium and light greens) camouflage pattern used by the ARVN airborne; called the *hoa rừng* (jungle flower).

ASAP As Soon As Possible. "A-sap" really meant "Get it done now."

As funny as a screen door on a submarine. Usually a satirical response to something not humorous or practical.

ash and trash Originally the daily fatigue detail of picking up barracks trash and heating stove ash. It came to mean any odd job or obscure, unpleasant, work detail. For aviators "ash and trash" missions were administrative—liaison, VIP, mail delivery, etc.

ass chewing Serious counseling session. Aka "ass reaming" or "butt chewing." "I've never had an ass chewing like that." "He reamed me out good."

asshole Jerk; someone who is irritating or contemptible. Aka "a-hole." A dipshit. It is said every platoon has a village idiot, a genius egghead, a gung-ho patriot, a psychopath, and a pig pen. It amazed some that they were so equally distributed within units.

assholes and elbows "I don't wanta see nothin' but assholes and elbows." Meaning be gone, get outta here, get busy, and do it pronto (q.v.).

ass-kicker 1) Officer or NCO known for verbally motivating subordinates: "He's a real ass-kicker."

2) Something difficult: "It was a kick-ass march."

assume Never assume anything. ASSUME is the acronym for, "Assuming makes an ass out of you and me." It is a stretch as an acronym, but makes the point.

Assume the position. A unit lined up to conduct a police call (q.v.) of their area and on the informal order, "Assume the position," the troops bent over slightly and moved through the area policing (picking) up anything that did not grow there.

As you were! 1) When an officer entered a room the first person seeing him shouted, "Attention!" As a common courtesy and to prevent disruption of activities the officer immediately shouted, "As you were!" meaning "Stay seated, continue with what you're doing." Alternatively he could say, "Carry on."

2) If a speaker makes a slip or error and catches it, he might say, "As you were," and then correct the error. "CHARLIE Company reported six… as you were, sixteen VC crossing the blue line."

Attitude check. "Fuck it!" The common response to the shouted mirthful command. When displeasure was directed at a guilty shamefaced individual, "He deserves a hymn." And in unison solemnly sung, "Hymn, him, fuck him."

audio letters Compact cassette deck tape recorder/players (aka "tape decks") became popular in the mid-1960s and were increasingly used to record "audio letters." The ⅛in tape cassette was mailed to the addressee; ¼in reel-to-reel recorders too were popular.

Aussies Australian Army soldiers, aka "Diggers" or "Ozzies." Australia (Oz) was pronounced "Oz-straylia," an allusion to the fantasy "Land of Oz" portrayed in *The Wizard of Oz* (1939). The main unit was the brigade-sized 1st Australian Task Force, 1966–72. Approximately 61,000 Australians served from 1962 to 1972, peak strength 8,500, with 415 KIA and 2,348 WIA.

AVGAS Aviation gasoline (AVGAS 100LL—100-octane low lead). Pronounced "av-gaz."

AWOL Absent Without Leave. Pronounced "a-wall." Absent from duty and unreported. The Marines/Navy use "Unauthorized Absence" (UA). After 30 days the errant serviceman is designated a Deserter and the case turned over to the FBI.

AWOL bag Small zippered handbag, aka "gym bag" or "travel bag." A piece of hand luggage sufficient for clothes and toiletries for a 2–3-day pass. Popular before the current day bag/small backpack. The AWOL bag moniker was given as it held what was needed to head home. It seemed apropos that they were available in the PX/BX.

B BRAVO

BA-30 Standard D-cell battery ("bat," q.v.) used in military and civilian flashlights and portable electrical appliances. (BA-42 is the smaller C-cell battery.)

baby killer An antiwar/military protester's severe and unfounded insult of all service personnel.

Back on the block. Returning to civilian life. Back at home. In the 'hood.

bad Something awesome or at least outstanding. "Awesome" as in today's over-usage was seldom heard.

badass Kick ass, hardcore, mo'fo. A belligerent troublemaker.

bagged and tagged Body placed in a "body bag" (q.v.) and tagged with a casualty tag for identification. While respect was shown for the dead, whatever means necessary were resorted to when evacuating the dead from the battle area.

bait tactics Process to lure an enemy force into an ambush or to become engaged by larger waiting forces. VC/NVA might attack a remote Free World firebase or defended village and ambush the relief force coming to its aid. Another method was for a few VC to plant indicators of extensive VC activity in an area—scattered equipment, shelters, and other signs of occupation—to cause Free World forces to waste time clearing it rather than going into an area actually occupied by the VC. Free World forces might establish a firebase in a remote area to entice the enemy to attack it and then airmobile in reaction and blocking forces.

Balls of the Queen Unofficial motto of the Field Artillery, referring to the infantry's nickname, "Queen of Battle." The Field Artillery is the "King of Battle."

bamboo Bamboo (*tre* or *cây tre*) grew in broad swatches of land throughout Vietnam. Growing in close-spaced clumps 20ft and higher made it particularly difficult and slow to move through. Bamboo was extensively used to construct all manner of buildings, houses, footbridges, fences, other structures, furniture, accessories, construction scaffolding, tools, utensils, and booby-traps.

banana peel Counter-ambush drill employed by reconnaissance teams. Aka "peel-back." In a chance contact (meeting engagement) the patrol's pointman engaged the enemy and threw smoke, WP ("Willie Peter," q.v.) and/or CS (teargas) grenades, emptied a magazine, and rushed rearward through the team—now alternating facing left and right. Each man rapidly repeated the maneuver until they all rushed rearward remaining in contact with each other. If the enemy pursued they repeated the maneuver until the enemy ceased pursuit or was lost.

bandoleers Cloth pocket shoulder belts to carry ammunition on the person. Designs varied to accommodate M1 and M14 rifles, M1/M2 carbines, M16 rifles, M60 MGs, 40mm grenade launchers, and Claymore mines (see "Claymore bag"). M3 bandoleers were often used to carry seven 20-rd M16 magazines rather than using standard ammo pouches. ("Bandoliers" is Australian spelling.)

BAR .30-cal M1918A2 Browning Automatic Rifle. Pronounced "B-A-R"—never "Bar." The Vietnamese called it a *súng trung liên* (rifle, medium rapid-fire).

barf bag Motion sickness bag, 3.5in x 6.5in buff paper bag complete with printed instructions. Available in transport aircraft, but seldom in helicopters.

barracks lawyer Self-proclaimed expert, especially in regards to regulations. In the Marines he was a "sea lawyer."

barracks party   Impromptu drinking party, usually held on weekend evenings after the officers and NCOs went home or to bachelor quarters. As long as things remained sane, such events were tolerated in-country. Most units on larger bases held occasional barbeques with grills converted from 20- or 55gal drums by the automotive maintenance shop.

barracks thief   Considered one of the most heinous crimes, stealing from buddies. Little forgiveness could be expected. When caught, sergeants cautioned, "Just don't kill 'im."

baseball cap   OG-106 field cap (hot weather) introduced in 1962 was extremely unpopular owing to its unmilitary look, with one officer describing its wearer as "looking like a garbage man or garage mechanic." Others described it as a "beanie" or "pinhead cap." Issue caps had a beanie-type crown with a small front stiffener. PX-sold and later 1969-issue caps had a more appealing raised front stiffener.

baseball grenade   Round (spherical) M67† fragmentation hand grenade slightly smaller in diameter than a hardball. Other versions were the M33, M33A1,* and M59.*†

* Extremely unpopular impact-detonated version.
† Safety clip factory-installed.

basecamp   Over two dozen major US basecamps were constructed throughout Vietnam, providing logistics and support facilities including artillery. Often they housed brigades and divisions or other major units with several hundred to over 10,000 troops.

Basic   The eight weeks of Army Basic Combat Training (BCT) undertaken by all male personnel entering the Regular Army, Army Reserve, and Army National Guard. Women undertook WAC Basic Training. Informally called "boot camp" (q.v.), but that is more properly the Marine (nine or ten weeks) and Navy (11 weeks) term. Air Force Basic Military Training was eight weeks. The length of each service's Basic has changed over the years. The preceding is for the Vietnam era.

Bat   Battalion. Little-used spoken abbreviation, mainly by the 173d Airborne Brigade: 1st, 2d, 3d, and 4th Bats, 503d Infantry. (Standard abbreviation for battalion was "Bn.")

bat   Batteries for radios, flashlights, night vision devices, and other electronic equipment. Plastic bat bags were highly prized for protecting personal items and covering radio handsets to repel dust and rain.

Bata boots   Lightweight jungle boots made by Bata, Inc. of Canada for the ARVN, RF/PF, CIDG, etc. Black rubber cleated soles and toes with black, brown, or OD canvas uppers.

battery-operated grunt   Marine backpacked field radio operator.

battery six   Typical barrage fired by a battery of six 105mm or 155mm howitzers; six rounds fired per tube to total 36 rounds. Rate of fire: 105mm—6 rds/45 seconds; 155mm—6 rds/90 seconds.

Bawouans   French term for *BPVN—Bataillon de Parachutistes Vietnamiens*, which remained in use by ARVN paratroopers. Aka *Nhảy Dù* (Airborne) or *Thiên thần mũ đỏ* (Red Hat Angels).

beans and motherfuckers   Meal, Combat, Individual ("C-ration") meat unit of "ham and lima beans" was the least popular of the meals. Aka "ham and muthas" or "ham and mo-fo's." Another meal, "beans with frankfurter chunks in tomato sauce," while satisfactory, was called "beans and baby dicks."

beehive rounds   Anti-personnel (APERS) rounds fired from tank guns, howitzers, recoilless rifles, and air-ground rockets, first used in 1966. The projectile was filled with small dart-like flechettes (pronounced "flā'SHet"), aka "nails"—French for "dart." The sound of the hundreds of flechettes passing overhead sounded like a buzzing bee swarm. A red pop-up flare (q.v.) was to be launched before firing a beehive round so friendly personnel could take cover—some units specified green. Not to be confused with canister rounds (q.v.) with shotgun-like pellets (40mm grenade launcher, 57mm recoilless rifle, 90mm tank gun). APERS rounds were identified by small white diamond-shaped markings. Some (APERS) "muzzle-functioned" like a shotgun spraying flechettes from the muzzle for a short range (*). Others had a mechanical time fuse (APERS-T) set to airburst just short of the target and spray the area (†). These were fitted with a red tracer (T). APER-T rounds could be set to muzzle-function without a delay. The aerial rocket was detonated by a proximity airburst fuse short of reaching the ground.

APERS Ammunition	Flechettes
40mm grenade launcher (test—not adopted)*	45
2.75-in aerial rocket (proximity fuse)	1,200
81mm direct-fire mortar (Swift boat)†	1,200
90mm recoilless rifle*	2,400
90mm tank gun (Patton)*	5,600
105mm howitzer†	8,000
106mm recoilless rifle†	9,500
152mm tank gun (Sheridan)* (called canister—CSTR)	10,000

beep   ¾-ton M37B1 lightly armored and armed gun truck augmenting convoy escort and used by some serial commanders.

beer can insignia Low-cost, locally made, painted thin sheet metal insignia, usually unit crests (q.v.) and larger insignia for commemorative plaques sold in mama san shops (q.v.).

Beetle Bailey The *Beetle Bailey* daily newspaper cartoon strip and comic books, running continuously from 1950 to the present, to be included in *Stars and Stripes*, never mentioned the Vietnam War.* It was even rare for a slack, lazy, hapless soldier in Vietnam to be called "Beetle Bailey" after PVT Carl James "Beetle" Bailey's personification.

* That said, a *Beetle Bailey* parody in *Mad* magazine (1952–2019) from the late 1960s depicts Sarge and Captain Scabbard wrestling the never removed cap off Beetle's face to reveal on his forehead the tattooed words, "Get Out of Viet Nam!"

berm 1) Bulldozed 2–8ft-high earth embankment surrounding firebases or other field positions or installations. Perimeter fighting positions and bunkers were incorporated into it and might be backed by a trench.
2) Earth parapet edging foxholes, trenches, artillery positions, mortar pits, and other open-topped fighting positions.

betel nut Berries and leaves of the betel palm (areca palm—actually a berry) are mildly narcotic and habitually chewed by many Vietnamese, especially older women, to relieve gum aliment pain. Over time this causes the teeth to decay and turn reddish-black. Betel nut is an important symbol of love and marriage with the Vietnamese using the phrase "matters of betel and areca" (*chuyện trầu cau*) to describe relationships.

Between a rock and a hard place. In a dangerous, difficult, or uncomfortable position. Facing a particularly difficult situation.

BFH Big Fucking Hammer. An implement recommended as the (figuratively speaking) solution to fixing things and resolving a variety of problems. "If nothing else works, use a BFH." Do whatever it takes.

big-ass... Anything that is real big. "That's a big-ass bomb."

Big Red One The 1st Infantry Division, owing to its OD patch displaying a red "**1**." The subdued patch had a black "**1**" which some soldiers refused to wear, preferring the namesake Red One. Aka "the B-R-O" or "the Big Dead One." "If you're going to be one, be a Big Red One."

big sky, little bullet While the direction and altitude of artillery fire supporting airmobile assaults and other operations were announced, there was little concern by helicopters and high-performance aircraft of being hit midair by supporting artillery. It did occur on rare instances.

billet 1) Quarters, where one lives.
2) In the Marines/Navy it is also a duty position/assignment.
3) In the Army the term used for a duty position is a "slot."

binos Binoculars or "field glasses." The Army used the 6x30 M13A1 and 7x50 M15A1, M16, M17A1, and M19. The Marine Corps used Navy binoculars: 7x50 Mk 28 Mod 0, Mk 32 Mod 7, Mk 39 Mod 1, and Mk 45 Mod 0 binoculars. (While commonly called "binoculars," a single unit is a "binocular" while two units are properly "two binoculars.")

Bird Dog Cessna O-1A/E/F/G observation airplanes used by airborne forward air controllers (A-FAC—pronounced "A-fak") directing air strikes for ground troops. Ground troops could not directly talk to USAF/Marine/Navy fighter-bombers and relied heavily on the FACs. They went by a variety of local call signs, but were commonly known as Bird Dogs. Designated the L-19 prior to 1962, they were sometimes still called that. The ARVN knew it as the *Chuồn chuồn* (Dragonfly).

birth control glasses Army-issue gray (prior to 1968) or black plastic-framed corrective eyeglasses. They were designed to fit inside gasmasks. They were "geeky" in appearance and by no means considered fashionably stylish. Many wore their own civilian eyeglasses and kept the Army issue as spares.

bitching Complaining severely, griping. Old maxims: "It's every soldier's right to bitch." "If a soldier ain't bitchin' he ain't happy." "Quit your bitchin'." A "bitch or gripe session" was an airing of complaints either among troops or with their lower level leaders.

black bar Subdued 1st lieutenant's (O-2) bar. Regular 1LT bars were silver.

Black Berets 1) Provisional (temporary) US LRRP companies and detachments were redesignated Ranger companies of the 75th Infantry on 1 February 1969; still with the LRRP mission. The Rangers unofficially wore black berets as did some pre-1969 LRRP units. (They were first unofficially worn by Rangers in 1951 and officially approved for the Rangers in 1975.)
2) ARVN Armor Corps.
3) US Navy River Patrol Force (unofficial).
4) Republic of Vietnam Navy.

black boxes Many new, sometimes still experimental, communications-electronics, fire control, detection, surveillance, navigation, and other high-tech add-on systems were rapidly being introduced for aircraft, combat vehicles, and weapons systems. An army of technicians were required to install, monitor, test, and repair these devices. While some were indeed black, there were other colors such as OD, gray, light green, and white.

black echo   The interior of a tunnel or cave system and the deep echoing of any sound experienced by tunnel rats (q.v.) while "running the hole"—exploring tunnels.

black gonorrhea or syphilis   Aka "Brand-X gonorrhea or syphilis" or "Saigon Rose." An "incurable" strain of gonorrhea ("the clap") or syphilis of which new arrivals were warned at the replacement battalions. They were told anyone contracting it would be quarantined on an unnamed island off the coast of Vietnam or the Philippines and their next of kin notified they were MIA or KIA. Supposed symptoms included rapid decay of the genitals. Treatment involved a whack on the male member with a hammer, which was of course completely fictitious. The term "sexually transmitted disease" (STD) term was not yet in use. Similar myths circulated in World War II and the KW.

Black, Gray, and White propaganda   The extent and aim of propaganda efforts is divided into three categories. The term "black ops" in regards to covert/clandestine operations was derived from black propaganda operations.

White propaganda: Omissions and emphasis—truthful and not strongly biased, where the source of information is acknowledged.

Gray propaganda: Omissions with emphasis and racial/ethnic/religious bias—largely truthful, containing no information that can be proven wrong; the source is not identified.

Black propaganda: Omissions of falsification—inherently deceitful information given in the product is attributed to a source that was not responsible for its creation, aka "false flag ops."

Black Hats or Caps   Jumpmasters wore black baseball caps identifying them in marshaling and rigging areas. Parachute instructors at jump schools also wore black caps.

black market   Illegal traffic or trade in stolen, officially controlled, or scarce commodities. In Vietnam this meant materials and items of all descriptions useful not only for civilian consumption, but sold or traded to the enemy. Sources were materials and items stolen, pilfered, resold, etc. by US and ARVN military personnel selling PX/BX goods to black marketeers, American and contract Vietnamese trucks delivering military and US State Department aid supplies into the wrong hands, stevedoring operations which virtually encouraged pilferage, and the fact that two-thirds of Vietnam's commercial import dollars came from US Agency for International Development (USAID) funds.

black ops   Little-used unofficial term for convert or clandestine operations.

Black Power   The Black Power or Black Pride Movement grew out of the early 1960s Civil Rights Movement and was active from 1965 to 1985. It encouraged racial pride, economic empowerment, solidarity, and creation of cultural and political bodies for Blacks. It also rejected traditional military life and a counterculture emerged. While estimates vary, less than 10 percent of Blacks in the Saigon area were heavily involved, mostly from service and other rear-area units. Elsewhere in the country only small groups formed, with most Black soldiers either not involved or only minimally involved in the movement. There were disputes over cultural identity and names, with "Black Americans," "Afro-Americans," and "African-Americans" gradually replacing "Negro" and "Colored." Similarly, other minority groups sought due recognition, with identities such as "Latino" and "Chicano" gaining usage, as well as "Mexican-American" ("Hispanic" was almost unheard of) and "American Indian." (The armed forces were officially desegregated on 1 October 1951.)

Black Power symbology This included "giving dap" (Black Power handshake, a form of bumping fists—said to mean "Dignity And Pride"). The "dap" was ritualized and specific within units and itself derived from "Gimme some skin"—one hand slapped down on the other. Other symbols were the Black Power sign (raised clutched fist), Afro haircuts (barely within regulations), Black Power bands or bracelets and necklaces (woven from black bootlaces or with black beads, aka "slave bracelets"), Black Power canes of elaborately carved ebony, "dashikis" worn off duty (brightly colored West African shirts), and Black Power flags of red, black, and green flown over or draped in self-segregated all-Black barracks. See "Soul Alley."

black rifle The 5.56mm M16-series rifles, replacing the 7.62mm M14 rifle in 1967, but was in use earlier. Aka "plastic rifle," "Mattel rifle" (rumored to be made by Mattel, Inc. toy company—a myth), ArmaLite (after the developing firm), "AR-15" from which it was developed, and simply "the 16."

Black Stetsons Some officers and men of air cavalry units informally wore traditional black Stetson hats in their bases. The design was based on the horse cavalry hat worn since the 1860s. Some aviators actually wore cavalry M1905 tan gauntlet gloves and yellow scarves.

bladder bird Transport aircraft carrying 500gal rubber (neoprene) fuel bladders to lift into forward bases. Aka "flying cow." See "elephant turd."

bladder canteen 2qt collapsible canteens and covers. Two types were used and proved none too popular. Also a 5qt "water bag" type canteen useable as a floatation device.

blanket party An internal form of punishment of an individual in a barracks by platoon members. Typically exacted on an individual causing difficulties, such as actions triggering group punishment—thievery, negative attitude, or being unsanitary ("scrub party"). A blanket was thrown over the sleeping victim, who was held down and beaten. Illegal, but sometimes encouraged by drill sergeants/instructors.

Blitz cloth   Blitz polishing cloth was packaged in a cardboard carton and used to polish brass and other metallic insignia. Insignia had to be removed from uniforms prior to polishing to prevent staining. The polish left a film, which was cloth-buffed off.

blood stripes   Marine officers and NCOs had worn red seam stripes on their blue trousers since 1840. From 1849 the stripes commemorated the 1847 Battle of Chapultepec in Mexico City where legend says large numbers of Marine officers and NCOs were lost assaulting the fortress—in reality, seven of the 40 Marines were casualties. Regardless, the issue of "blood stripes" to corporals and higher ranks was considered an honor. The hazing "corporal's blood stripe ceremony" did not originate until the mid-1970s.

blood trail   Path of dripping or freely flowing blood indicating the trail of a wounded VC/NVA or a dead man being carried/dragged. A "foamy blood trail" indicated the casualty was bleeding out. Blood trails were often reported, but not necessarily assuming any KIAs.

Blooper, the M79 grenade launcher nicknames

They made a "Thump" sound when you dropped a round in the chamber.
They made a "Thump" sound a little distance away from them when you shot them.
They only "Thumped" your shoulder when you shot them with very little recoil.
And they sure as heck "Thumped" whatever you shot with them pretty good enough!

Anonymous soldier, 1968

The 40mm M79 grenade launcher was bestowed numerous nicknames. Those after its firing signature included "blooper" ("spelled "bluper" or "blooker"), "bloop tube," "thumper," "thump gun," and "burp gun" (little used). Others were "elephant gun," "chucker," "M-Seventy-Nine," or "Seventy-Nine." Australians tagged the M79 according to its short-barreled shotgun appearance: "shottie" (shotgun), "sawnoff" (sawed-off shotgun), or "wombat gun"—possibly because of its stubby rotund appearance. The Vietnamese called it the *súng phóng lựu M79* (grenade launcher M79), the *súng M79* (launcher or rifle M79), or *Em bảy chin* (M-seven-nine). The M79 was developed under Project Niblick— the nickname for the high-lofting No. 9 iron. The projectile—"blooper ball," "egg," or "golf ball"—looked like a golf ball, was almost the same diameter, and had about the same velocity.

blousing rubbers   Rather than blousing (tucking) trousers cuffs into boot tops, the cuffs could be folded under with (originally) a couple of condoms tied end-to-end to hold the trousers in place. Large rubber bands could be used or PX/BX "blousing garters" were used—elasticized cords with small fastening hooks on the ends. "Jungle fatigue" trousers had integral tie-tapes in the cuffs.

blow away   To blow up, to zap, waste, fire up, blast, hose, grease, shoot, or bust caps. To "light up" means the same, but more specifically at night owing to muzzle flashes and tracers.

blue line   River or stream as indicated on a map. Term used in radio traffic.

Blues (air cav)   Nickname for aero rifle platoons organic to air cavalry troops. Light blue is the infantry branch color. Aero rifle platoons conducted ground reconnaissance, downed aircraft security and recovery, aircrew/passenger recovery, and small-scale strikes and raids.

Blues (uniforms)
1) Army Blue uniform or "Dress Blues." Dark blue coat Shade 450 and sky blue trousers Shade 451.
2) Marine Blue Dress uniform.* Coat is midnight blue—almost black—and trousers sky blue.
3) Navy Blue uniforms. Navy blue is actually black, providing more consistent coloration and reduces fading effects.
4) The Air Force wore Medium Blue Shade 1084 service uniforms.

* Most Marines were *not* issued dress blues, with the exception of recruit platoon honor graduates, Marine Corps Band, ship's detachments (formally), embassy guards, drill instructors, Washington DC area guards, and recruiters.

Blue, Yellow, and Red Areas   Quantitative classification rating for enemy and friendly controlled areas. See "contested areas."

Blue: Free World or friendly forces controlled day and night or when occupied.
Yellow: Free World forces controlled during daylight—typically highways and major roads and certain villages.
Red: Enemy controlled when occupied.

"Bobbie the Weather Girl"   There were actually two blonde, pixie-cute, personable "Bobbies" presenting weather forecasts for RVN, Stateside, and the R&R centers on Armed Forces Television Network, both varyingly dressed from stylish to provocative. The first was Barbara "Bobbie" Oberhansly, a Red Cross girl who launched the program in 1967 and performed only a short time—"First in war, first at the bar, first in line for an R&R." She succumbed to illness in 1968. Bobbie Keith, a USAID staffer, took over from 1967 to 1969. She also visited troops throughout Vietnam and signed off her program wishing her audience a pleasant evening, "weather-wise and otherwise."

Bob Hope Bob Hope (1903–2003) was a comedy performer extremely supportive of the armed forces. He performed in countless USO shows, more than anyone else, through WWII, KW, Vietnam War, and the Gulf War, receiving esteemed accolades for his efforts. He was instrumental in convincing other performers to join the tours.

bobtail 5-ton truck-tractor tasked to recover semi-trailers from damaged/broken down tractor-trailers in a convoy or simply a truck-tractor without a semi-trailer attached.

body bag Official designation is "pouch, human remains." A black rubber (neoprene) zipper-closed bag not unlike a civilian sleeping bag in shape and size. Aka (crassly) "Glad bag"—the first mass-marketed plastic trash bags in the late 1960s. Vietnam was the first time body bags were used in combat. When not available, bodies were wrapped in ponchos. Indigenous troops did not like keeping body bags on-hand, considering it a bad omen. Also a little used term for a prostitute. See "bagged and tagged."

body count The extremely controversial practice of quantifying military success according to counting enemy KIA found on the battlefield was standard practice. This was not a military generated practice, but established by Secretary of Defense McNamara. Unfortunately it was abused as it became a "rating" system of the "success" of unit commanders. Actual body count (the statement "by body count" was a validation it was an actual count) found on the ground was sometimes inflated. If abandoned enemy weapons were found they were each sometimes counted as representing a KIA without a body present (e.g. finding two KIA with weapons plus three abandoned weapons might be counted as five KIA). There were also estimated body counts submitted in addition to actual counted KIAs and that too was invariably inflated along with estimated enemy WIA. This was due to the normal enemy practice of recovering their own KIAs to deny Free World forces an accurate body count and "trophy photos." Another issue was if an installation occupied by multiple units was attacked and, e.g., four enemy KIA were found in the wire, then most units on the installation each reported the kills as their own and the totals were compiled and reported. There was also a category of "KIA by Air" in order to give credit to air support. This figure too was largely "guesstimated." From the civilian standpoint it sounded crass and callous and its validity rightfully questioned. Likewise captured weapons, equipment, pounds of documents, and supplies were reported, but tended not to be overinflated as the materials were unquestioningly actually present. Generally the troops on the ground turned in accurate enemy body counts—verified by physical count. Special Forces required an American to verify the body count and not indigenous troops. It was at higher headquarters that it might be inflated. Overall, though, admitted North Vietnamese post-war casualty figures were higher than total Free World forces reported.

boonie boots   Jungle boots (q.v.) or field boots. It was derived from "boondockers," long a Marine term for field boots. See "boonies." Also made in ARVN sizes.

boonie hat   Tropical field hat with a full brim. Aka "jungle hat" or "slouch hat." Several variants were issued from 1966. OG and many camouflage pattern models were purchased from "mama san shops" (q.v.) and personalized with patches, badges, and inked markings similar to "helmet cover graffiti" (q.v.). Early policy was for issue headgear to be turned in when departing RVN, which would not to be reissued. Personalized boonie hats were highly valued and the policy was changed allowing their retention after troops complained.

boonies   "The bush," the woods, the jungle, the field, and the boondocks—from which derived. Boondocks is derived from the Tagalog* word *bundok*—mountain— and came to mean a remote rural area. The term came into use by US soldiers serving in the Philippines from the turn of the century.

* Principal language in the Philippines.

Boot   Soldier, marine, or sailor attending Basic training, aka "pogue" or "pog." A "basic trainee" in the Army, the lowest common denominator, a "raw recruit" ("'cruit").

Boot Camp   Nine- or ten-week Recruit Training at Marine Corps Recruit Depot, Parris Island, SC and Marine Corps Recruit Depot, San Diego, CA. "Boot camp" was informally applied to Army Basic Combat Training. The Navy also conducted "boot camp."

boot socks   Cushion-soled wool and rayon or cotton blend socks with reinforced (thicker) toes, soles, and heels. Black socks were initially issued and lint stuck between the toes and turned white underwear dingy gray when washed together. OG socks were first issued to troops in Vietnam and then Army- and Corps-wide.

Bought the farm.   KIA or non-combat death. Serviceman's Group Life Insurance (SGLI) paid $10,000 from 1965 and $15,000 from 1972 to the designated beneficiary upon the insured's death. The monthly premium was $27 deducted from the serviceman's base pay. There were instances when a small number of buddies listed the others as beneficiaries to receive a percentage of the money in the event one was killed. This was later prohibited. "Bought the farm" originated in WWI (War Risk Insurance then $4,500) when the insurance payout could pay off the family's farm mortgage.

Bouncing Betty   M16-series antipersonnel mines. When activated, it projected a HE/fragmentation charge to chest-level and detonated, reaping devastation. The nickname was borrowed from the German WWII *SMi-44 Schrapnellmine* ("shrapnel mine" or "S-mine"), which influenced the M16's design. See "I stepped on a mine."

brain housing group One's head. "Put on a helmet and protect your brain housing group."

brass 1) Officers, aka "brass ass."
2) Uniform brass, i.e., "collar brass" denoting a soldier's branch of service plus belt buckles.

brass hats Officers, owing to the gold-colored braid and adornments on their service caps.

Brasso Metal polish in 7oz cans. Excellent for brass.

B-rats B-rations were canned (mostly No. 10, 1gal cans), packaged, and preserved foods served in garrison and the field when mess (cooking) facilities were available. They were served alongside A-rations (garrison rations, fresh foods) as well.

BRAVO-FOXTROT Buddy fucker. One who betrays or fails a buddy. "Thanks for ratting on me and telling the Top I was at the PX."

BRAVO-ZULU "Well done" by the Marines/Navy. "Good job," complimenting a person or unit. From the naval signal flag code of "BZ" meaning "well done."

breakbone fever Unpreventable dengue fever is a mosquito-borne tropical disease caused by the dengue virus. Symptoms begin 3–14 days after infection with high fever, headache, vomiting, muscle and joint pain—hence "breakbone fever." Recovery takes 2–7 days. Unlike malaria it is non-recurring.

break squelch Squelch is the radio carrier wave, the rushing background sound. The RTO could "break squelch" by quickly depressing and releasing the push-to-talk button on the handset. This "broke squelch" and he could respond to the station attempting to contact him. Breaking squelch once was the same as an acknowledgement—"I hear you, send your traffic." Sometimes the RTO's voice could not be heard, but squelch breaks were. One was for Yes/ROGER and two for No/ NEGATIVE. Two squelch breaks also informally meant OVER.

break starch Donning a starched khaki uniform. Shoving one's leg into the trousers leg caused a smooth ripping sound as the starch "broke."

brew, brewski, suds Beer. Common American 3.2 percent "G.I. beers" were Budweiser ("Bud"), Miller, Schlitz, Carling Black Label ("CBL"), Pabst Blue Ribbon, Ballantine's, Lucky Lager, and Griesedieck ("Greasydick"). San Miguel beer was sometimes imported from the Philippines. Australian beers ("piss") were Foster's Lager, Victoria Bitter (VB), and Reschs. See "3.2 beer." Beer was provided in "flattop" cans (q.v.). Local Vietnamese beer was available in bottles. Being under 21, many soldiers couldn't buy a beer.

brig   The confinement facility aboard a ship or on a Marine or naval installation. On an Army base it is known as the stockade.

bring smoke   Direct fire at a target or area. Blow stuff up. "Bring it on."

bro   Term of familiarity and bonding between Black soldiers with a common experience. Derived from "soul brother." Blacks were sometimes referred to as "bros" by Whites in a condescending manner. Vietnam veterans regardless of race now commonly refer to each other as "brothers" owing to their common experience.

Broken Arrow   Reputed to be a radio code warning that a US unit was in danger of being overrun. All available artillery and air support were dedicated. While this code was used in the Ia Drang Valley in 1965, it was not an Army- or country-wide code and not formally used elsewhere.

Brown Boot Army   The "old army" prior to the Vietnam War. Footwear and other leather items were brown prior to 1958 and uniforms were OD rather than Army Green with black leatherwear.

brown-noser   "Ass-kisser," one who "sucks up" to a superior at any cost for favoritism or to improve his advantage. A "yes man."

Brown Water Navy   As opposed to the Blue Water Navy, the big ships of the fleet. US Navy and Coast Guard coastal patrols (Operation *Market Time*) and "riverine" (q.v.) operations in the Mekong Delta (Operation *Game Warden*). They employed a wide range of coastal and river patrol boats plus modified landing craft for troop transport and support.

BS   Bullshit, disbelief. A variant is "horse shit" or "horse caca."

BS'ing   Bullshitting:
  1) Exaggerating, stretching a story. Giving a line of BS.
  2) Small talk. "Jawing." "We were BS'ing about the Top when he walked in."

bucket, the   Marine recruits were issued a 3gal galvanized bucket in which clothes were washed and packed with cleaning items, toiletries, and other necessary personal items.

buck private   Private (E-1), Army and Marines. Aka "slick sleeve private."

buckshot round   40mm XM526E1 multiple projectile cartridge with 20 No. 4 (.24-cal) buckshot pellets for M79/M203 grenade launchers for close-range engagements.

buck sergeant   Sergeant (E-5). "Three-striper." The lowermost of the sergeant grades.

Buddy Plan Army and Marine Buddy Programs allowed two or more friends to enlist together and ensured they would undertake Basic Combat Training and Advanced Individual Training together, if they were in the same military occupation specialty (MOS) and one wasn't recycled. There were no guarantees of staying together after AIT as they would be assigned to units according to the needs of the service.

BUF *or* BUFF Big Ugly Fellow or Big Ugly Fat Fucker. Pronounced "buff." Boeing B-52D/F Stratofortress bombers—"Big Bellies" modified to carry more bombs for Arc Light (q.v.) strikes. Less used terms were "bomb trucks" and "[bomb] dump trucks." First used over RVN in June 1965 with the final mission in August 1973. The first raid over North Vietnam was in April 1966. "Buff" also referred to the Sikorsky CH-53A Sea Stallion cargo helicopter.

bug juice 1) Insect repellent, applied on the body or clothing. A 2oz translucent or OD plastic bottle.* Aka "mosquito repellent" also repelling flies, gnats, chiggers, fleas, and ground leeches.
2) "Bug juice," a fruit-flavored mess hall punch.

* OD bottle introduced in 1968.

bugout To retreat or evacuate, to hit the road. Beat feet, hook it, book it, take off.

bullshit bomber Psychological operations aircraft dropping propaganda/surrender leaflets.

bummed out Depressed or upset, feeling down and out. "It's a bummer."

bunk Bed. Aka "rack." "Hit the bunk, rack, or sack." "He's racking out." The Marines do not use the term "bunk" except for "junk on the bunk" (q.v.).

bunk adapter Four 26in-long tubular adapters that fitted on the head and foot stands of steel bunkbeds to allow a second bunk to be stacked ("double-bunk"). They were occasionally used as a weapon in barracks fights.

bunker Any temporary field fortification built of local materials for defense or shelter from mortar, rocket, or artillery fire. They were built of sandbags, earth-filled wooden ammunition boxes, earth-filled 55gal drums, planks, and timbers. In rare instances they were made of reinforced concrete or of sandbags "capped" with a layer of concrete to prevent deterioration of sandbags by weather and foot traffic. There were fighting bunkers on base perimeters plus bunkers protecting TOCs, communications centers, fire direction centers, aid stations, ammunition, etc. It generally replaced the term "pillbox" as a covered fighting position. The VC/NVA used local and salvaged materials for bunkers, essential for protection from artillery and air strikes.

bunker bombs Satchel charges contained in demolition bags or large ammunition cans intended for throwing into firing ports and entrances of bunkers or tunnel/

cave mouths. Aka "bunker buster." Any large aerial bomb used to destroy bunkers. Another type of bunker bomb, an incendiary version, consisted of a large ammunition can three-quarters full of thickened gasoline with the lid sealed and taped to prevent leakage and 15 wraps of detonating cord turned around the can. An incendiary grenade was taped to the handle and a free end of the detcord (q.v.) taped under it, with a short time-delay firing device attached to the other end. They could be hand thrown like a satchel charge or dropped from a hovering helicopter.

burn barrel   A 55gal drum with air ventilation slits cut around its circumference near the bottom. Expired and unneeded classified and sensitive documents were destroyed by saturating with gasoline and burning. A stirring stick was used to ensure the layered papers/pages were separated and burned to ashes.

Burn before reading.   An exaggeratedly fictitious high-level security classification, a wordplay on equally fictitious "Burn after reading." Actual security classifications were (lowest to highest): CONFIDENTIAL, SECRET, and TOP SECRET. Unclassified, but sensitive materials, were designated: For Official Use Only (FOUO). Documents marked No Foreign (NOFORN) were restricted to US nationals with certain exceptions for Australians and New Zealanders.

burp gun   Little used in Vietnam, but slang for a Soviet 7.62mm PPSh-41 (ChiCom Type 50) submachine gun (SMG). Name originated during the KW owing to its firing signature. North Vietnam modified it as the K-50M* SMG with a shortened barrel jacket and replaced the wooden stock with the metal telescoping stock from the French MaT-49 SMG (q.v.).

* For North Vietnamese-made weapons "K-" means *Kiểu* (type).

bus driver cap   The visored, round-topped service cap worn with all services' Class A and B uniforms. Aka "saucer cap," "flying saucer cap."

Bushmaster operations   This tactic saw the insertion of platoons into sparsely vegetated areas in the last two hours of daylight. The platoons established ambushes after dark to interdict VC. A central command post was established and the platoons were within 750m of each other to provide mutual support. An offshoot of the "bushmaster" was "checkerboard." The next day the platoons would break down into squads occupying a grid square pattern. Squads patrolled continuously from square to square to locate small enemy elements. Since it was only a two-day operation they carried only ammunition and rations, allowing them to move easily. This technique was practical when the VC divided into small parties to evade the US sweep.

bust ass   To work extra hard. "We busted ass filling sandbags." "The company was busting ass through the bush."

busting brush Aka "breaking brush," "crunching brush," or "humping in the bonnies." Conducting operations in the jungle.

butter bar 2d lieutenant's (O-1) gold bar. The subdued version was brown, a "Hershey bar."

butterfly bomb These were M83 bomblets copied from the WWII Luftwaffe SD2 delivered in cluster bombs. The US made copies in WWII using them through Vietnam. The M28 was a 100lb cluster bomb with 24 bomblets and the M29 a 500lb bomb with 90 bomblets. The "butterfly" name was derived from the bomblets being OD with yellow markings and roughly wing-like panels opened to retard their descent. (The WWII German models, from which the nickname originated, were yellow with black and red markings.)

butt pack Small combat pack worn on the back of the equipment belt, aka "ass pack." Good to carry a day's ration of three MCIs (q.v.), pair of socks, and toilet kit. Little used in Vietnam due to its insufficient load. Rucksacks (q.v.) were much preferred.

butt can No. 10 (1gal B-ration) can usually painted red with a half-inch of water. May have been stenciled BUTTS in black. They were placed in barracks, offices, and work areas to extinguish cigarettes and emptied daily. Indoor smoking was allowed at the time. Marines called it a "buttkit."

Buzz Number Three-digit number (the last three digits of the five- or six-digit aircraft serial number) painted a vivid color. It allowed aircraft to be identified without recording the entire serial number. Derived from the old practice of identifying cadet pilots violating safety requirements, particularly buzzing the control tower.

By the book. Following Army regulations and manuals to the letter. No deviation or exceptions. Often used to describe individuals who rigidly and inflexibly followed regulations—"rigid flexibility" in their minds. Such inflexibility could be dangerous or counterproductive rather than adapting to local conditions, especially in a country with such varied terrain, climate, and the ever-changing characteristics of a counterinsurgency environment. "He plays by the book." Field manuals (FM) were not required to be followed strictly. They were guidelines, not unchanging rigid regulations.

By the numbers. Task to be accomplished step-by-step sequentially, the most efficient way.

C CHARLIE

C-4 Composition 4 plastic explosive. Aka "Comp-4." A widely used explosive for demolition projects. It generated less dangerous fumes and would not detonate when struck by bullets or fragments. Explosive relative effectiveness value is 1.59

(baseline TNT is 1.00). It was mainly issued in 1¼lb (1kg) blocks. M18A1 Claymore mines (q.v.) contained a 1½lb slab of C-4 that could be removed in emergencies for demolition work. It was widely known that ingestion of a very small amount of C-4 caused a "high" similar to ethanol. There was no "safe" amount as it depended on the individual's physical condition, weight, water content, temperature, existing stomach contents, etc. Others consumed a bit of C-4 in hopes of showing the symptoms of illness and be placed in convalescence. Ingestion of C-4 was extremely harmful and could result in stomach perforation and kidney damage.

C-5 Mythical plastic explosive more powerful than C-4. Myth had it that C-5 rolled into a small ball and lit to heat a canteen cup was so hot it burned through the cup—not true; C-5 did not exist.

C&C bird Command and control helicopter. Aka "CHARLIE-CHARLIE" or "Chuck-Chuck." Usually Hueys modified with a console (later factory-made) mounting radios for battalion and higher level COs, staff officers, and fire coordinators to oversee air assault and ground operations. The higher the command echelon the more elaborate the radio arrangements and sometimes additional niceties like cushioned seats and a 3gal coffee thermos.

cache French for "to hide." Pronounced both "ka-shay" (like "cachet") and "kash." A hidden spot or a stock of hidden items. They "cached" ("cashed") a stock of weapons in the cave. The VC/NVA established caches throughout base areas and in the vicinity of planned operations. They could range from a platoon's spare ammunition to tons of food, supplies, ammunition, or weapons found in caves, tunnels, dugouts, hidden structures, and buried pits.

call signs Radio call signs to identify individuals, units, and facilities varied greatly. In conventional warfare they were normally changed every 24 hours. In Vietnam they might be changed monthly or never changed over lengthy periods. They might consist of three-character alpha-numeric codes, a word followed by a number, or one- to three-word call signs. Any words may or may not have in some way been linked to the unit—e.g. an official motto.

Cambodes Cambodians or Khmers. Ethnic Khmers, many of whom fought in the Special Force-advised CIDG, were born and raised in RVN's Delta region, but were not considered Vietnamese citizens. See "KKK."

camo *or* **camie** *or* **cammie** Camouflage. Referred to vegetation-patterned uniforms, equipment, vehicles, and aircraft. Also the act of camouflaging—"camie-up," "camo'ed," "camie-paint."

camo cover Camouflage cover on the M1 steel helmet. They were reversible with five-color green pattern on one side and four-color brown on the other. Green-side out was worn almost exclusively in Vietnam. Aka "helmet cover."

Note: Green-side was light, medium, and dark green plus a small amount of tan and brown. Brown-side was dark earth, light brown, tan, and sand. In black and white photos the "brown-side" appears noticeably lighter shaded than the green-side.

camo *or* **camie stick**   Two-color camouflage makeup sticks contained in sheet metal tubes. While available in desert and winter colors, woodlands sticks in loam (very dark green) and light green were used in Vietnam. They were little used except by some reconnaissance units owing to discomfort, rubbing and sweating it off, and the annoyance of repeated application. The VC referred to SEALs in the Mekong Delta as "men with green faces."

Canadian base plate   The 81mm M29 mortar's 48lb M34A1 base plate was gradually replaced by the Canadian-designed 25.4lb M3.

candy ass   "Wimp" or "pussy." Does not refer to a coward, but someone lacking toughness.

canister rounds   These rounds were loaded with steel slugs or balls sprayed from the muzzle like a shotgun—"muzzle-functioning"—different from dart-like "beehive rounds" (q.v.).

Canister Ammunition	Slugs
12-ga shotgun (00 buckshot)	9
40mm grenade launcher	20 *or* 27
57mm recoilless rifle	154 *or* 176
90mm tank gun (Patton)	1,281

cannon fodder   Traditionally, low-quality troops thrown into combat—fed to the meat grinder. In the modern sense they were generally considered poorly trained and motivated usually owing to poor leadership. There are no bad units, just bad leaders.

Canuck   Canadian. The Canadian Vietnam Veterans Association estimates 20,000 Canadians served in the US Army and Marines. Some estimates reach 40,000. An estimated 12,000 served in Vietnam. There are 147 KIA and seven MIA inscribed on the Canadian Vietnam Veterans Memorial (aka The North Wall) in Windsor, Ontario. An anonymous US Marine said, "The worst of ours are going north, and the best of theirs are coming south." (In the first half of 1973, 240 Canadian troops served in the International Commission of Control and Supervision alongside Hungarians, Indonesians, and Poles monitoring the Paris Peace Accords.)

CAP   "Combined Action Program" was a successful Marine Corps village security effort in I CTZ. Marine rifle squads were attached to Vietnamese Popular Force (local militia—*Nghia Quan*) platoons to secure small villages. Operational from 1965 to 1971, the program at its height in 1970 included 2,100 Marines and 130 Navy medical in 114 CAPs (Platoons) and 20 CACOs (Combined Action Companies*) with over 3,000 militiamen. In 1970 it was redesignated the Combined Unit Pacification Program (CUPP).

* For a time CACOs were designated Combined Action Companies (CACs). *Cặc* is Vietnamese slang for the male sex organ and the abbreviation was changed. Additionally, the motto *sức mạnh*, which means "strength or power," was found humorous.

CA/PO   Civil Affairs and Psychological Operations. (Pronounced "kay-pol"). A convenient lumping together of two different activities and one confused with Civic Action (CA—military assistance to civilians). CA/PO involved aspects of both Civil Affairs (military government) and Psyops (q.v., pronounced "sigh-ops"), which dealt with propaganda activities against enemy forces. This resulted in many combat arms officers having little understanding of the three disciplines. CA/PO officers and NCOs were assigned to unit staffs.

CAR-15   Colt Automatic Rifle. Generic commercial term for shortened models of the AR-15/M16 rifle, the 5.56mm XM177-series SMGs. Pronounced "car-fifteen." Aka "shorty M16" or "Colt Commando." It replaced the Swedish K (q.v.) in 1967 when Sweden halted arms sales to the US in protest of the war. It was used by MACV-SOG, SEALs, Special Forces reconnaissance projects, MIKE Forces, and some LRRP units. The XM177E2 SMG may look similar to the modern 5.56mm M4 carbine, but they are almost entirely different weapons.

carbine   When "carbine" was mentioned in relation to US military weapons it invariably referred to the .30-cal M1 and M2 carbines widely used by the ARVN and other Vietnamese forces. The seldom seen M1A1 had a folding metal stock for paratroopers.

Note: Carbines fired a much smaller and less effective .30 Carbine round than the .30-cal (".30-06") used in M1 rifles, BARs, and MGs. Two other carbines encountered in Vietnam were the Soviet M1944 (ChiCom Type 53) and the SKS (ChiCom Type 56) (q.v.).

card-carrying   "He's a card-carrying dipshit (insert any other appropriate word)," meaning "He's 'officially' registered as an SOB." Whether spoken in a derisory, admirable, or indifferent manner, it meant the subject was widely recognized as such.

care package   A carton or box sent by a soldier's family containing snacks, food delicacies, personal hygiene and comfort items, and other minor luxuries. Often the contents were cushioned with stale popcorn in lieu of Styrofoam peanuts. Etiquette called for the contents to be routinely and expectedly shared with buddies. To hoard it for oneself led to ridicule and scorn. Of course the addressee could keep items specifically sent for him. Small health or sanitation "ditty bags" ("little red Christmas bags") were distributed through the American Red Cross, being assembled and donated by volunteer groups. The name was derived from "CARE Packages" distributed by the humanitarian organization Cooperative for Assistance and Relief Everywhere, a program launched for refugees and displaced persons in Europe in 1946, itself influenced by WWII International Red Cross POW food parcels.

CAS Close Air Support—basically jet fighter-bombers, "tac air." The Army's view of the Air Force was such that in listing fire support means in five-paragraph operation orders, they relegated an entire branch of service between two supporting weapons systems:

Fire Support

Artillery

Mortars

CAS (*Air Force*)

Air defense artillery

CASEVAC Casualty evacuation. Airlifting casualties for non-emergency transport, i.e., moving recovering patients from a field hospital to an out of country hospital—"evac'd." Pronounced "case-vac."

Castle Branch of service insignia of the Corps of Engineers was a two-turret depiction of a castle—"Corps Castle"—used officially since 1902, but can be traced back to 1840.

casual Personnel rated as "casuals" were attached to casual companies/detachments to await reassignment to another unit, depart for an overseas assignment or return to the States, or were recovering from wounds/injuries/illness. Marine term.

Catch 22 *Catch 22*, Joseph Heller's satirical WWII novel, was released in 1961 and widely read by servicemen. In simplest terms a "catch 22" refers to a paradoxical situation in which there is no clear or easy course of action due to contradictory rules or regulations. A simplified example: One could not have his photo taken for an ID card while sporting a mustache. Some sergeants major allowed the wear of mustaches, but only if your ID card photo showed a mustache.

cat eyes Typically two lieutenant bar-sized luminous tape tabs (with a faint pale green glow) stitched to the back of patrol caps or helmet camo bands. This allowed a following individual to keep up with the man in front of him; more effective than gripping the rucksack of the man in front. Widely practiced in the States (originated in the Ranger Course, aka "Ranger eyes"), it was little used in Vietnam, there being few night movements. When night moves were made, some stuck a white C-rat spoon under the back of their helmet band as a visual aid.

cat hole   Small hole dug with an e-tool (q.v.) or kicked with a boot heel in which to relieve oneself and then covered. Not unlike how a cat relieves itself and scrapes dirt over its waste.

cattle truck   Two-wheel semi-trailer enclosed box van for transporting 80 troops in training centers. Aka "cattle car." It possessed bus-like folding doors and troop seat benches.

Caught in an L-shaped ambush.   A particularly deadly ambush formation in which the main ambush force parallels the enemy route of march into the "kill zone" (q.v.) with an additional small force at the far end of the kill zone able to place enfilading fire down the length of the kill zone. The phrase also means finding oneself in a dire situation. For example, "I walked into an L-shaped ambush when I reported to the 1st sergeant's office." "We walked into an L-shaped ambush and had our asses handed to us."

C-Day   Conversion Day. A highly classified unannounced date when an MPC currency exchange was conducted. Several currency conversions occurred during the war in which existing Military Payment Certificates (MPC—Monopoly money, q.v.) were exchanged for a new MPC issue. Servicemen were limited to exchanging only US $200. If a soldier had more than US $200, he was out of luck. If in the field, US $200 MPCs were left with rear HQ. US troops were confined to bases on C-Day so they could not aid Vietnamese friends. This was an effort to control the black market and illegal money-changers. It was extremely crippling to illegal money-lenders, laundering operators, and black marketeers as there was a limit of how much could be converted. The hoarded stocks of unconverted MPCs were worthless and Vietnamese legally could not own MPCs. The announcement created a great deal of grief and even riots among Vietnamese.

CEV   M728 Combat Engineer Vehicle built on an M60 main battle tank chassis with a turret mounting a British-designed 165mm demolition gun (for breaching obstacles), hoisting A-frame, dozer blade, and winch. Assigned to engineer combat battalions. In spite of it having a tank chassis with a turret and main gun, high command emphasized it was not to be employed as a tank.

Chaffee tank   M24 light tank with 75mm gun used by the ARVN since 1950 until replaced by the M41A3 Walker Bulldog light tank (q.v.) in 1965. It was the only US tank used in Vietnam with a bow MG. Named after Major General Adna R. Chaffee, Jr. (1884–1941).

Chairborne Rangers   Derived from "Airborne Rangers." Staff officers and administrative personnel. Aka "Remington Raiders," referring to typewriters. Aka "Basecamp Commando," one who managed to remain behind with the company rear echelon in a firebase.

Charlie Nickname for the Viet Cong (*Việt Cộng*) derived from the phonetic alphabet for VC = VICTOR-CHARLIE. Aka Charlie or Charles, Mr. or Sir Charles, Chuck, Clyde, and the Cong. The ARVN disparagingly called the Viet Cong the *vit con*, a "duckling" or "small duck," meaning the VC were smaller game than the NVA. VC and Charlie were by far the most used nicknames, as well as "Those shitty little motherfuckers." Some say these nicknames were derogatory and demeaning, but it is certainly not unusual in wartime for opposing forces to refer to one another in less-than-flattering terms.

Note: Some revisionists claim US Information Agency (USIA) officials coined Viet Cong as a pejorative term early in the war intended as a demeaning propaganda label. They claim that by including "Cong"—Vietnamese for communist—it tied Vietnam's nationalist uprising to North Vietnamese, Soviet, and Chinese control, which it was. The true origin of the term Viet Cong evolved in the early 1920s and '30s. Vietnamese nationalists frequently fled the French to southern China and mingled with the *zhonagona* (Chinese Communists), which was translated to Vietnamese as *Trung Cong*. The Vietnamese nationalists began to be called the *Viet Quoc*. By the late 1950s South Vietnamese newspapers and President Ngo Dinh Diem were more frequently calling the communist insurgents the *Việt Cộng*. The term was well ingrained and widely used before major American involvement.

CHARLIE boat Command and Control Boats (CCB) or C&C Boats were modified monitors (aka MIKE boats, q.v.) deleting the 81mm direct-fire mortar and installing a tactical operations center (TOC) shelter. Hull numbers were prefixed by "C."

CHARLIE-CHARLIE Convoy commander. A convoy consisted of three or more vehicles departing from the same point at the same time for the same destination.

Charlie owns/rules the night. Resigned belief that "outside the wire" (q.v.) during the hours of darkness the VC controlled the ground and had relatively free movement, which was largely true. However, they too had to occupy terrain to control it and they seldom did other than possibly villages and their own base areas. When moving at night they sometimes imprudently used flashlights and intensely feared snakes, sometimes making noise to scare them off.

chateau general A term referring to a general maintaining a high standard of living (e.g. air-conditioned quarters, regular meals) who seldom saw his troops. This lifestyle applied to other senior officers too, especially some colonels. This does not by any means imply this was common. It was not.

Check fire! The command given over the radio by the unit receiving artillery support when it is necessary to immediately cease firing because the friendly fire is falling on or too close to the supported unit, is missing the designated target, or is now unnecessary.

checkerboard search   An area suspected of containing enemy forces was divided into 4km x 4km sectors (16 square kilometers), sometimes smaller. Rifle and reconnaissance platoons were airmobile inserted in sectors to search for the enemy. At different times throughout the operation platoons would be extracted and reinserted into different sectors in no discernable pattern to keep the enemy off balance.

cherry   The first-time soldier who attempted or qualified for an event. A "cherry grenade thrower." "Pop or bust one's cherry"—to do something for the first time. Also refers to a newly assigned soldier lacking experience. "We just had a cherry assigned." Derived from the slang phrase, "lost his/her cherry"—virginity.

cherry jump   Parachute students make five jumps to qualify for the Novice Parachutist Badge. His "cherry jump" is his first jump with his new unit. Many will exchange their originally awarded jumpwings—"cherry wings"—for a new pair of Wings. Within Special Forces a "cherry" was an individual who had not yet been awarded a beret regardless of how many jumps he had completed.

Chickenhawk   Marine helo (helicopter) insertion tactic using four UH-34s on standby with ARVN troops inserted to pursue withdrawing enemy elements.

chicken shit   Meaningless harassment and intentionally annoying treatment of the troops; anything considered time-wasting and unproductive by the troops. "Make-work details" to keep the troops occupied. A "chicken shit officer" or NCO—a practitioner of such antics and poor leadership.

ChiCom   Chinese Communist—People's Republic of China (PRC). Anything related to or originating from Communist China. Most of the weapons and equipment used by the VC/NVA were Soviet-designed, but ChiCom-made. Also written "Chicom" or simply called "Chinese."

ChiCom Claymore   The DH-10 (Soviet MON-100) was a directional anti-personnel mine. Aka MDH-10. It was a circular-shaped directional fragmentation mine set on a two- or three-legged mount. Larger than a Claymore (q.v.): 9.2in diameter, 11lb, 450 fragments (fewer, but larger than Claymore's). It was used for vehicle ambush, blasting gaps through barbed wire, ambushing LZs, and anti-personnel. It was command-detonated or trip wire-activated. The Soviet MON-200 saw some use in Vietnam: 18in diameter, 55lb.

Chief   Common name for various supervisory positions and ranks. See "crew chief" and "chief of smoke."

1) The ranks of Army chief warrant officers (CWO) 2, 3, and 4. CWO pilots did not like to be called, e.g., "Chief Smith" owing to the enlisted helicopter crew chief being informally called "chief." WOs were formally addressed as "Mister."
2) Army CWOs in technical and service positions, but not pilots.

3) Army aircraft crew chiefs were informally addressed as "Chief."

4) USAF chief master sergeants (E-9), the equivalent of Army sergeants major. They were not referred to as "chief."

5) Navy chief petty officers (CPOs) were NCOs in grades E-7 through E-9 and informally referred to as "Chief." "Chief of the Boat" was the senior CPO aboard a submarine.

Chief "Chief" was a common nickname for American Indians. It was not considered derogatory. "Geronimo," "Tonto," and "Cochise" were common too. (The term "Native American," just coming into use, was virtually unknown to soldiers and did not come into widespread use until the late 1970s.)

chief of smoke Chief of firing battery, the senior NCO (SFC)—aka "Smoke"—in the "firing battery HQ," which directly oversaw the howitzer sections and was a separate element from the "battery HQ."

Chieu-Hoi *Chiêu Hồi* Program was a Vietnamese and American psychological warfare campaign from 1963 to 1975. It correctly translates to "a call to return" (or to "regroup"), loosely translated to "Open Arms," (aka "chu hoi"). Various propaganda tools such as aerial loudspeaker broadcasts, aircraft-dropped and artillery-delivered leaflets doubling as safe conduct passes, and posters were used urging the VC to turn themselves in and be well treated Hoi Chanh or "returnees" or "railleries" rather than POWs. It folded at the end of the war, but over 100,000 VC and some NVA defected, although estimates vary greatly. Some would fight almost to the end and then surrender, shouting "Chieu-Hoi!" and waving a Chieu-Hoi leaflet they conveniently carried. Almost 7,000 defectors (*Hồi Chánh Viên*) joined the Kit Carson Scouts (q.v.) successfully working with US units as scouts and guides. Others were trained as mechanics for Free World forces.

China Lake grenade launcher 40mm (no designation—named after Naval Air Weapons Station, China Lake, California) pump-action repeating weapon used by the SEALs from 1969 to 1971.

Chinese fire drill Disorganized undertaking with no identifiable leadership, plan, or objective. "The S-3 shop is a Chinese fire drill." (This emerged from a high school prank in which a carload of teens stopped at a traffic signal, everyone exited the car, ran around to its opposite side yelling and waving arms, and reentered on the other side.) See "clusterfuck."

Chinook Boeing CH-47-series medium cargo helicopter. Named after an Indian tribe, Chinook also refers to the powerful Chinook winds of the Northwest Pacific Coast because of its double rotors' strong downdraft and the massive hot air blast generated by the dual-engine exhaust. One took a deep breath before boarding or exiting the tailgate ramp. Aka "Shithook" and "Forty-Seven."

choggie   Move out quickly, get going. It originated in the KW with the Korean Service Corps which built field fortifications and backpacked supplies to the front. They used a pack frame called a *chige*, which evolved into "choggie." Korean "choggie boys" were expected to move out quickly and finish jobs fast.

chopper   Helicopter, helo, bird, ship, or rotary-wing aircraft. So named as the whacking rotors chopped through the air. Fractiously, all helicopters were said to be Italian because they went "wop wop."

chopper pad   Helicopter landing pad or "helo pad." A designated landing site on a base or installation often marked with a large white "H"—sometimes within a white circle. MEDEVAC pads at hospitals usually had a red cross on a white square. Helicopter parking pads at large bases might have white squares or circles with 1- to 3-digit numbers within to identify the pads. On more developed bases the pads were covered by metallic airfield planking and oiled or asphalted to reduce dust.

chow   Food, meals, grub. "What's for chow?" "Ya got any chow left?"

chow line   Single-file line dishing out chow cafeteria-style in a mess hall with normal tableware or plastic or metal mess trays (q.v.) or a similar arrangement in the field with hot chow being served in mess kits or on paper plates. Traditionally, officers and senior NCOs were served after the enlisted men.

Christmas Truces   Temporary three-day ceasefires were agreed on each year between 1965 and 1972. Both sides reported violations during each ceasefire, principally the VC/NVA relocating troops and firing on aircraft. It was more advantageous to the VC/NVA than for Free World forces, who accepted truces to placate world opinion.

cigs   Cigarettes. Aka "smokes" or "coffin nails." Cigarettes were no longer included in MCIs (C-rats) from 1972, but remained in earlier lots. No cigs were packed in LRP rations. One does not smoke on patrol. Common PX/BX brands were Benson & Hedges Menthol,* Camel, Chesterfield, Kent, Kool, L&M, Lucky Strike,* Marlboro, Newport, Old Gold, Pall Mall,* Parliament, Salem,* True, and Winston.* Since many did not smoke, the four-cigarette pack in MCIs became a form of "trade currency."

* Issued in MCIs.

clacker   M40 firing device used to electrically detonate an M18A1 Claymore mine. Sometimes spelled "klacker" and compared to a staple gun in appearance.

Class VI   Class of supplies including personal use items such as toiletries, sanitation materials, tobacco, stationery, etc. It also includes alcoholic beverages, and Class VI (aka "Class 6") can refer to alcoholic beverages only; e.g. A "Class 6 store" is a liquor store.

Claymore   M18A1 anti-personnel directional mine. A command-detonated mine fired via an electrical wire and firing device ("clacker," q.v.). It could also be detonated by a tripwire ("mousetrap") or rigged as a booby trap using pull-type firing devices. It contained 704 steel 6mm pellets and 1½lb of C-4. Friendly personnel had to be at least 18m behind the mine and undercover. The mine was marked FRONT TOWARD ENEMY which led to such jokes as "We shall meet the enemy, and not only may he be ours, he may be us."* See "ChiCom Claymore."

* From 1953 in the *Pogo* comic strip (1948–75) by Walt Kelly and later came to refer to the Vietnam War's turmoil. Derived from Commodore Oliver Hazard Perry's (1785–1819) description of a naval victory: "We have met the enemy, and they are ours."

Claymore bag   M7 bandoleer for an M18A1 Claymore and accessories. Often used as a utility bag or to carry different types of ammunition. Two-pocket bag with an integral shoulder strap.

climbing rope   Several issue rope diameters were available, but the most common was the 120ft-long, $7/16$ in-diameter OD nylon rope used for climbing, helicopter repelling, rope bridges, etc. 3,849lb breaking strength will stretch one-third its own length.

Close to the flagpole.   The unit headquarters where everything was rush-rush and more "army" than elsewhere. The place where authority reigns.

clothespin bipod   M3 bipod for the M16A1 rifle. Every man was to be issued one, but it was rarely used, as it could not be folded out of the way while attached to the rifle and snagged on vegetation. It was unnecessary to support the lightweight rifle. When not needed it was inconveniently unclipped and carried in a pouch, often with an integral cleaning kit.

clover-leafing   A patrolling technique when a company was moving through an area and periodically halted, with each platoon establishing a perimeter and dispatching small patrols to loop out to the flanks to search the area and then return by a different route. If engaged the patrols would be reinforced by the rest of the platoon and even the company.

club tokens and chits   There were hundreds of variants and denominations of metal tokens, slot machine coins (aka "slugs"), paper credit checks ("chits"), and wooden nickels issued by various military clubs. They were intended to protect, regulate, and control Military Payment Certificates (MPC, see "funny money"). MPCs were exchanged for club chits and tokens to prevent MPCs falling into Vietnamese hands.

cluster bomb *or* bomblet   Aka "cluster bomb unit" (CBU), "sub-munitions," or COFRAM (COntrolled FRAgmentation Munitions). Numerous bomblets delivered from air-bursting aerial bombs or artillery projectiles (see "Firecracker"). They might detonate on impact, airburst after expelling, or deactivate or self-destruct on a preset delay time. Extremely dangerous to pass through an area with bomblets scattered about as duds might detonate if disturbed.

clusterfuck A disastrously misguided situation or undertaking involving numerous persons. "That mortar squad is a clusterfuck." "The entire operation was a clusterfuck from the get-go." Aka "gagglefuck," a panicked gaggle of geese. See "Chinese fire drill."

CMH "Casket with Metal Handles"—the cynical name for the "Congressional Medal of Honor," which is not its official designation, but simply the Medal of Honor. Aka "The Medal" or "The Big One." A total of 261 medals were awarded: 174 Army, 57 Marine Corps, 15 Navy, 14 Air Force, and one to the Vietnam War Unknown Soldier; 163 were posthumous.

CO Commanding Officer, the "unit commander," "the Old Man" (q.v.), "The Six" (q.v.). The number "6" designated unit commanders in radio call signs.* General officers in command positions were referred to as Commanding Generals (CGs).

* "6" was also used to designate the CO's M151A1 "jeep" in the unit's HHC (HQ-6).

coax The coaxial MG mounted alongside a tank's main gun on its right side—an important secondary weapon—aimed using the main gun's sight. These included the .30-cal M1919A4/A4E1/A5; M37; and the problem-ridden 7.62mm M73 MGs on M24, M41A3, M48-series, and M551 tanks and LVTH-6 landing vehicles, howitzer.

Cobra Bell AH-1G Hueycobra helicopter gunship. Aka "Huey Cobra," "Snake," and "skinny helicopter," a name bestowed by the VC/NVA (fuselage width 38 inches). They also called it a *Kobra* in Pidgin English. One of the few Army aircraft not named after a Native American tribe. The AH-1E Seacobra attack helicopter was used by the Marines.

cocked and ready Not just ready, but anticipating the command to launch an attack. Raring to go.

cocoa-coffee A three-quarters-full canteen cup of water was heated and an MCI ("C-rat") 1½oz cocoa beverage powder packet was stirred in with one or two each instant coffee, dry (powdered) cream substitute, sugar packets, and even crumbled chocolate discs, providing a "wake-up" drink on a chilly morning. The Vietnam soldiers' version of a modern-day specialty coffee shop's caffè mocha.

collar brass Officially, enlisted branch of service (BoS) insignia, aka "collar discs." 1in-diameter brass discs bearing the unit's branch of service device regardless of his MOS (Military Occupation Specialty) except for medical and a few others. Also worn was the U.S. enlisted collar insignia. On the khaki and Army Green uniforms' collars the U.S. brass was worn on the right side ("U.S. is right" as an immodest aide-mémoire) and the BoS insignia on the left. Basic trainees wore U.S. brass on both collars. Officers wore their rank on the right collar and the BoS insignia on the left.

collateral damage The term emerged early in the war, defined by the USAF as unintentional or incidental damage to non-combatant casualties and non-combatant property.

Combat! This 1962–67 WWII TV series had nothing to do with Vietnam other than troops taking R&R in Sydney might boast they saw a popular *Combat!* re-run episode there.

combat acetate Clear flexible plastic acetate sheeting with a clear adhesive on one side—protected by peel-off paper. It was applied to map sheets to protect them from rain and sweat and allowed marking with grease pencils. Aka "sticky acetate," it was sometimes applied to both sides of maps for better waterproofing. Paper posters, signs, and ID cards were similarly acetate-protected. (Regular non-adhesive acetate for map drop sheets was thicker and less flexible.)

combat and cargo field packs Marine pack system with a combat pack (aka "haversack") on the upper back and a detachable cargo pack ("knapsack" or "leave-behind-pack") on the lower back.

combat flight hours Initially Army aircraft crews were awarded an Air Medal (AM) for 25 flight hours for direct combat, 50 hours of combat support, and 100 hours of service flights. As a mix of missions were flown it was impossible to calculate actual hours. In 1968 the criteria was changed from equivalent flight hours' conversion to "typical" flight mission profiles regardless of actual duration: administrative flights counted for ¼ hour, support flights (such as reconnaissance or resupply) counted for ½ hour, and combat flights (combat assaults or extractions, fire support) counted for 1 hour. 24 hours warranted an AM. Pilots and aircrew could log over 1,000 "flight hours" in a tour and earn over 40 AMs indicated by brass numbers on the ribbon. Other services' AM requirements differed. The apparent highest number of AMs was earned by CW4 Armit C. Tilgner (1933–82) during six tours—136 AMs.

combat patch The "shoulder sleeve insignia of a soldier's former wartime service" unit in which he saw combat in Vietnam, Thailand, Laos, or Cambodia: 1 July 1958 to 28 March 1973. Worn on the right shoulder rather than the left as his current unit's. If authorized two or more combat patches, he could wear whichever he preferred or a different one on different uniforms. The Marines did not practice this.

Combat Pay Officially Hostile Fire Pay —$65 per month tax exempt for those assigned to a designated combat zone. This included flights over the war zone originating out of country or off-shore areas.

combat refusal A situation in which a small unit (company and below) refused to depart from a base for combat operations until some degree of "negotiation" with the leadership occurred and an agreement to examine the complaints. It might be due to morale issues caused by a loss in confidence in the unit's leadership, excessive duration in the field, prolonged abhorrent living conditions, and a change of mission deemed excessively dangerous or unnecessary, etc. This was usually manifested over a prolonged period and repeated requests by the spokesmen to the leadership failed to improve the situation. This always stopped short of mutiny. One combat refusal situation involved a unit in the States. The California National Guard's 1st Squadron, 18th Armored Cavalry, was Federalized in 1968 and some troopers refused to deploy to Vietnam. Negotiations eventually led to MACV canceling its need for the unit.

Combat Skyspot   Complex system of remote targeting for B-52 bomber Arc Light (q.v.) strikes in remote areas in RVN and Laos. It allowed B-52s, as well as other aircraft, to make accurate strikes on remote targets. The radar sites could be on large US bases or extremely remote peaks within enemy territory. The main radar employed was the AN/MSQ-77 bomb directing central radar (aka "Miscue-77"),* an automatic tracking radar/computer system for guidance of aircraft making bomb runs at night and in foul weather. It was accurate enough to bomb within 250–900m of friendlies. MSQ = Ground, Mobile-Special-Combination.

* "Miscue" being a play on words for "missing the cue"—a signal to an actor to enter or begin a performance; in this case, missing the target.

ComBloc   Communist Bloc. Weapons, ammunition, and equipment originating from Communist China, USSR, and Warsaw Pact states. Also written "Combloc."

comm center   Communications center, aka message center, "commo bunker." A unit HQ's facility for radios, radioteletypes, telephone switchboards, and message processing and distribution.

commo   Communications. Communications/Electronics (CE) was an all-inclusive term for all things related to signals and electronics. Aka little used "comms." As a verb, "make commo," to establish communications, principally via radio.

commo wire   Two-strand WD-1/TT field telephone wire, "landline wire," or simply "wire" (not to be confused with barbed wire, also called "wire"). Used for a number of non-communications purposes: clothes lines, substitute tent and antenna guy lines, tie-downs, and tripwires.*

* One strand was sometimes used for tripwire, but it was largely ineffective, being too thick and glossy black making it easier to detect.

Company D Packets   In late 1967 fourth rifle companies (Company D) were authorized for infantry, light infantry, airborne, and airmobile battalions, allowing for more flexible operations and increased operational tempo. Organized in the States, they were deployed in the fall of 1968. They were typically broken up, with three-quarters of the new troops going to the existing companies and those companies giving up a quarter of their men to the new company.

company-level   Command, administrative, maintenance, etc. activities performed at company/battery/troop-levels. Maintenance wise, 1st echelon was operator-level and 2nd echelon was company- and battalion-levels.

compass man   The soldier designated, often a squad or team leader, who navigated by map and compass. Aka "navigator." He kept the pointman (q.v.) ahead of him on course. The pointman was alert for signs of the enemy and could not be distracted by navigation. A "slackman" might be positioned between the pointman and compass man to cover the pointman. Land navigation was accomplished by terrain association using a topographic map, lensatic compass, and sometimes pace-counting. (The development of GPS commenced in 1973 for use by the US Armed Forces. While partly operational in the mid-1980s for military and civilian use, it did not become fully operational until 1995.)

complimentary steak   It was widely heralded that returnee processing stations in Oakland, California and Ft Lewis, Washington served a steak-to-order with all the trimmings. All troops signed a roster confirming they received the meal and those declining signed a statement that it was offered but rejected to prevent malcontents from complaining to the media. It was a treat.

concertina wire   "Concertina roll or coil" was 3ft 3in (1m) in diameter and about 50ft long when stretched out (varied). It could be made of spring steel barbed wire or "razor wire" (q.v.). Sometimes misspelled "Constantine."

concussion grenade   Mk 3A2 offensive hand grenade generating heavy blast (½lb TNT), but little fragmentation owing to the black asphalt-impregnated fiberboard cylindrical body. Aka "demolition or demo grenade."

CONEX   Steel corrugated shipping container, CONtainer EXpress box introduced in 1952. Pronounced "conn-nex." Aka "Conex box." They measured 8ft 6in long, 6ft 3in wide, and 6ft 10in high with double doors on one end, mounted on skids, and lifting rings. Over 300,000 were shipped to Vietnam with most remaining in-country and used as the "foundation" for MG bunkers, TOCs, FDCs, comm centers, aid stations, quarters, storage, etc. and heavily sandbagged. The CONEX led to today's ISO (International Organization for Standardization) intermodal shipping containers. ISO containers began to appear in Vietnam in 1968.*

* Regardless of the organization's English spelling, ISO is the formal abbreviation.

Connie Rodd   Cartoon character in *PS, The Preventive Maintenance Monthly*. She was a civil service maintenance management technician narrating the magazine with MSG Half-Mast, an old done-it-all maintainer. The Lauren Bacall look-alike blonde often wore provocative clothes exuding sexual appeal. (Her sensuous persona and dress were toned down in the mid-1970s.) Name derived from "con rod," slang for piston "connecting rod." *Preventive Maintenance* magazine originated in 1951, replacing *Army Motors*, and is still in circulation. (*PS* in the title derives from it being a "postscript" to technical manuals, or TMs.)

contact   An engagement with the enemy, a firefight. "Make or made contact." Not to be confused with communications contact—"make commo."

contested areas   Areas and routes that neither side effectively controlled unless they physically occupied it. Realistically, most of RVN was a "contested region." Even friendly villages were "contested" if security troops were not present. "Contested" was an attempt to throw a positive light on what were realistically uncontrolled/ unoccupied areas the enemy could move more or less freely through. See "Green, Yellow, and Red Areas."

cook off   1) Pulling the pin on a hand grenade, releasing the arming lever, retaining it for 1–3 seconds, and then throwing it. This allowed insufficient time for the enemy to recover the grenade and throw it back or escape the detonation. It might also be done to achieve an airburst over open-topped fighting positions or troops in the open. US casualty-producing grenades have a 4–5-second delay. A dangerous practice, it was discouraged or prohibited in some units.

2) Automatic weapons firing long continuous bursts could overheat and a round in the chamber unexpectedly detonate. It might set off a continuous uncontrolled burst, resulting in a "runaway gun." Extremely dangerous to friendlies in the vicinity. The belt was grabbed and twisted, breaking the links to halt it.

cordon   To "cordon off a village" was to surround and block all routes to and from a village or other site/area, to entrap the enemy or to search the area for hidden enemy, contraband, and tunnels. Derived from the French *corde* (cord), implying to "tie-off."

Corps   Operationally, the RVN was divided into four Corps Tactical Zones (I–IV CTZ)—*Quân Đoàn (QD)*. While these were RVN commands, the US recognized them as convenient regional control areas. US corps equivalent commands were I and II Field Forces, Vietnam (I and II FFV) controlling US forces in II CTZ and III and IV CTZs, respectively. III Marine Amphibious Force controlled US Marine and Army forces in I CTZ with the Army elements directly under XXIV Corps. "Corps" is both singular and plural usage. CTZs were redesignated Military Regions (MR 1–4) on 30 April 1971.

corrugated iron   Corrugated galvanized steel sheets widely used for temporary structure roofing and other construction purposes. Aka "G.I. sheets."

COSVN   Central Office for South Vietnam (pronounced "CŎS vĭn"), the Central Executive Committee of the People's Revolutionary Party (*Văn phòng Trung ương*

Cục miền Nam) operating from 1962 to 1976. The "mysterious" combined military and political HQ of the NVA, VC, and People's Revolutionary Party. The mythical VC HQ, the "Bamboo Pentagon," was part of COSVN. Some doubted its existence. There was speculation of COSVN's location ranging from the Cambodian Mimot Plantation to various areas in northern III CTZ north of Saigon, mainly the Fishhook area on the Cambodian border or War Zone C (q.v.). Regardless, there is little doubt its elements were widely dispersed and frequently relocated. From 1967 continuing efforts were made to locate and destroy COSVN to include Arc Light bombings (q.v.) and ground operations and was the objective of the 1970 Cambodian incursion. COSVN was never neutralized.

country boy Soldiers born and raised in rural or small town settings and assumed undereducated or naive. Aka "grit," "hick," "farm boy," "goat roper" (cowboy), "redneck," "cracker," "hillbilly," "dirt farmer," and "hayseed."

Country Fairs Marine/ARVN civil affairs operations in which villages were cordoned off, residents gathered, identified, given medical treatment and political and morale talks. Meals were provided and games for children. The village was searched for hidden VC and contraband. The force withdrew, leaving stay-behind elements to ambush returning VC.

country stores General nickname for small "mama san shops" (q.v.) catering to any and all soldiers in towns and villages. Vaguely reminiscent of American country stores, the most common merchandise were soft drinks, beer, cigarettes, batteries, and similar goods, mostly obtained through the black market.

cover Headgear in the Marines, a hat or cap. "Square away your cover, Marine."

cowboy Rambunctious, brash, reckless, or careless soldier who might be construed as overly gung-ho, but needs to be reined in. The term "hot shot" is derived from the days of wooden sailing ships, referring to the naval practice of heating solid cannonballs and firing them to set ships afire. See "Saigon cowboy."

crack troops Veiled phrase for Women's Army Corps (WAC)—pronounced "Wacks" or "Wax." A play on "crack troops," a phrase dating from the 1700s to denote "top-notch or superior troops," "crack shots," superior shots. Aka "split-tails." The Nurse Corps was separate from the WAC. A total of 7,484 women from all armed services served in Vietnam, of which 6,250 were nurses. Women Marines (WM) totaled 36. Eight nurses died in Vietnam, one KIA. The others were mostly lost in non-combat-related aircraft crashes. (The WAC was abolished and female soldiers integrated into previously segregated units on 1 October 1978.)

"C-rations"—Meal, Combat, Individual (MCI)

C-rations, aka "C's" were actually a category of packaged field rations. Actual C-rations adopted in 1938 were replaced by the MCI in 1958 and also informally called "C-rations." Some pre-1958 C-rations were issued early in the Vietnam War. Sometimes it is claimed WWII K-rations were issued in Vietnam, but the remaining K-rats were consumed in the KW. A "ration" is actually one day's meals. When packing for the field C-rats were "broken-down" or "stripped," removing packing materials and items the individual disliked to save weight and space. To prevent rattling, up to four cans were often carried in socks ("C-rat sock"), sometimes tied to the rucksack or web gear. Everyone had their favorite items and those they loathed. A common complaint was that the bread, cakes, and crackers were too dry.

MCIs or "C-rats" were issued in cases of 12 different meals in 3in x 5½in x 6in cardboard cartons. The top lid of the carton could be used as a postcard and mailed home. Instead of a postage stamp one wrote FREE. Each held a white plastic spoon, accessory packet (q.v), and three OD-painted cans containing different combinations of meat (M Unit), fruit or dessert (D Unit), and B Unit (candy, crackers, spread, etc.). The carton's lid indicated the M Unit by entree name and the B-1, 2, or 3 Unit. The B-1 was one of the more popular as it came with fruit.

B-1 Unit:

Meat unit—chicken or turkey loaf, beefsteak, chopped ham and eggs, or sliced fried ham.

Fruit unit—applesauce, apricots, fruit cocktail, peaches, or pears.

B unit—7 crackers, peanut butter, candy disc (chocolate, solid chocolate cream, coconut).

B-2 Unit:

Meat unit—spaghetti and meatballs with tomato sauce, or beef slices and potatoes with gravy, ham and lima beans, beans in frankfurter chunks with tomato sauce, or meatballs with beans in tomato sauce.

B unit—4 crackers, caraway or pimento processed cheese spread.

Dessert unit—fruitcake, pecan roll, pound cake, or orange nut roll.

B-3 Unit:

Meat unit—boned chicken or meat loaf, chicken and noodles, or spiced beef.

B unit—4 cookies, cocoa beverage powder; apple, grape, berry/mixed fruit, or strawberry jam.

White bread

Note: MCIs were adopted in 1958, replacing the original WWII C-rations, which were much different than the Vietnam-era "C-rats." MCIs began to be replaced by Meals, Ready-to-Eat (MRE) in 1981.

C-ration case opening   C-rat cases were secured by two wire bindings. These were cut by various means, often by shoving an e-tool's or bayonet's blade under the binding wire and sharply snapping it up to break it. If one had an early XM16E1 rifle with the "three-prong" flash hider it could be used to twist and snap the wire. The three-prong flash hider caught on vines and twigs and was replaced by the closed type "birdcage" flash hider, which could not be used for wire breaking. It was not until after the war that plastic strapping bands secured 26lb C-rat cases.

C-ration cookbook   *Charlie Ration Cookbook: Or No Food Is Too Good For The Man Up Front.* A 10-page pamphlet with 21 recipes concocted from C-rats and minimal condiments and additions. It was distributed free by the Macilhenny Company of Louisiana, the makers of Tabasco sauce (q.v.). A soldier's family could buy a cookbook and a 2oz bottle of Tabasco for $1.00 for inclusion in "care packages" (q.v.).

C-ration stoves   While MCIs could be eaten cold from the can, they were far more appetizing heated. A simple field stove could be made from a C-ration can, the most common being a squat B-unit or the taller M-unit, aka "bonnie stove." The lid was cut off and close-spaced holes punched around the bottom edge and top opening (top opening slits could be deleted). These were made by a church key (beer can and bottle opener) or pocketknife to provide ventilating air. A single Trioxane heat tablet (q.v.) or a ball of C-4* was placed in the can and lit. A canteen cup or a C-rat can was placed on top and quickly heated. A pair of ¼ to ½in-diameter 5–6in-long green sticks laid across the stove top proved more stable, especially for a canteen cup. The meat unit was densely packed and impossible to heat evenly without burning. The meat content could be emptied into a canteen cup, broken up to heat faster and more evenly, a dash of water added, and then heated. Tabasco sauce enhanced the taste.

Another method was a C-rat can with slits cut only around the top, an inch of sand added to the bottom, saturated with diesel, gasoline, or JP-4, and lit to heat a C-rat can or canteen cup. Yet another technique was to tear up the MCI cardstock carton and spacer in strips, coil it in a C-rat can with slits, and light it to heat a meal. The cardstock could be soaked with a little fuel or lighter fluid. Small cans of Sterno ("canned heat") jellied alcohol were sometimes sent in care packages.

* A ball of C-4 (q.v.) the diameter of a nickel with a small tit pinched on it to which a match was applied. Unburnt C-4 could be tipped out of the stove can and rolled on the ground with the green sticks to extinguish it for reuse. It was never stomped on to extinguish it as it could explode. Its burning fumes had to be avoided.

crest   Small enameled metal badge based on the design of the unit crest embroidered on unit colors. Officially designated a Distinguished Unit Insignia or "DUI." Worn on the shoulder straps of Class A and B uniforms and on the left front of enlisted garrison caps. Battalions and larger units, formations, commands, and organizations were authorized DUIs. Smaller units wore their parent command's DUI. Company/battery/troop-sized combat arms units wore the DUI of the parent regiment whose lineage they carried.

crew chief   There were several types of crew chiefs, aka "NCOIC" (Non-Commissioned Officer In Charge). See also "chief of smoke."

1) A helicopter crew chief is the enlisted mechanic responsible for its maintenance. Also served as a door gunner in most models of helicopters.
2) Gun truck commanders were aka crew chiefs or NCOICs.
3) In the USAF the crew chief was the senior NCO aboard a multi-crewed aircraft or assigned to maintain a one/two-seat aircraft. Loadmaster in cargo transports.

crispy critter   Burnt corpse. Aka "roasted peanut." "Don't eat the Zippo barbeque." Crispy Critters was a cereal brand with animal cracker-shaped bits marketed 1962–69. TV cartoon series ran 1964–69.

critically dead   Macabre term for an incinerated, dismembered, mutilated, or decomposed corpse. The lack of a pulse was unnecessary to confirm death. Aka "seriously dead."

crossed cannons   Crossed muzzle-loading cannons have been the Artillery insignia since 1834. In 1917 the Artillery split into Field and Coast Artillery,* the latter including antiaircraft artillery. In 1950 the Coast Artillery, now solely antiaircraft, and the Field Artillery merged into a single Artillery branch which used the crossed cannons insignia. In 1957, with air defense entering the missile age, a Nike Ajax missile† was added in the center and worn by both field and antiaircraft artillerymen. In December 1968 the Artillery again split into the Field (FA) and Air Defense Artillery (ADA), but the latter units did not begin to be redesignated ADA until September 1971. The crossed cannons with the missile were assigned to the ADA and the bare crossed cannons restored to the FA.

* The Coast Artillery used crossed cannons with a projectile set on a red oval in the center.

† The world's first operational surface-to-air missile of 1954.

crossed pistols   The crossed muzzle-loading pistols collar insignia of the Military Police Corps was approved in 1922. They were the Harper's Ferry .54-cal Model 1805, having been the first US-made military pistol.

crossed rifles   Crossed rifles collar insignia of the infantry branch. Early insignia displayed different types of muskets and rifles as standard models changed. The Springfield .69-cal Model 1795 has been the traditional musket for infantry branch insignia since 1924. It was selected as it was the Army's first American-made mass-produced musket. Marine lance corporals through master sergeants displayed crossed Garand .30-cal M1 rifles on their rank chevrons since 1959 as a visual reminder that Marines were riflemen first.

crossed sabers   Crossed sabers collar insignia of armored cavalry (reconnaissance) and air cavalry units, especially worn by officers. They were actually armor branch and unofficially wore the crossed sabers of the old cavalry branch (dating back to 1851) instead of the crossed sabers surmounted by a head-on M26 Pershing tank adopted in 1950.* While the saber model was not specified in official descriptions, it was the Model 1860 light cavalry sabre.

* Armor became an official branch on 22 June 1950, absorbing the cavalry branch.

crotch rot   "Rotcha-crotch-off" (spoken as a single word) is medically called "tinea cruris." Aka "crotch itch" or "jock itch." See "jungle rot."

culvert pipe   Corrugated metal pipe (CMP). 1–6ft-diameter half-sections (arch) of galvanized steel pipe 2ft in length bolted together in the desired length and diameter. Often used in constructing fortifications and small shelters. A man could rack out inside a 6ft-long, 3ft-diameter half-arch shelter covered with two layers of sandbags.

cunt cap   The garrison cap was the most nicknamed headgear. The following were little used: "fore and aft cap," "overseas cap," "piss cutter," "side cap," and "envelope cap." Adopted in WWI to replace the bulky campaign hat ("Smokey Bear hat", q.v.) that could not be carried in duffle bags, thus, the term "overseas cap." "Garrison cap" originated because prior to WWII only the M1911 campaign hat could be worn off-post, with the garrison cap restricted to post.

Cut some slack.   "Give me a break." A typical response might be, "I cut no slack for anyone." "Slack" refers to excess rope, to loosen up: "Give me more rope."

cutting charges   Most types of artillery rounds and all mortar rounds were provided a number of separate propellant charges, usually in small cloth bags contained inside 75mm and 105mm artillery projectile cases or attached between mortar round fins. 75mm pack and 105mm howitzer cartridges were semi-fixed, i.e., the projectile removed from the case, the desired number of charges removed ("cut") from the case, the "projo" refitted ("marrying") on, and loaded. 155mm and larger rounds have separately loaded bagged propellant changes. Graphic firing tables (a manual) provided the angle of elevation and number of charges to achieve the desired range. All rounds were provided the maximum number of necessary charge bags or "increments." In preparing for a fire mission the number of unnecessary charges were "cut." Excess charges were burned in pits.

cutting Zs   Sleeping, snoring, sawing logs. "I'm going to rack-out and cut (as in sawing) some Zs."

CYA   Cover Your Ass. Actions taken to ensure one is protected from criticism, violating regulations, or other transgressions, often with bureaucratic cover up connotations.

cyclo   Three-wheel peddle taxi. Pronounced "psych-lo." Aka "pedicab." Commonly called a "three-wheel bicycle," rightfully a "tricycle," but seldom called as such. Pronounced "sick-low" from the French *cyclo pousse* (rickshaw). Two passengers, third wheel in the back under the peddler.

D   DELTA

Daisy Cutter   USAF's BLU-82B "Commando Vault," or "Big Blue," 15,000lb blast bomb parachute-dropped from C-130 transports. They flattened jungle areas in order to clear helicopter LZs and firebases and to destroy high-value targets. Most were dropped by the US in Laos in 1970. The Vietnamese dropped some in 1975 in efforts to halt the NVA onslaught. (In WWII "daisy cutter" referred to small ground-bursting fragmentation bombs "cutting down daisies.")

danger close   A warning that friendly troops were within the danger area for the impact of aerial munitions (cannon fire, bombs, rockets) or artillery or mortar fire. There was no one standardized distance as it depended on the specific ordnance: helicopter MGs—100m; helicopter rockets—200m; aerial bombs—300m; mortars and artillery—600m; naval guns 5in and smaller—750m; larger than 5in—1,000m. The ordnance could have been adjusted closer once the initial rounds were delivered.

Darvon 65   Dextropropoxyphene, a popular analgesic (opioid painkiller) for mild to moderate pain. The 65mg capsule was a common dosage. (Its effects were questionable and in the late 1970s it was associated with suicide. It was finally banned in the US in 2010.)

date-time group (DTG) Official manner of presenting the date and time in military documents using the 24-hour clock with the date shown by day, month, and year (DD/MMM/YYYY), not the usual civilian month, day, and year. The time and time zone preceded the date. Example: 1600Z02FEB1968 = 4:00 PM on 2 February 1968 ZULU Time Zone. See "ZULU Time." Days were shown as two-digits, the month always in three upper case letters, and the year in four digits. To determine military time between the hours of 1300 to 2400 (1 PM to 12 AM) subtract 12 hours; e.g. 1800 Hours equals 6:00 PM civilian time. (Leap years [366 days] were 1960, 1964, 1968, and 1972.)

deadlined Vehicle or aircraft mechanically disabled and undergoing repair. Destroyed or unrepairable vehicles and aircraft might be cannibalized for repair parts, which were always in short supply. See "hangar queen."

Dear John letter Letter from a girlfriend, fiancée, wife, or mother (just kidding) terminating a relationship. Shattering to say the least, there was little a serviceman could do in response other than write his own letter back, which seldom changed the situation. In some units men posted their Dear John on a bulletin board and the first sergeants awarded the best of the month a case of beer.

Delayed Entry Program DEP allowed volunteers to sign a contract formally enlisting in the service with up to a 90-day delay. He was not sworn in until he reported for enlistment on the agreed date. Being a volunteer, he could withdraw with no ill consequences. The time did not count toward time in service or grade.

Delta, the Mekong River Delta region of RVN; operationally the same general area as IV CTZ containing 12 provinces. *Đồng bằng Sông Cửu Long* (Nine Dragon River Delta). The over 15,600 sq mi of the mostly flat and open Delta is crisscrossed by over 2,000mi of rivers and streams and 2,500mi of manmade interconnecting canals.

demo Demolitions: explosives, detonating cord, blasting caps, fuses, and firing devices.

demo pit Excavation or crater in which defective, dud, and captured munitions and materials were destroyed by detonating demo charges and/or burning.

Dentyne wrapper. Army Good Conduct Medal. The name derives from the cinnamon-flavored chewing gum's red and white package—the medal's ribbon is red and white. Usually pronounced "Dintine." Awarded for exemplary behavior, efficiency, and fidelity during a three-year hitch. Some called it, "I didn't catch the clap award."

Depuy fighting position/bunker Two-man fighting position championed by MG William E. Depuy (1919–92) commanding the 1st Infantry Division 1966–67. Pronounced "De-pew." It featured a frontal berm and overhead cover with firing ports angled on the ends to achieve overlapping fields of fire around a perimeter.

WORDS OF THE VIETNAM WAR: ALPHA TO ZULU • 47

Unpopular owing to the time and effort to construct, often taking half the night and limiting sleep. Troops also complained it prevented fire and observation to their direct front. Aka "Hay Hole," renamed after MG John H. Hay, Jr. (1917–95), commanding 1st Infantry Division 1967–68. The position itself was the same, but on firebase perimeters they were positioned in two lines with one second-line position covering two perimeter positions. The positions offered improved protection and after the war were adopted Army-wide as "frontal berm fighting positions."

DEROS   Date Eligible for Return from Overseas. Pronounced "dee-roes." The end date of the Army 365-day tour of duty ("the lost year"), when a soldier should return to the States as an "overseas returnee." The Marines had a 13-month (395-day) rotation with the return date called the Rotation Tour Date (RTD). The Army tour date began on the day the soldier departed the States, even if by ship. The Marines counted it from the day they arrived in Vietnam.

detcord   Detonating cord. Fuse-like high-velocity (6,400 meters/second) explosive contained in a ¼in flexible plastic tube to link multiple demolition charges for simultaneous detonation. Aka "Cordtex" and "Primacord."

deuce and a half   2½-ton 6x6 M35-series cargo trucks built by REO Motor Car, Kaiser, and AM General from 1950 to 1971. The most widely used cargo truck could transport 2½ tons cargo cross-country or 5 tons on improved roads.

dictator   Demanding and over-controlling CO or other leader who truly means it when he says the Army is not a democracy. Autocratic, authoritarian, oppressive, dictatorial, tyrannical, domineering, draconian, and iron-fisted. A "Little Hitler" for extremists.

Dig it?   "Do you understand?" "Yeah, I dig it." "Can you dig it?" "I get it." When one "digs it," it is usually a positive thing. "I dig it"—I like it. It has nothing to do with "digging in," i.e., digging a foxhole.

dime-nickel   "10-5," radio slang for 105mm howitzers.

dipshit   1) Brimmed field or bush hat with one side of the brim turned down. Australian Digger hat, aka "slouch hat." The Australian-style bush hat was often worn by Air Commandos and was never properly called a "boonie hat."

2) Much disliked person. "He's a card-carrying (q.v.) dipshit." A "dipstick," an unessential person.

Dirty Thirty/Third   General term for a platoon or detachment of approximately 30 men. Usually prefixing a unit designation if bearing "thirty" in its designation, e.g., "The Dirty Thirty of Thirty-Three" meaning Special Forces Operational Detachment B-33. The term "Dirty Third" was also used by some units designated the "3d."

ditch guns   M14 and M16A1 rifles, handheld M60 MGs, M79 grenade launchers, and pump shotguns carried aboard "gun trucks" (q.v., armed convoy escort trucks) to defend against close-in attacks, thus "ditch guns," as the enemy sought cover in roadside ditches to be under the arc of fire of truck-mounted MGs.

ditty bopping   Traipsing through the jungle or up a road or trail without a care in the world. Implied lax security and inattention, haphazardly carefree individuals with weapons not at the ready. Believed derived from the Vietnamese *Đi đi* (to go away) and the 1950s bop-style dancing.

DivArty   Division Artillery, the artillery command controlling a division's organic and attached artillery units—4–6 battalions. Commanded by a colonel. Pronounced "div-arr-tee."

DMZ   Vietnam Demilitarized Zone, aka "17th Parallel"* or "the Zee," which was mostly north of the DMZ, although the Parallel ran through the northeastern portion of the DMZ on the coast and at the mouth of the Ben Hai River. The Ben Hai served as the dividing line for some three-quarters of the DMZ's length. The DMZ was just over 100km long and roughly 10km wide, its width varying as it ran from the South China Sea westward to the Laotian border. North Vietnam ignored the DMZ, and Free World Forces, while not entering it, did bombard it. Established 21 March 1954, dissolved 1975.

* Actually 17 degrees 0 minutes 54 seconds North latitude.

Doc   Doctor. Could informally refer to any medical personnel, not only unit surgeons. Platoon medics/aidmen were frequently called "Doc," as well as "Bones," "pill-pusher," "pill-roller," or "bandaid." In the Army they were officially designated "medical or company aidmen," and commonly called "aidmen" or "medics." The term "corpsman" was used by Navy medical personnel (officially "pharmacist's mates") assigned to the Marine Corps. "Corpsman" was not used by the Army. "Corpsman up!" was the call for help. To the extent possible, the same aidman was attached to and became part of a specific platoon.

dog and pony show   Full-fledged staff briefing designed more to impress than provide information. Nothing like today's over-produced PowerPoint slide presentations. These were simply big white paper flip charts or the backs of old map sheets and felt markers.

dogfight   1) Particularly vicious and/or confused firefight (q.v.). (Was there ever an "organized" firefight?)
2) Another use describes an unattractive or unrefined date: "She's so ugly I wouldn't take her to a dogfight." "She fell out of the ugly tree."

Doggies   Marine name for Army soldiers. From the WWII "Dogface."

dogleg   Sharp bend in a road. A possible convoy ambush point on an improved road as it slowed traffic and blocked the convoy's intra-visibility. Also used as a visual landmark/reference point by helicopters owing to its distinctive shape. "We're two klicks south of the dogleg."

dog tag   Identity tags or "ID tags." Each serviceman was issued two stainless steel ID tags on a ball-and-chain necklace; the second, smaller, tag would be turned into headquarters if an individual was deceased. The other tag remained with the body. ID tags were to be worn on the person at all times. A religious symbol, memento, locker key, and/or P-38 can opener may have been on the necklace, technically prohibited. Some individuals threaded a dog tag on the lowest boot lace on one or both boots. The theory was that if one was decapitated the tags around the neck would be lost; in fact, there was a higher probability of losing one or both feet. Earlier production tags still in use had a notch in one end. It was rumored the notch was jammed between the front teeth of the deceased—entirely untrue. It was a positioning notch for an obsolete handheld tag stamping machine. Data included full name, serial number or Social Security number (from March 1968—required on all tags from July 1969), date of birth, and blood group. Today Vietnamese vendors sell "found" G.I. dog tags and other paraphernalia. Gullible tourists buy up all they can in hopes of returning them to veterans' families. The tags are fakes.

dog tag silencer   To prevent any noise from ID tags, commercially made clear plastic slip-on covers plus a ¼in-diameter clear plastic tube for the necklace (often discarded) were available. Another type consisted of a pair flexible plastic rectangular pieces stretched around both tags' rims. Others wrapped their tags in black plastic electrical or 100-mph tape (duct tape).

Domino Theory   The political theory that the downfall of a country overtaken by communism would lead to the fall of a neighboring country, followed by others. It mostly identified with RVN and the subsequent fall of neighboring countries if North Vietnam prevailed. The theory was prominent from the 1950s into the 1980s. It was partly realized with the subsequent rapid fall of Cambodia and Laos. It stopped at Thailand.

donkey dick   Flexible nozzle for 5gal fuel cans. Aka "filler nozzle," "neck," or "gooseneck."

Do Not Boil   Precaution printed on nylon air-ventilating "jungle boot" (q.v.) insoles leading to grunts saying, "Don't boil 'em, peel and eat 'em."

Don't call me sir. I work for a living.   The usual response by Army drill sergeants when accidently addressed as "Sir" by recruits, or for that matter, any NCO called "Sir." However, through initial training Marine drill instructors were addressed as "Sir."

"Don't know shit from Shinola." Truly dumb person. Another way of putting it was, "Doesn't know his asshole from a hole in the ground." Shinola was formally a popular shoe polish brand. The use of the brand did not reflect on its quality, but was used simply because of the alliteration and its familiarity to soldiers. The phrase emerged in WWII when the Army wore brown footwear prior to 1958 as opposed to the current black. Another version was, "Don't know shit from floor wax." The firm operated from 1907 and folded in 1960. Regardless, the catchy phrase remained in use through the Vietnam War.

Don't sweat it. "It's no sweat," meaning, "Don't worry about it; it's no big deal. It don't mean nothin' (q.v.)." Many Vietnamese understood the meaning of "no sweat" and it became part of the vernacular. ("Don't sweat the small stuff" idiom did not emerge until 1979.)

Donut Dollies Female American Red Cross (ARC) volunteers serving refreshments and providing recreational activities and entertainment to troops in bases and hospitals. Officially known as Supplemental Recreational Activities Overseas (SRAO) and Service to Military and Veterans Hospitals (SMVH). Aka "biscuit bitches"—tongue-in-cheek nickname rather than derogatory. They were much appreciated. Three of the 1,120 women died in Vietnam.

donut reel MX-306 A/G telephone wire dispenser with a half-mile of WD-1/TT field telephone wire. A donut-shaped, canvas-covered wire spool. See "commo wire."

door gun Free-mounted MG in the side doors of certain helicopter models: M1919A4, M60, M60D, M2 (.50-cal), and M134 minigun.

door gunners Huey UH-1 helicopters and others had an MG mounted in both side doors. One was manned by the assigned crew chief, but the other was unmanned according to T/O&Es (q.v.). They were manned by unrated volunteers from all units. Scores of what were designated MG, aerial gunner, automatic rifle, or door gunner platoons under Operation *Shotgun* were organized in Hawaii from 1963 to 1966 by the 25th Infantry Division for 90-day temporary duty tours. Aka "Shotgun platoons" as they rode as escorts as did Old West stagecoach shotgun guards. They made per diem, combat pay, and flight pay, all tax exempt. Later dedicated door gunners were assigned on regular tours.

double A bats AA 1.5-volt batteries for pen flashlights, portable transistor radios, cassette tape recorders/players, cordless electric razors, and other portable electrical devices and appliances. There always seemed to be a shortage in the PX/BX. (BA-3058 military number.)

douche bag Obnoxiously despicable person. Aka "shit bag," "shit bird," "shit brick," or "dipshit."

dove   Peace-seeking opponent of the Vietnam War. Aka "peacenik" or "peace lover." See "fence-sitter/rider" and "hawk."

downrange   1) Portion of firing ranges forward of the firing line or firing positions. The area containing the targets and impact areas—"range fan." Prior to opening fire on a range the safety NCO shouted over the PA, "Is there anyone downrange?" three times.

2) "I'm going downrange" referred to an individual with orders for Vietnam. Marines on Okinawa referred to Vietnam as "down south."

dozer tank   M48-series Patton main battle tank mounting an M8 dozer blade for obstacle breaching, vegetation and rubble clearing, berm construction, and mine clearance. Allotted one per tank company.

Draft, the   Males were conscripted for two years under the Selective Service Act of 1948, reestablished after the WWII induction act expired in 1947. There were over 8,700,000 service members serving between 1964 and 1975. 3,403,000 had been deployed to Southeast Asia. Roughly one-third had been inducted, aged 18–26. Some 2,594,000 actually served in Vietnam. In 1965 some 20 percent of the troops were draftees. By 1970 they were comprised of 70 percent draftees. The Air Force and Navy did not accept draftees. The eligible age was raised to 35 in 1967. Married men were ineligible for the draft until August 1965. One could "volunteer" for the draft through his draft board for a period of his choosing rather than wait to be selected. 2,215,000 were drafted into the Army and Marines during the Vietnam War. Only 42,600 were drafted into the Marines and not all deployed to Vietnam. The draft ended on 27 January 1973 and the draft registration requirement was eliminated in 1975.

Draft Card   Officially the *Selective Service System Notice of Classification* (SSS Form No. 110) with revisions on 05/07/63, 11/10/65, and 05/25/67. Men were required to register for conscription at age 18. During the war it became a common form of protest to burn or tear up draft cards; the first such "mass" burning took place in New York City on 12 May 1964. There were instances when protesters gave the appearance of destroying draft cards when they were, in fact, folded index cards. Card burning was outlawed in August 1965. Upon conscription or voluntary enlistment, recruits turned in their card, although some managed to retain theirs as a memento.

draft dodger   An individual failing to register for conscription; someone who actively sought deferments, evaded authorities, and sometimes resorted to fleeing overseas (estimated 100,000), especially Canada. Amnesty was granted 16 September 1974 and a pardon on 21 January 1977 regardless of circumstances. Men joining the National Guard or Reserves were sometimes accused of "draft-dodging," but in reality they contributed to national defense and were obligated to complete six years' Guard/Reserve duty. See "Weekend Warriors."

Dragon Wagon   50-ton M15A2 eight-wheel tank transporter semi-trailer (aka "low-boy") towed by a 10-ton M123 tractor-trailer. The nickname originated in WWII with the M26 tractor-truck towing the 45-ton M15A1 trailer.

drive on   Press on, keep going, push yourself, never give up.

drive on rag   Scarf or towel draped loosely around the neck to wipe off sweat and pad slings and shoulder straps. This could be an issue OG (olive green) bath towel, triangular bandage, or issue neckerchief.

Drop a dime.   Sometimes "Drop a nickel." This was directed by a radio speaker telling the receiver to change the radio's frequency by dropping it 10 or 5 megahertz (MHz) to an unauthorized frequency for a brief "private conversation." Upon its completion they would return to the primary frequency. This was done informally as opposed to using assigned alternate frequencies. It might also be used because of static, interference, or weak signal on the primary. Of course anyone on the net could change frequencies and listen in, but this was seldom done.

dry hole   Area or point reconnoitered by reconnaissance elements or swept in a search and clear operation and no enemy or "caches" (q.v.) found. Indications of the enemy may have been found, but none were present. (Originally an oil well driller's grievance.)

dry season   The November to April dry season or northeast monsoon with little or no rain. Soldiers insisted there were actually three seasons: wet, dry, and dusty, which occurred at one-hour intervals. See "wet season."

dry shave   A recruit neglecting to shave or failing to shave properly might be required to dry shave without the benefit of water or shaving cream. (Straight razors were prohibited as dangerous weapons.)

dual-hatted   Commanders or staff officers of usually larger commands with responsibilities for two different organizations/duties. One example: MG John Hay was Commanding General of "Hurricane Forward"—the forward tactical HQ of II Field Force, Vietnam during the Tet Offensive; he was also the Commanding General of Task Force HAY, conducting IIFFV tactical operations in and around Saigon. This occurred too at lower echelons. For example, an infantry battalion's communications officer (part of the staff) was dual-hatted as the communications platoon leader.

dud, misfire, and jam   There is a difference. A "dud" projectile or other explosive ordnance device is one that fails to explode on impact or other ignition. A "misfire" is a cartridge or some other ordnance propellant system failing to fire, launch, or ignite. A "jam" is a mechanical failure or malfunction of a weapon, especially if caused by the cartridge or a damaged part.

Duffle Bag Platoon   Individuals in Army Basic experiencing physical or less than adequate weight loss difficulties were detailed to the "Duffle Bag Platoon." They remained in their normal platoons, but afterhours were given remedial training to bring them up to standard. "Duffle bag" sometimes referred to an overweight person.

Dumb as a rock.   Pretty stupid. "Lump on a log." "Dumb as a brick" or a "stump."

Duster   M42A1 full-tracked twin 40mm Bofors air defense gun used for ground fire support, firebase defense, and convoy escort. Its nickname originated in Vietnam where it "dusted off" ridge and hill sides. Some say its name was owed to the columns of dust fast-running M42s made in the desert at Ft Bliss, Texas and New Mexico, where crew training took place.

DUSTOFF   Code name for medical evacuation (MEDEVAC) helicopters (q.v.). Originally the call sign for the first such unit, 57th Medical Detachment (Helicopter Ambulance) in 1963, but adopted by all MEDEVAC units as a universal call sign.

DX   Direct Exchange. When a damaged piece of equipment or weapon is turned in for repair/salvage and immediately exchanged for a working one. "DX'ed" came to mean replace or exchange. "He DX'ed his girlfriend."

E   ECHO

E-1 through E-9   In the Army an enlisted man's pay grade was often used in lieu of the formal rank title. "He was promoted to E-5 (SGT)." E = Enlisted. However, Specialists 4 through 7 were referred to as "Spec 4," for example, rather than by their pay grade. (All armed services had the same pay scale for E-1 to E-9.) Marines did not use pay grade designations, but formal rank titles only.

Eagle Flight   Small airmobile reaction forces formed by Special Forces in 1965. Consolidated with the growing Mobile Strike Forces in 1966.

eagles   1) The spread-winged eagle rank insignia of a colonel (O-9) (silver full-color, black subdued) (Captain in Navy).

2) US Coat of Arms-style spread-wing eagles were displayed on Spec 4–7 rank insignia. Aka "birds" or "squashed mosquitos." It was also displayed on the "Unassigned to Branch" (aka "Branch Immaterial") collar insignia worn by Special Forces EM (Enlisted Men) from 1953 to 1987.

Easter Offensive   The 30 March to 22 October 1972 NVA offensive (*Chiến dịch Xuân Hè 1972*) was an effort to seize key regions from which to launch future offensives. Most US ground forces had departed. The NVA deployed significant conventional forces attacking across the DMZ, into the Central Highlands, and north and east of Saigon. The ARVN fought well, receiving significant air and logistical support from the US. The invasion was repelled with heavy losses in personnel and equipment on both sides.

eat it "Bite it, bite me, eat me, you know what you can do with it." It could simply imply, "eat the lead or eat the pain."

eight-inch *or* **eight-incher** 8in (203mm) M110 self-propelled howitzer, the most accurate and second longest ranged field piece in the US artillery inventory. The 8in M55 self-propelled howitzer saw limited use with the Marines.

eighty-one 81mm (3.1in) M1 and M29 mortars widely used by Free World forces.

eighty-two 82mm (3.2in) Soviet BM36 (ChiCom Type 53) mortars.*

* US/NATO 81mm ammunition was the one type of ammunition that could be fired in ComBloc weapons, but not vice versa. This led to rumors of several other types of ComBloc weapons which could fire using US/NATO ammunition, but we could not fire theirs in ours. With the exception of the 81mm and 82mm mortars, no other US/NATO ammunition could be fired in ComBloc weapons.

elephant grass This dense 4–8ft and taller grass (*cỏ voi*) of the bamboo family covered vast swatches of the lowlands and highlands. Foot movement was slow and visibility only a few feet. Helicopters could not land in it as it hid obstacles such as tree stumps, logs, and termite mounds. It was so dense it could not be determined if the surface below was water covered. Difficult to move through owing to its density, it did not offer shade from the sun, it blocked any breeze, harbored ants, and the feet-long serrated leaf blades could give "paper cuts."

elephant turd 500gal black rubber (neoprene) fuel bladders carried in 2½-ton cargo trucks and CH-47 helicopters (see "bladder bird"), or positioned on airfields and motor pools for refueling. 500gal = 3,200 pounds.

11 Bulletstopper 11B was the MOS for a light infantryman. Aka "11 BRAVO," "11 Bush," "11 Bang-Bang," "bullet catcher," "bullet magnet," "grunt," and the little used "jungle bunny." 11Bs could be small unit leaders, riflemen, grenadiers, automatic riflemen, machine gun and recoilless rifle gunners, and RTOs.

Note: Other 11-series infantry MOSs were 11C (mortarman), 11H (antitank gunner), and 11F (operations and intelligence sergeant). Prior to 1965 the rifleman MOS was 11110. A Marine rifleman was MOS 0311, which also included "11."

engineer tape White textile tape, 2in wide, 500ft roll. Intended for marking minefields, cleared passage lanes, obstructions, booby-traps, and any other hazard. On bases it marked tent guy lines, barbed wire, open holes, and other nighttime trip-obstructions.

e-tool Entrenching tool; a small folding shovel carried by individual soldiers. One learned *never* to call it a "little shovel." The M1943 lacked a folding pick head, which the M1951 possessed. The M1967 collapsible "tri-fold" e-tool was all-metal; no pick.

expedient Expedients were non-standard methods of using materials and equipment to overcome some seemingly insurmountable problems in a variety of situations. It meant the adaptation or modification of existing items, materials, and techniques to overcome a problem or fulfil a shortage. The Infantry School sold (for 30¢ plus 5¢ postage) an 88-page *Field Expedient Handbook* (1964) of examples to encourage further ideas.

exploding booby-trapped ammunition In 1968–69 MACV-SOG reconnaissance teams covertly left single cartridges or clips of 7.62mm AK/SKS, 12.7mm MG, and 82mm mortar rounds on trails or in VC/NVA ammunition caches. Known as Project Eldest Son, Italian Green, or Pole Bean (depending on the period), these rounds were modified to explode when fired, destroying the weapons and killing or wounding the operators. Some VC/NVA units refused to use ammunition that had not been under their control. Casualties are unknown, but it is known to have affected morale. American authorities warned US troops not to use captured ammunition, it being "defective."

extract To pick up a reconnaissance team or an infantry unit from within enemy territory by helicopter or watercraft. An extraction. See "insert."

extraction ladder Two types of 80ft ladders with 12in- or 36in-wide aluminum rungs with thin side cables were lowered from Hueys for reconnaissance teams to climb into the hovering helicopter when vegetation and obstacles prevented landing. The team could clip themselves to the ladder with snaphooks (q.v.) and ride it out during a hot extraction. A danger was dragging the ladder-riders through treetops. If necessary, teams could be inserted by climbing down the ladder, although this was slow and seldom practiced, with rappelling being preferred.

Eye Corps I Corps Tactical Zone, the northernmost of the four regional corps tactical zones (CTZs) and abutting the North Vietnam DMZ and Laos. Pronounced "eye core." Included the five northernmost provinces.

F FOXTROT

F6 From the Intelligence Sources Reliability Rating. It rates the reliability of information sources considering two factors: source reliability history and estimated information reliability. "F6" was sometimes used as a humorous nickname: "reliability unknown and probability and validity of information cannot be determined." Actually "E5" is a less credible rating, meaning "source unreliable and information improbable." A specific intelligence report could be rated as "B4," for example.

Source Reliability	Information Reliability
A Reliable	1 Confirmed by independent sources
B Usually reliable	2 Probably true

C Fairly reliable	3 Possibly true
D Not usually reliable	4 Doubtful
E Unreliable	5 Improbable
F Reliability unknown	6 Difficult to say

faggot (fag)   Homosexuality was prohibited in the military and admitting homo-sexuality prevented one from enlisting or resulting in an "other than honorable discharge" if discovered. Generally, at this time homosexuality was not widely accepted nor condoned by society. Common terms were "homo," "queer," "fairy," "sissy," and "pervert." The term "gay" was just coming into general use and still sounded strange in the homosexual context. Even "queer" was still used to say one was odd or unusual or that something felt queer (different). "Dyke" and "Butch" were used to describe lesbians, who were generally rejected by heterosexual feminists. Considered offensive today, in the 1960s many lesbians preferred "dyke" while "straights" thought it rude.

Farmer by day, guerrilla by night.   A literal description of VC Local Forces.

farts   Take a bunch of guys, with poor to marginal diets, plus illnesses, etc.—yes, there was a lot of farting. One could be a "fart face," "fart head," or simply a "fart." "A fart in a hurricane" meant a feeble, pointless effort. "A fart in the dark. There's no one to blame." Someone might say, "Keep talking lieutenant, we'll find you." "He who smelt it dealt it."

fart sack   Sleeping bags were virtually nonexistent in Vietnam. In the northern mountains night temperatures could be chilly. Rather than sleeping bags, a poncho liner or wool blanket might be placed inside a poncho if rainy.

fast-mover   High-performance jet fighters flown by "zoomies" as opposed to helicopters and prop-driven aircraft—"slow-movers."

fatal hookup   Incorrect manner of threading a rappelling rope through a carabiner (aka "snap-link," q.v.) when rappelling down a cliff or from a helicopter. If threaded incorrectly the rope will slip out of the carabiner and the individual goes into a brief freefall.

Fat Farm   If recruits couldn't make it through the Marine physical fitness program they could be sent to the Physical Conditioning Platoon for however long it required to lose weight and get in shape.

fatigues   Army Olive Green Shade 106 (aka "OGs") field and work uniforms. Pronounced "fa-tigues." Satirically pronounced "fat-i-gues." (The Marines used the term "utilities," q.v.).

Fayettenam   Fayetteville, North Carolina, outside of Ft Bragg. Known for its Hay Street bar fights and other shenanigans.

Federal Holidays

The recognized dates of Federal, public, or "legal" US holidays changed during the Vietnam War. These were days on which Stateside Federal and usually state and county offices were closed for business along with banks and other financial institutions. The closure of businesses depended on the specific holiday and commercial practices. States occasionally recognize different dates. While the holidays were celebrated in different ways (especially special dinners on Thanksgiving and Christmas), in Vietnam there were no "days off," but holidays were recognized to the extent possible. Near the war's end, the days on which certain holidays were recognized were changed by the Uniform Monday Holiday Act of 1968 and took effect on 1 January 1971 to increase the number of three-day weekends.

Holiday	Date before 1971	Date from 1971
New Year's Day	1 January	1 January
Washington's Birthday*	22 February	3rd Monday in February
Memorial Day	30 May	Last Monday in May
Veterans Day†	11 November	4th Monday in October
Columbus Day	12 October	2nd Monday in October
Labor Day	1st Monday in September	1st Monday in September
Thanksgiving Day	4th Thursday in November	4th Thursday in November
Christmas Day	25 December	25 December

* Aka Presidents Day.
† Veterans Day was known as Armistice Day prior to 1954. It was moved back to its traditional 11 November in 1978. The Marine Corps' Birthday is celebrated on 10 November.

Feel for the ground. The developed awareness of the nuances of the terrain a unit is on. The gradation of slopes, vegetation, water courses, terrain features, and how it effects movement and visibility, all coupled with the changing local weather conditions. The man on the ground develops a feel for terrain and understands terrain can vary drastically even within a small area. Commanders in the rear or orbiting at 1,500ft in helicopters may think they understand the terrain. They do not and should accept the appraisal of the man on the ground.

fence sitter/rider One who wasn't really for or against the war; an "undecided voter." See "dove" and "hawk."

fever of undetermined origin Fevers of undetermined origin were found in Vietnam and FUOs made up one-fourth to one-half of all fever cases. Few resulted in death. Most identified fever cases were malaria and dengue ("break bone fever," q.v.).

field commissions NCOs could be granted field ("battlefield") commissions by MACV as 2d lieutenant (O-1) and no higher in spite of rumors of higher ranks being granted. It was required that applicants possess at least one valor decoration.

field dressing Troops were issued two field dressings to carry in their first aid pouch for entry and exit wounds or multiple fragmentation wounds. Often only one dressing was carried. Medics/aidmen carried additional. Aka "bandage." The VC recovered discarded US dressings then washed and reused them. Vietnamese girls used dressings as sanitary napkins, trading with soldiers for them. The VC would use sanitary napkins as field dressings, buying them up prior to operations.

field 1st sergeant Unofficial temporary duty position. In training or combat the "field first" was usually a platoon sergeant appointed to undertake 1st sergeant duties in the field while the actual 1st sergeant remained in the cantonment area/firebase, overseeing company administration, discipline, and supply. In some units they were employed as "operations sergeants" or "training NCOs." In the Marines the "company gunnery sergeant" (aka "company gunny") performed similar duties.

field strip a cigarette After extinguishing a cigarette, if there was no "butt can" (q.v.) available the cigarette was "disassembled" by hand-shredding the paper, remaining tobacco, and the filter into tiny bits and dropped it on the ground if not thrown in a wastebasket. No bits were to be large enough to require pick-up during police call (q.v.).

field strip a weapon Extent the weapon's operator was authorized to disassemble a weapon for cleaning and minimal maintenance. "Field strip" can mean to disassemble anything.

fifty-cal Browning .50-cal M2 MG. Aka "ma-deuce" (deuce = two), "fifty," and "Number 50" (the Vietnamese term along with "M50"). Often called the HB M2, HB = heavy barrel.

fifty-one cal Soviet 12.7mm DShKM-1938/46 MG (ChiCom Type 54). Myth had it that US .50-cal ammunition could be fired in the DShKM, but ComBloc ammunition could not be fired in the US .50-caliber. Not true. Both weapons were

.511-cal, but the US cartridge was shorter, and case dimensions and feed links were much different. Neither round could be fired in the other weapon.

fifty-seven   The 57mm (2.2in) M18A1 recoilless rifle used by the ARVN, CIDG, and VC/NVA. They also used the ChiCom 57mm Type 36 RR, a copy of the M18A1.

fighting camp   Later Special Forces camps were "hardened" with more effective perimeter barbed-wire barriers, bunkers for key facilities, more crew-served weapons, increased perimeter MG bunkers, and a fortified inner perimeter to better withstand attacks and sieges.

fighting knives   A wide variety of privately purchased hunting or sheath knives were used. They were more commonly used as utility knives, i.e., as tools rather than for fighting. Randalls and Gerbers were very popular, as were the Marine Ka-Bar (q.v.), Army M3, and Air Force survival (q.v.) knives as well as many other low cost "hunting knives" with 5–7in blades.

final protective fires   Final concentrations of fire in an established defensive (perimeter) to include around a firebase or other defended installation. This includes mortar and artillery defensive concentrations (DEFCONS) fired into or on the outer edge of the barrier wire. When signaled, MGs would fire along their FPF lines interlocking diagonally and crisscrossing around the perimeter. Riflemen and grenadiers would increase their un-aimed volume of fire.

fire arrow   Arrow-shaped wooden frame 8 or so feet long that rotated 360 degrees. Emplaced in Special Forces and some other bases. Several cans were attached to the fire arrow's shaft and V-shaped arrowhead. Electric lights or candles were set in each can. If the camp was attacked the arrowhead was lit and between one and seven lights on the shaft were lit, indicating the range and direction of the attacking enemy—each light indicating 100m range. They fell from use as radio communications improved.

firebase   Fire support bases serving as unit basecamps and secure positions for artillery fire support plus support for neighboring FSBs. Also designated forward operating bases (FOBs) or landing zones (LZs). The Marines called them "combat bases." They were identified by numbers, boastful names, local terrain features, names/terms associated with the unit, Vietnamese place names, fallen heroes, etc. They could be temporary or "permanent." They could be occupied by as little as a firing battery with security to a massive divisional base.

firecracker   The 155mm M449 and 8in M404 improved conventional munition (ICM) projectiles. They would airburst, ejecting 60 and 104 sub-munitions (HE-frag cluster bomblets), respectively, which bounced 6ft on impact to detonate with a firecracker-like ripple of fragmentary explosions. They were particularly lethal to troops in the open and in open-topped positions. Dud bomblets were hazardous to people moving through an impact area.

firefight   Short-term close-range engagement between small units. They could be over within minutes or escalate into a large-scale engagement as additional units were committed. It might be called the "15-second war," that being a typical duration.

Firefly   Seven C-123 aircraft landing lights were mounted on a traversable frame in the door of Huey gunships. Forward-firing MGs and rocket pods engaged detected ground targets. It proved to be too bright, reflecting glare from vegetation and making it difficult to detect personnel and small objects. See "Nighthawk."

Fire for effect!   Once artillery or mortar fire had been adjusted or "walked" onto the target the order was given, "Fire for effect!" The specified number of rounds were fired to neutralize the target. Informally, it can mean, "Finish the job or clobber someone"; e.g. "The Ol' Man fired for effect when I walked into his office."

Fire in the hole!   A warning shouted three times by demolition men prior to detonating an explosive charge. A traditional dynamite blaster's warning adopted by the Army.

Fire on the tree line.   Suppressive fire from ground units aimed at a wood line occupied by the enemy. Also refers to fire placed on a tree line by gunships. The phrase can mean any dire situation.

fire team   The smallest fire and maneuver elements of a rifle squad.

> Army—Two FTs (ALPHA and BRAVO) per squad, one five-man and one four-man overseen by a SSG squad leader. SGT FT leader, SP4 automatic rifleman,* SP4 grenadier, and one or two PFC riflemen. Mechanized rifle squads possessed an SP4 APC driver.

> Marine—Three FTs (No. 1, 2, and 3) per squad overseen by a SGT squad leader with a LCpl grenadier. Cpl FT leader, LCpl automatic rifleman,* and two PFC riflemen.

* When M14 ARs were replaced by M16A1 rifles the auto riflemen became "designated automatic riflemen," i.e., an M16A1 armed rifleman with an M3 "clothespin bipod" (q.v.) and "authorized" to fire full-automatic. Ineffective, they became just additional riflemen.

fire watch   Temporary wooden barracks built in WWII continued in use on most posts. They were highly susceptible to catch fire. One could become fully engulfed within 5 minutes owing to aged dry lumber, no insulation, and flammable materials. Fire guards walked one-hour shifts, pacing both floors or polishing their boots from retreat to reveille.

Firm, The   Central Intelligence Agency. (Aka "The Agency.") The CIA ("spooks") controlled many of the Special Forces operations through its US Operations Mission prior to June 1963 when operations were placed under US Army Special Forces,

Vietnam. The CIA still controlled national intelligence operations and most covert combat operations in Laos.

First In, Last Out. Motto of the Pathfinders—paratroopers trained to be inserted to guide airdrops and act as tactical air traffic controllers managing helicopter traffic. Three-week course earned Pathfinders the "winged torch badge." See "Black Hats."

1st Up… 1st Up, 2nd Up, and 3rd Up were the order of commitment for standby MEDEVAC helicopters. When the standby 1st Up was launched the 2nd Up became the new 1st Up and a new 3rd Up aircraft and crew were put on standby.

fishhook Reconnaissance team technique used to occupy a RON (q.v.) position. The team moved past the site the patrol leader designated as the RON, hooked or doubled back to the by-passed position, and occupied it quickly in a "wagon wheel" formation (q.v.). If the team was being tracked the pursuing enemy would bypass the RON rather than follow directly into the RON. The team could either withdraw or ambush the following enemy depending on circumstances.

five-by-five "I hear you five-by-five" ("5x5"). "Five-by-one" means a strong radio signal is present, but the vocal (intelligibility) cannot be understood. "One-by-five" means the vocal is understood, but the signal is weak. "Five-by-five" means loud and clear. See "LIMA-CHARLIE." The "in-between" strength codes were seldom used. This International Telecommunication Union practice is not an official military means of reporting signal strength/intelligibility, but was often used informally.

five-five-six 5.56mm (.223-cal) cartridges for M16-series rifles and XM177-series SMGs. "I need a case of five-five-six." Aka "five point five-six." Deficiencies in the "5-5-6" cartridge propellant were the cause of many of the M16's problems.

550 cord Type III 550lb tensile strength, $\frac{5}{32}$ in (4mm) in diameter nylon cord used as parachute suspension line, tie-down cords, "dummy cords" (q.v.), rifle sling substitutes, boot laces, and general use to include repairing web gear. Aka "paracord." OD nylon sheath with 7–9 core nylon yarns. White 550 cord suspension line was used on reserve and training parachutes with white canopies.

Five o'clock Follies Daily MACV press briefing conducted at 1700 hours by the Joint US Public Affairs Office.

five-quarter-ton The 1¼-ton 4x4 M715 cargo truck. Unpopular, underpowered and less-than-robust partial replacement for the ¾-ton M37B1 truck. Built from 1967 to 1969 by Kaiser-Jeep and based on their Gladiator. 1¼ tons = "five ¼ tons." Began to be replaced in 1976.

five-tonner A 5-ton 6x6 truck: "5-ton cargo" (M54) or "5-ton tractor" (M52) differentiated cargo trucks and truck-tractors for semi-trailers. The many variants were built by Diamond T, International Harvester, Kaiser, Kaiser-Jeep, and Mack, 1951–65.

flagpole, the   Higher command headquarters owing to possessing a flagpole and rated to fly the American flag. Only the senior headquarters on a base rated a national color. "You don't want to be near the flagpole. You'll get nailed with extra details."

flak vests   Two types of body armor, aka "armor vests," were issued for ground troops and aviators. Ground troops used the M1952 fragmentation protective body armor (Army), M1955 armored vest (USMC), and M1969 fragmentation protective body armor (all services). Most Army infantrymen did not wear vests in the field, as they were heavy, caused wearers to overheat, restricted movement, and made noise moving through vegetation. Marines were required to wear vests at most times. Aviators wore heavier and more restrictive vests. Aviators employed a number of experimental vests, which hampered aircraft operation and amplified fatigue. The aircrew body armor set was adopted in 1965 and included an insert ceramic chest plate, known as the "chicken plate" or "bullet bouncer." Many door gunners scrounged a second vest and sat on it, but more fire hit choppers slanting upward from the sides.

flare fight   An impromptu, usually good-natured "firefight" within a base using pop-up flares, pen flares, and smoke grenades. Damage and injuries were minimal during such un-condoned pressure-release antics. Also conducted during certain holidays such as New Year's Eve and 4th of July with some degree of tolerance.

flare ship   Helicopter or fixed-wing aircraft fitted with aerial flare dispensers to drop parachute-suspended flares around friendly positions under attack and illuminate the attackers. This allowed the friendly base to fire HE from its mortars and artillery rather than flares, which required different firing calculations. On-call aircraft were on station in high-risk areas, either on ground alert or airborne alert at key times. Aka "flare bird" or "Smokey." The USAF employed C-47s, C-123s, and C-130s for Blind Bat and Candlestick missions.

flashback   A movie plot device depicting an event or scene taking place before the present time in the narrative and inserted into the chronological structure of the work. "Flashback" originated in 1916, but it was not until the early 1970s that the term emerged to describe a stress-induced psychological phenomenon in which an individual had a sudden, vivid re-experience of past events. Related to PTSD (q.v.).

flattops   Beer and soft drinks available through commissary sales and the PX/BX were in cans without ring pull tabs or pop tabs* ("flattops") and were just being introduced in 1964 along with aluminum cans, which were not shipped to Vietnam. This is so they would not pop open in transit in hot cargo ship holds, trucks, and warehouses. A "church key," pocketknife, or "P-38" (q.v.) was necessary to open them. Beer and soda were shipped in pasteboard cases of 24 cans with 48 cases to a pallet (1,152 cans). Beer was $2.40 a case.

* Pop tabs at the time completely detached from the can and did not remain fastened as today's stay-on-tabs.

Fleasville   Leesville, Louisiana, outside of Ft Polk. Aka "Diseaseville." Implies it was a small town and/or possessed infested prostitutes. Some think it should have been memorialized as the stereotypical 1950s and 1960s military town.

flight pay   Aviation Crewmember Monthly Incentive Pay. The pay rate varied depending on pay grade and time in service, ranging from $55 a month for an SP4 under two years to $165 for a CPT over four years. A WO1 helicopter pilot with over two years drew $105.

flip-flops   Rubber shower sandals or thongs. The Vietnamese called them "Japanese slippers" or *dép tông* or *dép xỏ ngón.* They were essential to protect the feet in funky showers and also worn in quarters when off duty. They were introduced to US soldiers serving in Japan after WWII, called *zōri* in Japanese.

floating camp   Many Special Forces camps in the Mekong Delta flooded during the wet season. They were surrounded by large high berms (q.v.), atop which were bunkers and fighting positions. Camp buildings, barracks, facilities, and mortar positions were built on earth mounds or stilt platforms and others on floating platforms using 55gal drums. Footbridges and sampans were used to move about the camp.

flower power   Referred to a vague, free-spirited, unstructured lifestyle intermeshed with casual sex and recreational drug use. Hippies, flower children, long-hairs. Peace-loving, environmentally protective, and antiwar by nature. See "Hippies."

Flying Leathernecks   Marine Aviation crewmen. Marine pilots were officially rated as Naval Aviators.

flying twenty-five $25 advance pay drawn against the basic trainee's first payday to purchase personal necessities. "Flying 25" referred to how fast it disappeared.

FNG   Fucking New Guy. Newly assigned green replacement, "fresh meat," a "green troop." In polite company he was a "Funny New Guy." Within a month or so they were like any other in-country soldier or marine.

"Hey new guy, go and get me a…"

As an FNG (q.v.) one might be ordered by someone in his new unit to go to supply, headquarters, such-and-such shop or office, or wherever and fetch a specific item ASAP:

spool of contour line or gridline;

6 feet of skirmish line;

box of grid squares;

bottle or bucket of rotor wash (helicopter units);

bottle of prop wash (fixed-wing aircraft units);

bottle of liquid squelch (communicatios);

left-handed monkey wrench or left-handed ratchet or left-handed screwdriver or left-handed cleaning rod or left-handed combination tool or damn near anything left-handed;

left-handed smoke-shifter (See what we mean?);

(Beware too of any really strange-sounding wrenches, tools, gages, or greases.)

metric crescent wrench (Aren't they all?);

metric hammer and/or nails;

keys to the parade ground or Area 3;

keys to the flagpole (To turn on the brass globe, which is supposedly a nightlight or aircraft warning light);

Cannon Report (artillerymen) (You may be asked specifically to bring the blue copy);

4-pound can of compression (aviators or mechanics);

can of dehydrated water (It weighs almost nothing);

box of sterile fallopian tubes (medical personnel);

box of tank traps (They are somewhat larger than mousetraps);

pair of pivot shoes (Helps you march better, make tighter facing movements);

compass batteries (They work just as well without them);

case of sky hooks (They attached antiaircraft targets to clouds);

1D-10-T Manual (It translates to IDIOT).

Whether you were fooled or decided it was a hoax, upon return you might tell the original requestor that you were to relay an order to him to fill out the appropriate request form.

Fort Beginning   Ft Benning, Georgia. The Infantry School. A place where so many beginnings began: OCS, NCOC, Jump School, Ranger Course, etc.

Fort Dicks   Ft Dix, New Jersey. The one non-Vietnam-oriented infantry training center. Aka "Fort Pricks." Some soldiers destined for Special Forces or OCS undertook infantry AIT there as they would later receive Vietnam-oriented training.

Fort Garbage   Ft Gordon, Georgia. A signal training school and the only airborne-oriented infantry advanced individual training center.

Fort Head Ft Hood, Texas. Alluded to the marijuana plants growing wild on the base. Troops were turned out to cut and burn the large fields.

Fort Hood 43 A group of 1st Armored Division Black soldiers, mostly Vietnam vets, confined for refusing to perform civil disturbance duty at the August 1968 Democratic National Convention in Chicago. Sentences varied widely.

Fort Lost in the Woods Misery Ft Leonard Wood, Missouri. Aka "Little Korea" owing to the climate. The combat engineer training center.

Fort Piss Ft Bliss, Texas. Air Defense Artillery School where quad-fifty and Duster crews were trained. Most of the post's less than blissful acreage is in New Mexico.

Fort Puke Ft Polk, Louisiana. An infantry training center. Long considered one of the least desirable posts in the US. Aka "Camp Swampy."*

* It is actually not swampy nor was it the namesake for "Camp Swampy" in the 1950–present *Beetle Bailey* cartoon strip, which was influenced by Camp Crowder, Missouri (1941–58) where Bailey's creator served in WWII.

Fort Smell Ft Sill, Oklahoma. The Field Artillery School. So named because of the extent of artillery firing on the base.*

* It is not cordite, which was not used in US propellant charges. Cordite propellant was used by the British and phased out after WWII.

Fort Turd Ft Ord, California. An infantry training center.

Fort Useless Ft Eustis, Virginia. The Transportation School.

forty-five Colt .45-cal M1911A1 pistol. .45-cal ammunition was also used in US SMGs.

Forty MIKE-MIKE Twin 40mm M2A1 antiaircraft guns mounted on M42A2 "Duster" self-propelled vehicles. A single 40mm was mounted on early riverine monitors and C&C boats.

fou gas Mispronounced and misspelled term for a flame fougasse weapon. 20 and 55gal drums filled with jellied gasoline were dug in at an angle around firebases. They were electrically command-detonated with a "kicker" explosive charge in the bottom and an igniter charge on top to ignite the expelled fuel, which would bellow outward in a fireball. Aka "fougas." In Vietnam a major US television network reporter enthusiastically claimed he had "proof" the US was using "chemical warfare agents" in the form of "fou gas." It might have been called "fool's gas" along the lines of "fool's gold." The employment of fougasse weapons are completely legal within the Hague Convention and are not classified as a chemical warfare agent; it is merely gasoline.

4x4 ¼-ton, ½-ton, ¾-ton, and 1¼-ton trucks with four powered wheels (aka "four-by") for improved cross-country mobility and traction. Power can be switched only to the back two wheels when all-powered wheels (4x4) are unnecessary and to reduce fuel consumption.

four-deuce The 4.2in (107mm) M30 mortar. Aka "four-point-two." Used by the US and some by the ARVN.

Four quicks, one slow, and three strongs. This VC tactical doctrine was followed in a logical sequence: slow plan (lengthy preparation), quick advance (movement to the objective from a safe distance), quick attack (rapid surprise attack), strong fight (violence of action), strong assault (concentrated attack), strong pursuit (follow-up attack and consolidation on the objective), quick clearance (collect captured materials, move off the objective), and quick withdraw (disengage and depart before enemy support arrives).

four-star general General (GEN) (O-10). Aka "full general."

Fourteen The 7.62mm M14 rifle replacing the M1 rifle in 1959. The 1st, 25th, and 4th Infantry Divisions arrived in Vietnam armed with M14s as did non-divisional support units. Most Marine units also arrived with the M14. The 5.56mm M16A1 rifle began replacing the M14 in 1967 and was eventually issued Army- and Marine Corps-wide. See "M14 AR."

foxhole One- or two-man fighting position, aka "fighting hole." Usually open-topped, but could have light overhead cover. Depending on its depth, soldiers might fight kneeling or standing, usually the former. The most common was a prone shelter, a slit trench large enough for a man to lie in 1–2ft deep plus the earth parapet surrounding it and called a "grave."

foxhole strength Actual field strength of a company—those actually present for duty—exclusive of those on R&R, leave, AWOL, confinement, hospitalized, ill in quarters, assigned to work details, detached special duty, etc. Aka "paddy strength" in the 9th Infantry Division operating in the Delta.

frag Fragmentation hand grenade inflicting casualties by fragmentation and blast. There were three main types: Mk 2 "pineapple," M26 "lemon," and M67 "baseball" grenades (q.v.). Their wounding radius was 15 meters and their kill radius 5 meters.

frag bag Canvas bag or pack holding fragmentation and other hand grenades stowed in observation helicopters and gunships to drop on targets of opportunity. Ammunition cans were also used.

fragging Fragging was the act of warning, harassing, threatening, wounding, or murdering an NCO or officer and, in some instances, victims were the same rank as the attacker. Sometimes unarmed fragmentation grenades (pin not pulled), teargas, or smoke grenades were used to warn and intimidate. Grenades were used as they are untraceable, unlike firearms. Only approximately 10 percent of fragging incidents were adjudicated. The cause of fragging could be personal grudges, abuse and harassment, overly aggressive and zealous NCOs and officers, inept leaders, and occasionally fragging was tied to drug and racial issues. There were approximately 900 suspected and confirmed fragging incidents in Vietnam between 1969 and 1972 among US forces, mostly in Army and Marine combat units. They resulted in 86 deaths and 714 wounded, including bystanders. Attacks were virtually nonexistent prior to 1969 and extremely rare since the war.

Freedom Bird   Chartered commercial airliners with regular passenger amenities returned troops to the "real world"—the States. Miniskirt-clad stewardesses (now "flight attendants") provided hot meals and cooled damp towels to place on foreheads. A cheer went up as the wheels lifted and another when the pilot announced they had cleared Vietnam airspace. The same occurred when entering US airspace and the wheels touched down. Some vets dropped to the tarmac and kissed USA soil.

Free Fire Zone   An area designated by the HQ responsible for the Tactical Area Of Responsibility (TAOR) in which there were no Free World forces nor friendly civilians present. Any personnel detected within such areas were assumed to be enemy. Regrettably there were incidents in which there still were civilians present who may or may not have been enemy sympathizers. FFZs were a fire control measure affected by rules of engagement. It may have allowed unidentified persons to be engaged at night without confirmation. Engaging units did not have to request approval from higher HQ nor coordinate with other Free World Forces near the FFZ. Aka "free strike zone." See "ROE."

French forts   In the early 1950s the French built hundreds of concrete pillboxes. Occupied by a squad, they protected highways, crossroads, bridges, and key towns. They restricted French maneuver warfare and gave the initiative to the Viet Minh, allowing them to attack where they wanted, and avoid the fixed fortifications. Though mostly abandoned, some were incorporated into Special Forces camps and firebases if favorably located. They were sometimes used as reference points for helicopters as they were easy to spot and prominently marked on maps.

freq   Short for frequency. Pronounced "freak." Radio frequencies calibrated by Megahertz (MHz). See "push."

Friendlies   Free World military forces: US, RVN, Australia, New Zealand, South Korea, Thailand, and the Philippines, plus Republic of China (Nationalist China/Taiwan) training elements.

friendly fire   Fire of any type from friendly elements—air or surface. Friendly fire could be caused by human error, misdirection, incorrect information, or being too close to the impact area.

Frontline is the direction you're facing. The point is there was no frontline in the conventional sense. Units had to prepare all-round (360 degrees, q.v.) defenses and expect the enemy to approach from any direction. The frontline was 18in wide. The term "behind enemy lines" is a misnomer. There were enemy-controlled areas to varying degrees (Indian Country, q.v.), but there were no frontlines with "two up and one back"—two subunits on the frontline and one to the rear in reserve. There was no conventional rear area either. The larger bases were reasonably safe, but a more appropriate name was "secure area."

front-seater The gunner/co-pilot in an AH-1 HueyCobra gunship as he was seated forward of the commander/pilot ("back-seater").

fruit salad 1) The garish award and decoration ribbons and badges worn on the left breast on service and dress uniforms.
2) A .50-cal belt combination of two incendiary (blue tip), two armor-piercing incendiary (silver tip), and one armor-piercing incendiary tracer (red tip, silver band).

Frying Pan Area Cantonment area on Ft Benning, Georgia, where paratroopers undertook training. It seemed to be a particularly hot area in the summer.

Ft Benning School for Boys The US Army Infantry Officers Candidate School (OCS) at Ft Benning, Georgia—5th–9th Student Battalions (OCS), The Student Brigade. Aka "Charm School."

F Troop A unit, regardless of its actual designation, suffering from poor leadership, morale, efficiency, and other problems. Derived from the satirical TV comedy series *F Troop* (1965–67) depicting a fictitious madcap cavalry troop in the mid-1860s. "Those clowns down in the 218th are another F Troop."

FUBAR Fucked Up Beyond All Recognition. Things aren't going well, more so than usual.

Fucking A! Fucking Army! An exclamation of anger or frustration, but in some instances, a declaration of approval. "Leave in Vung Tau? Fuckin' A!" "FTA" (Fuck the Army—seldom spoken phonetically).

Fuckin' Nam "Fucking Vietnam." Self-exclamatory; the ultimate blame for all troubles and woes.

fuck you lizard Named during the Vietnam War, the tokay gecko's (*gekko gecko*) cry sounds distinctively like a chirpy "fuck yooou." The *fuck* sound is quite clear and followed by a half-second pause and an elongated *you*. The gecko's cry may have been in response to the green-colored blue-eared barbet bird which sang REEEE-UP… REEEE-UP, sounding somewhat like "re-up," the offer to reenlist. Many debate if it really sounded like "re-up."

fueler   1,200gal 2½-ton M49 fuel service truck. Aka "fuel truck."

fuel tanker   5,000gal M131 four-wheel semi-trailer towed by a 5-ton M52 truck-tractor. Aka "tanker truck."

full-bird   Colonel (COL, O6). Aka "full-colonel," "bird colonel," or "full-bull." Colonels commanded divisional brigades, regiments, groups, DivArty's, support commands, and served on division and higher staffs.

full field layout   All of a soldier's web gear and field equipment laid out on a poncho or shelter (half of a pup tent, q.v.) on the ground for inspection. See "junk on the bunk."

funny papers   Military topographic map sheets, 1:50,000 scale. The standard tactical map, "topo maps." See "pictomaps."

G   GOLF

G-2   The intelligence officer on a general staff. To "G-2" something was to look into it, examine it, check it out. The term "S-2" was used in the same manner. "I'll G-2 it and see what's going on."

Gama Goat   1¼-ton 6x6 M561 amphibious cargo truck. The double-hulled articulated vehicle was unpopular owing to extensive and difficult maintenance requirements. If loaded with heavy equipment or communications vans, e.g., it might be too heavy to swim. Produced from 1969 to 1973 by Consolidated Diesel Electric Company (CONDEC). "Gama" derived from its designer, Roger Gamaunt.

Garand   .30-cal M1 semi-automatic rifle used by the ARVN up to 1968. There are many weapons designated "M1," but when saying simply "em-one" without further distinction, it customarily meant the M1 rifle, a "soldier's rifle." Some Stateside and overseas Active, Guard, and Reserve units outside of Vietnam still had M1s into the 1970s. Named after its Canadian-American designer, John C. Garand (1888–1974).

garbage can rockets   NVA 107mm and 122mm rockets modified with large over-caliber warheads looking somewhat like garbage cans fitted atop rockets. While delivering a significantly larger payload, they were less accurate and shorter ranged than unmodified rockets.

gasmask   Officially the "M17 and M17A1 protective masks." In some units one would be scolded for calling it a "gasmask." They were used in Vietnam for teargas protection.

gasmask puff   An M17 protective mask that had its cheek filters removed, duct-taped over, and a small hole made in one. The mask was donned, a lit joint (marijuana cigarette) was inserted in the hole, and the wearer inhaled filling the mask with smoke. It could cause one to pass out owing to oxygen displacement.

gear in the rear "The gear in the rear" refers to rear echelon service and support elements on firebases and other installations. "I'll be with the gear in the rear." Popular because it rhymed nicely. "Life in the rear" on the major bases was not significantly different than life in a Stateside base except for the rare rocket attack, being largely restricted to base, various shortages, and the alien environment. A variant was, "I'll be with the beer in rear."

General Giap *Đại tướng* (General) Võ Nguyên Giáp (1911–2013), Minister of Defense of Vietnam (1948–80), the legendary leader of the NVA and mastermind of the North Vietnam victory.

General Orders There were 11 General Orders for Sentries. They were boiled down to a more practical:

1. I will walk my post in a military manner.

2. If there's fire I'll ring this bell.

3. If there's trouble I'll run like hell.

Geneva Convention Card *Armed Forces of the United States Geneva Convention Identification Card* (DD Form 528). A white or off-white card carried in the field rather than the usual Branch of Service Identification Card with a photograph. The Geneva Convention card did not have a photograph and included only the individual's full name, rank and pay grade, branch of service, service number, and date of birth, the only information a prisoner of war was required to report according to the Geneva Convention of 1949.

Get out of jail free card Special identity cards were issued to selected personnel such as the Army Security Agency, Criminal Investigation Division, and MACV-SOG. They included a photo of the bearer, the usual identifying characteristics, and some statement on the back such as: "The possessor of this document is on a classified military assignment. Do not detain or question him. He is authorized to wear civilian clothing, carry a weapon, or pass into restricted areas." Examples of most such cards sold on the Internet are bogus.

Get your head on straight. Get it together, start doing the right thing. Stop being stupid.

"Get your head out of your fourth point of contact." "His head's up his fourth point of contact." Synonymous with "Get your head out of your ass." The "fourth point of contact" is the fourth body part to come in contact with the ground during the side roll of a parachute landing fall (PLF): 1) balls of the feet, 2) side of the calf, 3) side of the thigh, 4) *side of the hip or buttocks*, and 5) side of the back (aka "pushup muscle").

ghost   A person avoiding attention and work details, keeping a low profile, hiding out, out of sight, out of mind. "He's always ghosting." "He's a spook." "Casper the Friendly Ghost,"* a cartoon character. He's "skating," "goldbricking," "lollygagging," and dodging work details. See "goof off."

* Casper dates from earlier cartoon strips, but the first film cartoon was in 1945 with new releases in 1963.

G.I.   Government Issue. Anything to do with the Army. It was not so much used as a term for soldiers as it had been in WWII. It was widely used by the Vietnamese in this manner, which might be pronounced "*jin.*"

G.I. coffeehouses   These coffee cafes were organized by civilian activists support-ing the antiwar movement by inflaming antiwar sentiment among G.I.s. They were opened in towns outside of many military bases. The shops hosted activist speakers and some printed antiwar newsletters. Many were short-lived owing to the pro-military sentiment of locals dependent on the bases for employment and soldiers' paychecks. The first was opened in January 1968 and the last closed in 1974.

gig   To receive a gig during an inspection is to get a black mark; given for any infraction on one's uniform, equipment, or weapon, e.g. it being dirty, damaged, worn, or missing.

gig line   Vertical uniform centerline with the edge of the shirt's front opening, the right end of the belt buckle, and the edge of the trousers' fly opening perfectly aligned. A misaligned gig line during an inspection resulted in a gig.

G.I. Joe   Boys' scale-model action figure introduced in 1964, disproving the conventional wisdom that "boys do not play with dolls." A wide variety of variants and accessories were available. The term quickly came to mean a dedicated overly gung ho soldier.

G.I. party   Detailed top-to-bottom total barracks cleanup in preparation for a coming Saturday inspection. Not a barracks party (q.v.). The Marines call it a "field day."

G.I. proof   Soldiers tended to treat weapons, equipment, and everything else with more than two moving parts roughly. Aka "soldier proof." The attitude seemed to be that gear was made to be treated rough; they have other things on their mind besides being gentle with gear, and there's "always" a replacement available. The point is that any military item used in the field had to be robust and reliable enough to withstand rough treatment, not just endure the environment and normal wear and tear.

G.I. soap   Officially, "soap, toilet (for fresh or salt water use), 4-oz cake." Strong smelling. Most service members bought popular commercial soap brands in the PX/BX.

G.I. town   A community outside of a military base catering to military personnel. At the time this could include numerous bars, pawn shops, tattoo parlors, camera stores, strip clubs (or whatever the local community permitted), and used car dealers. True to the era, while the community relied on the installation for income (including employing local civilians and contractors, selling food, and other goods and services), many in the community exploited service members, doing everything they could to separate G.I.s from their meager salaries, and often looked down on them.

Give him a 5-minute break…   and he'll need to be retrained. Someone perpetually behind the learning curve. Little retention capability. Sometimes self-deprecating: "Give me a 5-minute break and I'll need retraining."

Give me ten!   "Stop what you're doing (usually something wrong) and give me ten good pushups." "Knock 'em out!" "You're not on the ground already?" Jump students when wearing a parachute harness could not do pushups so did ten squat jumps ("Beat your feet/boots!" as the boot tops were slapped at each squat), made more difficult by its weight and restraining straps. An alternative was knocking out 20.

Give the [Vietnamese] barber your firebase's coordinates and he'll give you a free haircut.   Implies that some "friendly" Vietnamese were VC sympathizers.

Glider Patch   Circular red, white, and blue embroidered insignia displaying a parachute canopy and an obsolete Waco CG-4A cargo glider. Worn on the forward side of the garrison cap's (q.v.) left side by enlisted, and right by officers. Aka "airborne cap." Worn by individuals assigned to airborne units whether parachute-qualified or not. Paratroopers only wore this cap with Class A and B uniforms and never the "saucer cap" (q.v.)—"leg cap." A traditional insignia, glider training was last conducted in 1947 and the requirement cancelled in 1951. Some paratroopers sewed a silver dollar coin under the patch for emergency funds and to deliver a hardy slap to the face of an opponent in a bar altercation. Obsolete in 2004.

Globe and Anchor   The "Eagle, Globe, and Anchor" is the USMC's official emblem since 1868 (earlier versions existed). Sometimes called the "EGA," an officially discouraged term. It was worn on uniform collars, headgear ("covers"), displayed on buttons, and black stenciled on the left chest pocket of utilities and the front of utility covers.

Goer   M520 articulated, amphibious 8-ton cargo truck and variants built by Caterpillar. Bored drivers would turn on the bilge pumps to douse oncoming and passing vehicles by "super squirting" them with rainwater accumulated in the cargo compartment.

Go-Go   Four ACH-47A "Guns A Go-Go"* or "Go-Go Birds," up-gunned Chinook helicopters employed from 1964 to 1968 by the 1st Cavalry Division.

* "Go-go dancers" were popular in nightclubs and discotheques from the early 1960s, entertaining crowds by lively dancing on small elevated platforms.

Golden BB   A random lucky shot from any weapon managing to down an aircraft.

golf suit   Wearing of the olive green fatigue uniform with mismatched shades, either the shirt or trousers being more laundered and sun-faded than the other.

good gook   "The only good gook (q.v.) is a dead gook." Derived from "the only good Indian is a dead Indian" Old West sentiment. A crass sentiment caused by the nature of counterinsurgency warfare—a difficult to define and identify enemy, apathy of the population, poorly motivated, undedicated allies, lack of support from home, and conflicting and changing alliances.

goodie box   C-ration or other cardboard box in the corner of an office, shop, bunker, or any workspace. Unused C-rats, accessory packet items, goodies from home, etc. were tossed into a communal box and taken by anyone needing them.

Good patrolling weather.   Informal term for weather conditions beneficial to patrolling. While undefined, most experienced soldiers fully understand the concept. Typically, it meant that the temperature was mild or cool enough to stay comparatively comfortable (although "cool" was seldom experienced in Vietnam) while moving with intermittent light showers or sprinkling or heavy mist/fog. The light rain muffled the sound of footsteps and other noises while moving through vegetation, but was not heavy enough to soak one's clothes. For the static enemy sentries, the light drizzle, especially when coupled with the slightest coolness, made them chilly and uncomfortable and more concerned with staying dry than staying alert. This only reinforced the dreariness and boredom of sentry duty. The fog and mist, while offering the patrol concealment, also limited the patrol's visibility and hampered navigation.

good to go   You're or it's good to go. Ready for action. Sometimes replaced the traditional, "Up!" shouted when a crew-served weapon was ready for action.

goof off   Habitually lazy person performing less than his fair share of work—a shirker, "goofing off," "shamming," "lollygagging." Such a person in the Marines was a "yardbird." See "ghost."

gook   The most common of the many negative and pejorative terms for Vietnamese people (*Kinh*) and other Asians.* Aka "dink," "dip" (from dipshit), "gooker," "goner," "ricebelly," "riceburner," "slant," "slant eye," "slope," "slope-head," "zip," "zipper-head," "Luke the Gook," and "chink" (little used, being reserved mainly for Chinese). The South Koreans referred to Vietnamese as *ddang kong* (peanuts) as Koreans were typically taller.

* "Asians" and "Orientals" were then used interchangeably.

gookaniese   Vietnamese language (*tiếng Việt*). Derisive contraction of "gobbledy-gook" and "Vietnamese."

gook grenades   VC homemade grenades (*luu dan*) made in field and village workshops ("jungle factories," q.v.) using locally available materials. Extremely crude and unsafe. Even expended US smoke grenade bodies and fuses were refurbished as casualty-producing grenades.

Gooks in the wire!   An alert that the enemy was attacking or infiltrating through a base/installation perimeter wire barrier. A dire warning striking immediate alarm.

Gooooood Morning, Vietnam!   The opening line of the AFVN morning radio show, *Dawn Buster*, from 1965 to 1966. The program's DJ was USAF SSgt Adrian J. Cronauer (1938–2018). The fictional movie *Good Morning, Vietnam* (1987) did not accurately reflect his experiences, as the movie was written for entertainment. Cronauer said if he had acted as portrayed in the movie he would have served time in the Ft Leavenworth, Kansas penitentiary. The idiom "Gooooood Morning, Vietnam" became a common greeting, frequently with less than earnest enthusiasm. VC/NVA radio intercept operators would scan through frequencies, enthusiastically saying, "Gooooood Morning, Vietnam!" in hopes of getting a response from an inattentive/bored US radio operator, thus indicating a particular frequency was in use by a US unit and they would monitor it. Cronauer was followed by SP5 Pat Sajak, future *Wheel of Fortune* host, who continued the classic opening line from 1968 to 1969.

Got his shit wired tight.   He has it together, on the ball, a good plan. "He's wired."

GP small, medium, and large   "Tent, general purpose, small, medium, or large." Widely used OD canvas tents for troop shelters/quarters, CPs, supply rooms, mess halls, and any other facility needing temporary weather protection "under canvas." The GP small was hexagonal-shaped (six-sided, "hex tent") and the GP medium and large were rectangular-shaped peaked-top pitch tents.

grab ass   Horseplay, goofing around. "Cut out the grab ass!" "Quit grab-assing around!" "Dicking around."

Grab their belts to fight them.   VC/NVA adage for a close battle tactic. Move in as close to the Free World positions as possible to prevent them from using artillery, mortars, air strikes, and gunships. Within "danger close" (q.v.) ranges.

grass   Marijuana. Aka "pot," "weed," "Mary Jane," "dew," "reefer," and "ganja." Normally smoked or "toked" in hand-rolled cigarettes—"joints." A "roach" was a partly smoked marijuana cigarette butt. A "Bong Son Bomber" was a large joint. The grass was grown and sold locally. Zig-Zag brand cigarette rolling papers were legal and sold in PX/BXs. Purchase or possession of a large amount would draw attention.

Zig-Zags were also brought back from R&R. Cigarette packs of 20 cigarettes being brought into Vietnam when deploying from the States or returning from R&R were required to have the top torn off and the alignment of the cigarettes was checked. Any joints substituted in the pack would be uneven. Specific regional types of grass included: Buddha, Delta Dust, Khmer Rouge, and Laotian Red.

gravel mines   BLU-44/B "Dragontooth" was a small (75mm x 45mm x 45mm) plastic bomblet with 120 loaded in CDU-2/B cluster adapters. Aka "button mines." These were dropped mainly on the Ho Chi Minh Trail and other infiltration routes. Being small, oddly shaped, and subtly colored made them difficult to detect in ground covering vegetation. They would blow off a foot and puncture truck tires. Unfortunately civilians were injured by them. The BLU-44 was one type; there were other models, some smaller.

grease gun   The .45-cal M3 and M3A1 SMGs. Name bestowed because of similarity to actual lubricating grease guns. They were mainly issued as on-vehicle equipment with two per tank. Some were used by MPs, the ARVN, and widely used by Marine Force Reconnaissance until largely replaced by the M16A1 in 1967. Few M3s were still in use. Only the M3 could be fitted with a silencer for use by reconnaissance teams, which was limited.

green beret   The initially controversial rifle (dark) green beret (Shade No. 297) worn by US Special Forces soldiers. The ARVN Special Forces (LLDB) too wore a green beret. Green berets were first worn unofficially from 1953 and approved by President Kennedy in 1961. (Aka "green beanie"—the term probably used more by "SF'ers" than others.)

Green Berets   Popular term for US Army Special Forces soldiers. They did not particularly like being called "Green Berets," which is a uniform component. Special Forces soldiers were trained in one or more skills: operations and intelligence, light and heavy weapons, communications, medical, and engineer/demolitions. They organized and advised the CIDG, MIKE Forces, and special reconnaissance projects. They were not assigned to a branch, but wore unassigned collar brass. See "eagles." It was not until 1983 that Special Forces became a branch and received the crossed arrows collar insignia (formerly worn by Indian Scouts).

Green Berets, The   *The Green Berets* by Robin Moore was released in 1965 as "fiction." It was a mix of factual and less than accurate information. In 1966 it was a bestselling paperback. The movie with John Wayne (q.v.) by the same title was released in 1968 and loosely based on the book. Filmed on Ft Benning, Georgia, Wayne wanted to initially film in Vietnam. Despite unfavorable reviews, it was a commercial success. "The Ballad of the Green Berets" sung by SSG Barry Sadler (Vietnam veteran, Special Forces medic) accompanied the movie and was a top-selling single on several charts in 1966. The single and album sold over 11 million copies, an anomaly considering the opposition to the war. *The Green Berets* was one of the few "pro-war" or "war justification" movies at the time. Over the years numerous variations of the song have been rendered by different units and organizations.

green eggs and ham   Powdered eggs served "scrambled" with a greenish or grayish tint owing to a chemical reaction between the naturally occurring sulfur in eggs and Mermite can aluminum insert containers. It was harmless to consume. The "ham" was cubed Spam. Cooks might mix in a dash of real eggshell bits to give the impression they were real eggs.

green hornets   Dexedrine amphetamine (dextroamphetamine) pills. Aka "Dex," "DEXAMIL," "stay awake pills," "go pills," "pep pills," "orange wedges," and "uppers." "Green hornet" was actually the carried-over name for a similar WWII pill. The pills were issued to keep a man awake and alert and were mostly used by aircrews, reconnaissance teams, sentries, and others when prolonged operations were demanded. There were several types available. A common pill was the small 5mg orange-colored three-sided shield-shaped tablet that could be broken in two wedge-shaped 2.5mg segments. Imprinted SKF E19. Directions recommended one tablet if sleepy and needing to stay awake or two if extremely fatigued. Doses should only be repeated no less than 6 hours apart. No more than six tablets should be taken per week. "Schedule 2 controlled substance: high potential for abuse and abuse may lead to severe psychological or physical dependence."

Green light, go!   Refers to the green lights affixed beside a jump aircraft's exit doors. It changed from red (No-Go) to green, signaling the jumpmaster to exit the paratroopers. It came to also represent that "green light" means approval. "The ol' man gave us the green light." Paratroopers cannot be red/green color blind.

Green Machine   The all-consuming Army or Marine Corps. "He was sucked into the Green Machine."

Greens   1) Army Green uniform, a Class A uniform. Army Green Shades 44 (wool—winter) and 344 (polyester/wool blend—summer, later all-season).

2) Marine forest green service uniform, aka "pickle suit."

3) Naval Aviation Working Green uniform for officers and chief petty officers. (Similar to Marine forest green.)

green-side out   The green side of the camouflage helmet cover. The reversed "brown-side out" (tan and brown) of the cover was seldom used in Vietnam. The phrases were mainly used by the Marines derived from WWII landing orders.

green skivvies   Army and Marine undershirts and shorts were white and boot socks black. Troops deploying or after arrival dyed their underwear dark green with Rit dye. From 1966 olive green underwear and socks were issued to deploying troops and

OG was soon issued Army- and Marine Corps-wide. Often in the field perpetually sweat/rain-damp underwear was not worn owing to chafing and rashes.

Green Tabber Army officers or NCOs in command or leadership positions were authorized to wear Combat Leadership Identification Tabs on Class A and B uniforms. These were Kelly green felt loops worn on shoulder straps. The distinctive unit insignia (crest) was pinned to the tabs. The individual had to be in a command or leadership position designated by T/O&E. This included fire team leaders and tank commanders and on up the chain-of-command plus section/platoon sergeants, 1st sergeants, and command sergeants major.

green tracers Most Soviet-made small arms ammunition used green tracers (identified by green bullet tips). ChiCom tracers for the same calibers burned red and still had green tips. US tracers were red (red or orange tips). It is a mistake to assume all red tracers were friendly and that the enemy only fired green tracers. Nor did the tip color necessarily indicate the tracer color.

grenade pin *or* **ring** Steel 1¼-in diameter split ring with a 1⅛-in cotter pin retaining the arming lever and spring-loaded firing pin. When pulled the arming lever (aka "spoon," q.v.) is held in place by the hand. When thrown the lever springs off the grenade and the spring-loaded "mouse-trap" firing pin strikes the primer to ignite the delay fuse (4 to 5 seconds for casualty-producing grenades, 1.2 to 2 seconds for smoke and chemical grenades). Many soldiers kept one or more grenade pins in their helmet camouflage band or elsewhere to disarm booby-traps and mines, many of which were based on grenades.

Ground Week First week of the Basic Parachutist Course, so named because of the simulated aircraft exits and the sawdust-filled pits for parachute landing fall drills at Ft Benning, Georgia. See Tower Week.

grunt The epitome of the Army and Marine infantryman in Vietnam. The name is derived from the low grunt one made when rising to his feet after a break with a full rucksack, weapon, ammunition, rations, water, and equipment. Besides his own gear he would carry a variety of ammunition and items for his squad and platoon: belted MG ammo, 40mm grenades, smoke grenades, LAW, Claymore mine, trip flares, and/or a mortar round. Grunt originated with the Marines and soon spread to the Army.

Guard, the Army National Guard (ARNG) and Air National Guard (ANG). (Known as State Militia prior to 1903.) Guard units were under the control of each state and certain territories, but funded, equipped, and overseen by the Army or USAF. As part of the Reserve Components, they could be Federalized for active duty or called up by the state for civil disturbances, disaster relief, and other emergencies. Guardsmen take a dual oath to the US President and their governor. Two ARNG artillery battalions, two companies, and several detachments were Federalized and served in Vietnam along with several thousand individual Guardsmen. Other units were Federalized, including 29th and 69th Infantry brigades, but remained in the States to replace deployed active units. The Guard was depicted as a haven for men enlisting to avoid conscription and Vietnam. Actually this had the advantage of filling Guard units in the event of conflicts elsewhere in the world, as Regular Army units outside of Vietnam were drastically understrength and under-equipped. Since 1963, Guardsmen undertook up to six months Basic and Advanced Individual Training alongside regular troops as part of their six-year obligation. Previously they received abbreviated Basic and MOS training within their unit or were already trained during prior active duty ("prior service"). "NG" was said to mean "No Good" or "No Guts." Guardsmen countered with, "Not Going!"

guerrilla warfare   While Vietnam is often characterized as a guerrilla war and there were significant insurgent warfare elements involved, it was more of a low-level conventional war with large-scale maneuvering. Granted, even the NVA used elements of guerrilla warfare and insurgency, but it was the nature of the climate, terrain, means of transporting logistics, and the close proximity of the population that forced widespread counterinsurgent and guerrilla tactics and techniques.

gun bunnies   Artillerymen. When conducting a fire mission the crew scampered about the gun position preparing ammunition, loading, and firing the gun. "Cannon cockers." See "Red Leg."

Gung Ho   *Gōng hé* is a shortened version of the Chinese phrase *gōngyè hézuòshè* (Chinese Industrial Cooperatives). Gung Ho is an Americanism derived from the Chinese term and not an accurate transliteration. Marine LtCol Evans Carlson (1896–1947) had been an observer with the Chinese Red Army in 1937–38. Claimed to mean "working together," Carlson adopted it as a motto for his 2d Raider Battalion in 1942. It spread through the Marine Corps and eventually into the Army as a term representing a strong military enthusiasm and dedication. In Vietnam it could refer to a seriously dedicated soldier or an overly enthusiastic soldier. See "hardcore."

gun jeep   Lightly armed (M60 MG) and sometimes partly armored ¼-ton M151A1 utility trucks used by infantry battalion reconnaissance platoons,* convoy and serial commanders, and MP escorts. See "Rat Patrol."

* Most battalion reconnaissance platoons eventually operated only on foot.

Gunner   Marine chief warrant officers (CWO) 2 through 4 designated as Marine Gunners—replacing the CWO titles—e.g. "Marine Gunner 2." They held the position of infantry weapons officers and specialized as battalion weapons training specialists. They had to at least achieve staff sergeant (E-6) for commissioning as CWO 2/Marine Gunner 2. From 1959 to 1964 no new Gunners were designated. They were again selected between 1964 and 1974.

Gunny Marine gunnery sergeant (GySgt) (E-7). Not to be confused with Marine gunner (q.v.), a warrant officer rank.

guns "Gun" can be a generic term for any firearm or artillery piece. However, "gun" in this context is frowned upon. It is properly a rifle, carbine, pistol, MG, SMG, etc. To call a rifle a "gun" is an unforgivable infraction and might result in pushups or endlessly reciting, "This is my rifle, this is my gun, this is for fighting, this is for fun," while grasping the weapons in question.

gunship 1) Army and Marine helicopter gunships included UH-1B/C/E gunships, UH-1B aerial rocket artillery, and from 1967, AH-1H and in 1971 AG-1J Cobra gunships. They were armed with 7.62mm MGs, Miniguns, 40mm grenade MGs, 2.75in rockets, and in some instances, 50-cal MGs or 20mm canons.
2) USAF attack aircraft converted from transports included the AC-47D Spooky (aka Puff the Magic Dragon or Puff), AC-119G Shadow, AC-119K Stinger, and AC-130A and AC-130H Spectre gunships employed for ground fire support and "truck hunting" on the Ho Chi Minh Trail. They were armed with combinations of 7.62mm Miniguns, 20mm Vulcans, 40mm automatic cannons, and 105mm howitzers.

Guns up. Helicopter gunships, usually with scouts, launched on fire support missions. Comparable to saying, "Cavalry to the rescue."

gun truck 2½- and 5-ton cargo trucks outfitted with numerous MGs in a "gun box" in the cargo bed, add-on armor, and other modifications employed as convoy escorts to counter ambushes and harassing attacks. The trucks were often painted black and decorated with gaudy symbols and slogans. The crews were known for their aggressiveness.

H HOTEL

halazone tablets Iodine water purification tablets (a misleading term, as halazone purification tablets are chlorine-based and were replaced in 1952 by iodine water purification tablets; the original name "halazone" stuck). Each man in the field was issued a 50-tablet bottle. Two were put in each quart of water and allowed 20 minutes to dissolve. It left a mild aftertaste.

half-assed Not fully involved, little effort made, incompetent, inadequate, a sorry job of it.

half-culvert Corrugated steel half-culvert pipe sections, the two halves being bolted together to form a full culvert pipe. A variety of diameters were available. Half-culvert sections were placed overlapping each other to cover foxholes, sleeping holes, and trenches and further covered by two or three sandbag layers.

hamlet *Xã* (hamlet) designates a geographical and administrative sub-unit of a village, which might be comprised of two to eight hamlets. By one account, there were 16,398 hamlets in RVN as compared with more than 3,000 villages. The number of villages and hamlets changed constantly with the winds of war. See "vil." Hamlets were identified by parenthesized numbers within, e.g., Lien Đa village comprised of Lien Đa (1) and Lien Đa (2) hamlets.

handheld mortar The 60mm M19 mortar with the M5 bipod, baseplate, and sight removed and fitted with an M1 "spade baseplate." The baseplate was set on the ground and the tube's elevation (angle of fire) estimated by the gunner gripping the tube. Its short range and limited accuracy saw it little used in this mode.

Hand Receipt DA Form 2062. Used to temporarily transfer property from one unit or individual to another. "Get a hand receipt for anything that's transferred."

hangar queen An aircraft that spends a great deal of off-line time being repaired owing to maintenance problems. Occasionally referred to ground vehicles requiring excessive maintenance.

hang fire When a weapon was fired and the primer or a mechanical malfunction caused a momentary delay of propellant ignition; e.g., when the trigger was squeezed, the lanyard pilled, or when the mortar round struck the firing pin there was a fraction of a second delay before it ignited. This could cause injuries or damage to the weapon as the crew responded to the malfunction.

Hang in there. Don't give up. Keep at it. Drive on. "I'm hanging." "He's hanging tough."

Hanoi Hannah Trịnh Thị Ngọ (1931–2016) (alias "Thu Huong"), a North Vietnamese radio personality broadcasting English-language propaganda programs for North Vietnam directed at US troops. She had broadcast for Voice of Vietnam's and Radio Vietnam's taunting English-language news from 1955 to 1975.

Hanoi Hilton The original French-built (late 1800s) Hoa Lo Prison ("fiery furnace") in central Hanoi as the *Maison Centrale* (Central [Prison] House) for Vietnamese prisoners. After the French ouster it served as a communist reeducation center. The first American POW was incarcerated in August 1964. An annex was added in 1967, "Little Vegas." Treatment, health, sanitation, and food were inhumane and included propaganda exploitation, torture, and brutal interrogations. After the 1973 Paris Peace Accords the POWs began to be released. Most of the prison was demolished in the 1990s and was replaced by a housing complex and museum. There were 12 other POW camps at one time or another in North Vietnam.

Hanoi Jane Actress/activist Jane Fonda after her imprudent and traitorous actions during her July 1972 trip to Hanoi, posing on an antiaircraft gun and making anti-American Radio Hanoi broadcasts.

hard-charger A highly motivated, aggressive self-starter. Does not know how or when to quit.

hardcore A "hard ass," tough and dedicated. Occasionally incorrectly spelled "hardcorps." The "hard core" refers to an apple core with the soft part chewed away, leaving a hard core. A related term is "hard ass"—a tough individual or someone who's hard on others. See "Gung Ho."

hardened convoy Line haul (q.v.) convoys from late 1967 with some hardened trucks, more escorting gun trucks, air cover, planned fire support available, and better trained drivers.

hardened truck Cargo trucks protected by add-on armor plate, sandbags, and planking. Usually unarmed and not to be confused with heavily armed "gun trucks" (q.v.).

hard luck bracelet Legend has it that crew chiefs and other Huey and Cobra crewmen wore a "hard luck bracelet," "shoot down," or "silent chain" wrist bracelet if they had survived a crash. This was fabricated from the tail rotor's pitch-change linked chain. It was by no means official and in some units any crewman might wear one whether they had experienced a crash or not. Other units ignored the practice.

hard-striper Army corporals and sergeants in pay grades E-4 through E-7. Hard-stripers wore NCO chevrons and rockers rank insignia rather than the Specialist 4 through 7's eagle and arcs insignia.

hash marks Embroidered Service Stripes worn angled on the left cuff of uniform coats. Their colors depended on the service. One stripe represented three years' service "hitch" in the Army and four years in the Navy and Marines. (Not worn by USAF or any branch's officers.)

hassle To give someone a hard time. "The LT's been hassling me." In use since the 1800s, it is believed derived from harass or to hack at. Its use became widespread in Vietnam.

HAWK The HAWK MIM-23A air defense missile system on the M192 towed triple-missile launcher. Two Army and two Marine Hawk battalions served in Vietnam's I CTZ to protect installations from North Vietnamese air attacks, which never materialized because of their presence and the huge presence of US interceptors on and off-shore.

hawk Supporter of the Vietnam War. Accused of being a "warmonger." See "dove" and "fence-sitter/rider."

Hawk's Claw Code for Huey UH-1B gunships armed with XM26 TOW missile launchers deployed in 1972 to blunt the NVA Easter Offensive.

head and head Headquarters and headquarters company (HHC), battery (HHB), troop (HHT), or detachment (HHD) of an Army battalion/squadron, regiment, group, brigade, division, and higher commands. (There is even an HHC, US Army at Ft Myer, Virginia.) The "headquarters and" part was comprised of the CO, XO, principal staff officers, and command sergeant major. The "headquarters unit" part consisted of other headquarters and staff personnel and supporting elements and had its own CO and 1st sergeant. Its composition varied greatly depending on the type of unit. The Marines employed "headquarters and service companies/batteries" (H&SC/B—"Heat and Steam Company"—they had hot water) at battalion-level and up. Marine divisions had an HQ battalion.

heads   Marijuana smokers. Aka "pot heads," "smokers," "dopers." The latter also referred to those using hard drugs—"dope."

head shed   A unit's headquarters building/bunker, "the HQ." On a firebase it is known as a "TOC" (Tactical Operations Center, pronounced "tock"). In the Marines it was a Combat Operations Center (COC). A command post (CP) was an HQ deployed to the field, usually with minimal staffing. A simpler name was "command bunker."

headspace and timing   Said of a person, "His headspace's off" or "His headspace and timing are off." Equates to "He's a little off," "He's nuts," "He's a goofball." "Headspace and timing" refers to the proper adjustment of a Browning MG barrel's breech and bolt interface and requires a headspace and timing gage to adjust it.

Heads up!   Pay attention, stay alert. Be on the lookout. Related to "Up!"—the signal given by the gunner or loader (depending on the type of weapon) that the weapon was loaded and ready to fire. Similarly, "Clear to the rear!" was the order given by the loader on recoilless rifles and rocket launchers, indicating personnel and obstructions were clear of the weapon's back blast.

hearts and minds   The psychological warfare goal of "winning hearts and minds," i.e., winning the spirit and support of the civilian population. A more crass philosophy was, "If you grab 'em by the balls their hearts and minds will follow," and the more daunting tongue-in-cheek, "Give me your hearts and minds or I will kill you," which was essentially the VC philosophy.

HEs   C-ration (MCI) chopped ham and eggs earned the nickname "H-Es"—high explosives—because of the bloating and gas they might cause.

heat tabs   Trioxane. Pronounced "tri-ox-sān." Compressed fuel tablets used to heat rations. Three foil-wrapped light blue oval bars in a carton. One-half to a full bar would heat a C-rat can or canteen cup of water for a beverage. Its chloroform-like flumes were to be avoided. It also created a sharp odor when burned. See "C-ration stove." (MRE flameless heaters were not issued until 1990.)

heavy drop   Parachuting heavy equipment, vehicles, supply pallets, etc. other than paratroopers. A "heavy drop" also referred to overweight women or men. "He came into the bar with this heavy drop following him."

heavy fire team   "Mission package" of two gunships and one observation helicopter for aerial fire support missions typically provided by air cavalry units. See "light fire team."

Heavy Hog   UH-1B Huey gunships with a 40mm M75 grenade launcher armed chin turret looking like a pig's snout. See "Hog." They also mounted forward-firing MGs and rocket pods.

He can't pour piss out of a boot…   with the instructions on the heel. Too stupid to accomplish the simplest tasks. "If he had a brain he'd take it out and play with it."

He'd fuck up a wet dream.   Can't do anything right. Can't close the deal.

helicopter pen   Helicopter revetment; a square structure large enough for a helicopter to park for servicing and offering protection from rocket and mortar fragmentation. Two or three sides were walled 4–6ft high built of sandbags, earth-filled 55gal drums, landing mats, and timbers. Similar revetments were built for fixed-wing aircraft.

Helmet cover graffiti

A variety of artwork, slogans, and verbiage was sometimes marked on steel helmet camouflage covers and camouflage bands with black felt markers, ballpoint pens, and colored grease pencils. This included, but was not limited to: first and/or last names, nicknames, hometown or state, girlfriend's name, rank, unit insignia, mottos, slogans, blood type, short-timer months checked off, cartoon characters, peace symbols, smiley faces, stars, Ace of Spades, crosses, dagger-pierced heart, skull and crossbones, and other symbols. Covers were seldom retained as souvenirs, but many soldiers kept a photo of their helmet. Some units prohibited the practice and it was rare among Marines. Some men considered it bad luck to do so or thought it provided an aiming point. Example slogans follow; there were hundreds.

Airborne! *or* Airborne All the Way!	In God we Trust
Bomb Hanoi	Just you and me, right, Lord?
Boonie Tunes	Kill a commie
Born to breed	Kiss my ass
Born to kill	No limits
Born to ~~kill~~ die	Not a tourist, I live here
	Peace
Bring 'em back alive	Pot is better than peanut butter

Death From Above (Airborne units)	Semper Fi *or* Semper Fidelis
Don't follow me, I'm lost	Shit happens
Don't shoot, I'm short	Short-timer
Dr. Death	Too young to vote, but not
Follow Me! (Infantry motto)	to die
Fuck everything	Unit mottos *or* nicknames
Fuck _____ (select object of spite)	Wake me when it's over
God walks with me	War is hell
Gooks go home	We were winning when I left
IHTFP (I Hate This Fucking Place)	Ranger! *or* Rangers Lead the
What, me Worry? (*Mad* magazine)	Way!

Make love not war (and other antiwar slogans)
Sat Cong (Vietnamese for "Kill Viet Cong")
FTA *or* FTW (Fuck The Army *or* World)
UUUU (We the Unwilling, led by the Unqualified, doing the Unnecessary for the Ungrateful)
Warning: Nam may be hazardous to your health
When I die bury me upside-down so the world can kiss my ass

hell box   Ten-cap Fidelity-type blasting machine used to detonate electrically initiated demolition charges. "Hell box" was its traditional civilian blaster's nickname. "Ten-cap" meant ten electric blasting caps could be detonated simultaneously. There were larger capacity models.

Hell no, we won't go!   Anti-Vietnam War protesters' chant originating in December 1967 during the "stop the draft week" demonstration in New York City. Anonymous.

helmet litter   This was not a slang term, but describes items commonly stowed on the steel helmet for easy access using the elasticized camouflage band. Usually only one to three items were carried: insect repellent bottle, chap stick, weapon oil bottle, field dressing, camouflage stick, cigarette package, book matches, cigarette lighter, P-38 can opener, foil-wrapped heat tablet, C-rat toilet paper roll, C-rat spoon, grenade arming pin(s), weapon cleaning brush, one or more loose cartridges, magazine charger adapter, and an M16A1 magazine. In dense vegetation, items could be snagged and lost. Many items could not be exposed to rain of course and some negated camouflage efforts. Some units prohibited the practice.

helmet radio   A "squad radio" seeing some use was the two-component AN/PRT-4 and AN/PRR-9. The AN/PRR-9 was a small receiver clipped on the side of the steel helmet with an integral speaker and a small antenna. The companion AN/PRT-4 was a handheld transmitter clipped on the web gear suspenders and had its own short antenna. It was considered awkward and inconvenient to handle. Intended to be carried by platoon and squad leaders and platoon sergeants. Sometimes only the platoon leader and platoon sergeant had transmitters and receivers and the squad leaders only receivers.

helo "Helicopter, "chopper," "bird," or "copter" (little used). "Choppers don't fly, they beat the air into submission."

Heresy squirts Diarrhea caused by dysentery, food poisoning (Salmonella or E. coli), or other illnesses. Aka "shits," "squirts," "runs," "trots," and "Ho Chi Minh's Revenge." One of the most discussed topics in Vietnam. Common treatment was Lomotil (loperamide) anti-diarrhea 2mg white tablets and plenty of fluids. "How can that tiny pill plug such a big hole?" (Imodium was not available until the mid-1970s.)

H-harness Web suspenders attached to the equipment belt to take the belt (aka "pistol belt") gear's weight off the hips and transfer it to the shoulders. Small equipment items could be attached to the suspenders. An "H-harness" is also a web strap system to secure rucksacks, weapons containers, and other gear to a paratrooper's parachute harness below the chest-mounted reserve parachute.

high and low birds Air cavalry helicopters operated in teams of one or two scout helicopters (Whites) and one or two gunships (Reds). Usually the scout chopper would fly "low" above the trees searching for enemy signs and to draw fire. They might mark the target with smoke grenades. The scouts sometimes had white markings painted on the upper fuselage so the "guns" could keep track of them against green vegetation. The gunships flying "high" a short distance away would roll in and attack the revealed target.

high and tight A crewcut haircut shaved clean on the sides and nape of the neck and extremely short on top. Favored by the Marines. Soldiers paid the barber 25¢ for the privilege of receiving a ⅛in to ¼in G.I. haircut, a burr.

Barber: "You want to keep your sideburns?"

Recruit: "Yes, sir."

Barber: "Hold out your hands."

higher Informal radio term for a unit's higher HQ or CO. "I have to clear it with my higher" or "Notify your higher ups." Even "higher HQs" have a higher, the "higher-higher."

high hat M577A1 command post vehicle. An M113 APC with a conspicuously heightened troop compartment used as a command vehicle in mechanized infantry, tank, armored cavalry, and self-propelled artillery units. They transported staff elements, providing standup workspace, map boards, typewriter, power generator, and radios. An expandable tent was attached to the rear. They were also used for artillery fire direction centers and mobile aid stations.

Hi-Power   Canadian-made FN-Browning 9mm Mk I Hi-Power pistol used by MACV-SOG. Also used by Australia as the L9A1. "Hi-Power" referred to the 13-rd magazine in an era when most automatic pistols had 7- or 8-rd magazines. "The Hi-Power can count to 13 faster than you can."—Advertisement.

Hippies   The hippie subculture emerged in the mid-1960s as a rebellious youth movement. It was somewhat influenced by the dissolving beatnik subculture of the 1950s. Hippie came from "hipster," a self-describing beatnik term. Also called "flower children," they embraced free love, the psychedelic drug culture, preservation of the environment, protest music, and generally rebelled against popular material possession culture. Clothing could be any style (including military), any condition, from revealing to modest, but unkempt, discarded looking or outlandish tie-dyed with headbands, "love beads," and bracelets—"anything goes." By the early 1970s the subculture began to fade in line with the withdrawal from Vietnam. By the late 1970s the subculture was a shadow of itself as devotees aged over 30. Any so-called hippies after the 1970s were "reenactors" at best.

Ho Chi Minh sandals   Practical durable sandals made from truck-tire treads for soles and strips from inner tubes as straps. VC/NVA often wore them in the field and called them "tire sandals" (*dep vo xe*).

Ho Chi Minh Trail   This infiltration trail network used existing paved, gravel, and dirt roads, bicycle paths, and foot trails running from central and southern North Vietnam through Laos, and deep into Cambodia to funnel troops, supplies, and munitions into RVN, via dozens of branch trails. The "Trail" itself was actually a corridor of interconnected trails and roads spanning some 600 miles. The name Ho Chi Minh Trail was bestowed by the Americans, but the NVA adopted it and also called it the Truong Son Road.* Thousands of NVA troops and impressed civilians expanded and maintained the trail network with truck, engineer, road construction, antiaircraft, communications, logistical, and security units. There were fuel pipelines, bridges, ferries, rest areas, supply and maintenance depots, aid stations, and even large garden plots. Weather, disease, and American attacks inflicted a toll, but never halted the southbound traffic. B-52 bombers, fighter-bombers, and gunships executed frequent attacks as did MACV-SOG with ground attacks and constant reconnaissance efforts. The Trail was instrumental to North Vietnam's victory.

* Vietnamese name for the Annamite Mountain Range, which the trail crossed.

Hog   Huey UH-1B gunships with rocket pods. Aka "Frog." see "Heavy Hog."

honey wagon   Cart used to transport human waste ("night soil") from village latrines to the fields for fertilizer. Workers were called "honey-dippers."

honor and color guards   Honor guards to greet VIPs and participate in formal ceremonies ranged from squad to company-strength; platoons were more common.

Color guards escorted national and unit colors consisting of two or three unarmed color bearers and two rifle-armed (bayonets fixed) guards. Uniforms could range from starched field uniforms to full dress in immaculate condition. Commonly seen accoutrements included chromed helmets, helmet liners painted white or branch/unit colors, branch-colored accosts (scarfs), white gloves, and white boot laces (q.v.). Military bands might use similar accoutrements. Guards were typically picked by 1st sergeants and sergeants major and were usually taller than 5ft 10 inches.

hooch   The word's origin as a shelter is unclear, but believed to be derived from the old Japanese term *uchi* (pronounced "ooh-chi" and evolved into "hooch"), meaning "inside one's home." It generally referred to any crude or simple shelter such as a Vietnamese hut, a soldier's shelter made from one or two ponchos, a canvas tarp, a sandbag bunker if lived in, as well as one- and two-story wooden barracks on bases. See "SEA hut."

hooch boy   Locally hired Vietnamese boy paid to polish boots and perform minor barracks chores. Aka "boot polish boy."

hooch maid   Locally hired Vietnamese girl officially employed as a barracks house-maid on a base for cleaning, making bunks, washing laundry, and other chores. Aka "hooch girl" or "hooch monkey" (derogatory). It was often assumed many hooch maids were prostitutes. They might flirt, but most shunned sexual relations. Only a small number of girls freelanced.

hooker   Along with "whore," the most common name for prostitutes (*mãi dâmn, điếm*). Aka "boom-boom girl" or "co," "body bag" (q.v.), or LBFM (Little Brown Fucking Machine), an ungracious nickname.

hop and pop   Parachute training jump without carrying combat equipment and conducted without a follow-on tactical exercise. Aka "Hollywood jump." Simply chute-up, board the aircraft, hop out, and pop (open) the canopy. Aka "admin jump," "pay jump" or "fun jump"—a jump solely to qualify for continued monthly "jump pay" (q.v.).

horn   A radio. "I just got off the horn with the ol' man." Derived from the old crank-style telephones with a bugle-like mouthpiece. "Hook" was another term for a radio.

horse pills   Chloroquine-primaquine anti-malaria pills, called "horse" owing to their large size and taken once a week—aka "Monday pills." Orange-colored, aka "big orange pill." Dapsone anti-malaria pills (diaminodiphenyl sulfone) were small white pills taken daily, aka "little white pills" or "daily-daily." Some soldiers avoided anti-malaria pills believing they caused diarrhea and other intestinal ailments. Troops could be punished for failure to take the pills.

hot LZ   A landing zone (LZ) or pickup zone (PZ) under effective fire by an enemy force. Landing helicopters were at their most vulnerable when flaring for a landing and as they took off. "Happiness is a cold LZ"—Philip Caputo, USMC.

hot on-load   Refers to "engines running hot." Passengers are loaded aboard aircraft while the engines are running. It implies it will only briefly be on the ground. Also "engine running off-load." Board or debark rapidly. There was also a "hot refuel," an "engine running refuel."

Howard Johnson's   Vietnamese street vendor's pushcart. (Howard Johnson's restaurant chain has since closed.)

How copy?   Did you hear my last transmission? When a word was spelled or numbers read the receiving station would say again* what he heard for confirmation and the sender would say, "Good copy" or "Copy that."

* "Repeat" was never used, but rather "Say again." "REPEAT" meant to repeat an artillery fire mission or air strike.

howtar   The 107mm (4.2in) M98 towed HOWitzer-morTAR used by the Marines from 1956 to 1967 when replaced by the 4.2in M30 mortar, which the howtar itself had earlier replaced. The howtar was a 4.2in mortar barrel mounted on a 75mm pack howitzer carriage.

HT-1 walkie-talkie   Low-cost Hallicrafters HT-1 handheld radio; used by Special Forces-advised CIDG for intra-company communications and for the CIA-supported Village Radio Program. The Village Radio Program under the Office of Public Safety (OPS) provided simple portable transceivers to report VC activities to district or provincial HQs. The radios were built by Hallicrafters: HT-1, HT-2, FM-1, FM-5, and TR-20. The first four were handheld radios and the TR-20 a larger base radio.

Huey   Nickname derived from the Bell UH-1 utility helicopter's 1960–62 designation, "HU-1A"; changed to "UH-1A." Its official nickname was the Iroquois, but it was seldom ever called that, with many soldiers unfamiliar with the moniker. The Huey was *the* iconic helicopter of the Vietnam War.

hug a tree   Punishment in which one was ordered to wrap his arms and legs around an abrasive tree truck and hang on without sliding down, which invariably ensued.

hump   To carry a rucksack. "We spent two weeks humping rucks." "A hump" is synonymous with "to carry" and "a march." "It was a tough hump."

"Hurry up and wait."   The race to get ready, be prepared, and report to the appointed place on time to be followed by an endless wait. Typically what occurred was that each echelon's CO moved up the report time 15 or 30 minutes in event of delays. The reporting time might be 0730 hours, but the troops were cocked and waiting at 0530 hours.

Hush Puppy   Smith & Wesson 9mm Mk 22 Mod 0 suppressed pistol with a 14-rd magazine used by the SEALs. SEALs also used the unmodified version, the S&W Model 39 (no military designation) with the standard 8-rd magazine. Its primary purpose was to silence dogs and sentries outside of basecamps/villages. (Hush Puppy casual shoes were popular in the 1960/70s, but had nothing to do with the silencer.)

Husky M116 (Army) and M116A1 (Marines) full-tracked 1½-ton amphibious cargo carriers seeing limited use. Aka "Hog," being squat and ugly.

hymn "Let's sing him a hymn." The response was a solemn, "Hymn, him, fuck him." A group response and display of disagreement or spite for someone's suggestion or comment.

I INDIA

I can't hear you! I still can't hear you! Shout it louder, from the heart.

I'd give my left nut for a... Something desperately wanted. "Sure. No you won't."

I'd rather be pissed off than pissed on. Take it easy and don't worry about it. Things could be worse. Also "chapped off," "chap" being something irritating.

idiot stick Vietnamese short yoke-like shoulder pole (*đòn gánh*) with a pair of balanced baskets or buckets for carrying goods/materials. Occasionally referred to a rifle.

If I had two... I'd shit on one and cover it with the other. Something with which one is unimpressed or finds to be of little use.

I have to pee so bad... my back teeth are floating. One really has to pee. Also, "I have to pee so bad my eyeballs are swimming or yellow or...I can taste it."

If I know your name... then you're either on my shit list (q.v.) or you're a star. Either way, it's not a good thing to be on the drill instructor/sergeant's, 1st sergeant's, or sergeant major's "shit list."

If it didn't grow there, pick it up. When running a police call (q.v.) of the company area the instructions meant if it was not naturally growing there, then pick it up—e.g. cigarettes, wastepaper, metal scraps, etc. Non-smokers complained of having to pick up cigarette butts from smokers who failed to "fieldstrip" (q.v.) their butts.

If the Army [Marines] wanted you to have a wife... they would issue one. Typical CO's response when requesting permission to marry. The appropriate comeback was *not*, "Where did you get yours, Sir—from supply?" (8,040 Vietnamese war brides came to the US from 1964 to 1975.)

If you ain't Cav, you ain't shit. Units carrying cavalry lineages were proud of their traditions, perhaps overly so, some considering themselves to possess a degree of "eliteness." This included air cavalry (attack and reconnaissance) and ground armored cavalry units, as well as the airmobile infantry battalions in the 1st Cavalry Division with traditional cavalry designations.*

* For example, 1st Battalion (Airmobile), 7th Cavalry was an airmobile infantry battalion.

If you don't pay attention in this class…   ya gonna die in Vietnam! After this had been shouted at trainees and students 40 or 50 times it went in one ear and out the other.

I hope your dog dies.   The worst insult one could give a Special Forces medical student—aka "dog killers." Phase III Special Forces medical training was referred to as "Dog Lab." If their patient (dog) died through neglect or fault, he was terminated from the course. The dogs were only referred to as "patients" and medical records kept the same as for human patients.

IHTFP   I Hate This Fucking Place. Seen chalked or painted mostly in I CTZ by soldiers to express their lowered morale. Another protest abbreviation was UUUU—We the Unwilling, led by the Unqualified, doing the Unnecessary for the Ungrateful. Oft said, "The only difference between the US Army and the Boy Scouts of America is the Boy Scouts have adult leadership."

I know nothing, *nothing!*   The catchphrase spoken with an obligatory German accent popularized by the affable *Hauptfeldwebel* Hans Schultz played by John Banner* in the *Hogan's Heroes* TV series (1965–71). A humorous denial of any knowledge or participation in an act.

* Equivalent to a 1st sergeant. Austrian-born Banner served as a supply sergeant in the US Army Air Forces in WWII.

I'll give you three guesses…   and the first two don't count. The answer is as obvious as the nose on your face.

illum   Illumination. Pronounced "il-lum." Parachute-suspended white illumination flares fired by howitzers, mortars, naval guns, grenade launchers, and ground "pop-up" signals (q.v.). (The Navy called them "star shells.")

illum grenade   Mk 1 Mod 2 illumination hand grenade used by the Marines. Its magnesium filler burned on the ground for 25 seconds at 55,000-candlepower, illuminating a 200m-diameter area.

I love you too much, G.I.   A "come on" teasingly uttered by prostitutes and "tea girls" (q.v.). "I love you too much. You buy me Rolex?"

I'm Alive in '65 Medal   National Defense Service Medal (NDSM) awarded to all military personnel serving between 1961 and 1974 in "time of national crisis." "65" is the year major combat units deployed to Vietnam. Regardless of what year(s) one served, "65" rhymed and stuck as a nickname.

I'm going to jail!   Dismal declaration by a 1st sergeant, drill instructor/sergeant, or other NCO because a subordinate committed such an unforgivable and grievous infraction that he is going to the stockade for murdering or seriously injuring the perpetrator.

impact awards Division commanding generals (and other designated senior commanders) were permitted to bestow "impact awards" to soldiers in combat. The idea was to provide immediate recognition and heighten morale with "on the spot" awards for valor. This included Silver Stars (seldom), Bronze Stars, Air Medals, and Army Commendation Medals.

Inbound Army troops departing the States were "inbound" for Vietnam and passed through US Army Personnel Center, Ft Mason, San Francisco, California. In 1964 it relocated to Oakland Terminal, California, and was renamed Oakland Army Base in 1966. To relieve the increasing load at Oakland, another transient personnel center was established at Ft Lewis, Washington in 1966. Both deploying ("inbound") and returning troops were processed at the US Army Personnel Centers, Oakland and Ft Lewis. They both possessed an Overseas Replacement Station, a Returnee-Reassignment Station, and a Transfer Station.

Marine replacements en route to Vietnam passed through Staging Battalion, Camp Pendleton, California. They undertook processing at West Camp Hauge (often misspelled "Hague") on Okinawa, flew to Da Nang, and were assigned to units.

in-coming Impacting enemy fire at the receiving end: small arms, MG, recoilless rifle, mortar, rocket, and artillery. Shouted as a warning or signaled by banging on a clanger. Whistling in-coming could not be heard unless it passed over. The opposite is "out-going" fire directed at the enemy.

in-country Anything or anyone within RVN. "I've been in-country four months." From the Marine aspect, "Ashore." "In-Country" was written on an envelope in place of a stamp if a letter was mailed to an addressee within Vietnam.

in-country R&R Three-day pass Rest and Recuperation facilities were located in Vung Tau and China Beach (Bac My An). There were four other minor locations. In-country R&R centers were in addition to the 5–7-day R&R outside of Vietnam. While decreed for all personnel, only a small number drew it, often as an incentive award. Divisions and separate brigades sometimes established their own recreation centers, like the 101st Airborne Division's Eagle Beach, where companies were rotated and stood down for a break.

Indian Country Enemy-controlled base areas and other rural areas with significant enemy forces present. Aka "Indian Territory." Also referred to as "Up country."

indig Indigenous. Identified low-cost field equipment designed for indigenous troops, especially the CIDG: indig rucksacks, ponchos, poncho liners, rations, etc. These were of marginal, but workable quality at very low cost made in Japan and Okinawa. The CIDG rucksack was modeled on the NVA rucksack and cost US $2.80. Also referred to indig (local) troops; usually ethnic minorities.

Indig rations/PIRs

The official designation for Packet Indigenous Rations (PIR) was often erroneously called Patrol Indigenous Rations or Food Packet and Indigenous Rations. Project PIR cases were peculiarly marked "Packet, Subsistence, Indigenous." PIRs were issued to Special Forces trained CIDG Camp Strike Forces, MIKE Forces, and reconnaissance projects, including the accompanying Americans. They were produced in Okinawa from 1965 to 1971 after development by the CIA's Counterinsurgency Support Office (CISO). They were packed in gray-green plastic-foil laminated bags, 24 meals of the same menu per case. Besides the dehydrated meat packet there was a plastic bag with instant rice. It was filled with hot water to a red line and the rice swelled to a full bag after 10–15 minutes. Some filled the rice bag with tepid water in the morning, tied it to the rucksack, and it would be sun-warmed by lunch. It included small packets of dehydrated vegetables and spices to mix in the rice; instant tea; sugar, salt, powdered soup, and candy, plus a vitamin pill. They were sometimes supplemented by canned mackerel, tuna, or sardines. Americans scrounged MCI meat unit cans to mix with the rice. There were five menus: beef (overly salted and left an oil slick after prolonged boiling), dried fish/squid (like chewing a mouthful of rubber bands), shrimp/mushroom (most popular), "boot heel" mutton (later beef jerky), and a "sawdust-filled" sausage.

The PIR packet was marked only with a menu number and there was no wording on any of the smaller packets, only pictographs indicating the contents. They could not be attributed to any specific country. Additionally, many CIDG spoke only obscure dialects or were illiterate. Some could not read the menu numbers so they were color-coded, allowing them to remember favorites. Some CIDG were suspicious of the vitamin pills and the SF told them they were fertility pills giving them more strength. They would save them and when returning to camp consumed them all to better pleasure their wives (CIDG families lived in the camp or an adjacent village).

No. 1—red	Beef	
No. 2—blue	Fish/squid	
No. 3—purple	Shrimp/mushroom	
No. 4—yellow	Mutton (or beef jerky)	
No. 5—black	Sausage	

Indochina A geographic region in Southeast Asia (SEA), its geographic coverage varying depending on era. The Indochinese Union (1887–1947, French *Union indochinoise*) and Indochinese Federation (1947–54, French *Fédération indochinoise*), which included Vietnam (what would become North and South Vietnam in 1954), Cambodia, and Laos. Indochina today as a geographic region includes the independent countries of Vietnam, Cambodia, Laos, Thailand, Burma, and Malaya (today's Myanmar and West Malaysia, respectively, but politically and militarily they were not involved in the war). The entire region of Indochina is now usually referred to as the Indochinese Peninsula or Mainland Southeast Asia (SEA exclusive of Indonesia and other off-shore regional states).

infantry blue   Official infantry color was robin's egg blue, a light blue. The infantry also used a medium blue with a secondary white; e.g., guidons, unit colors, and Dress Blue officer shoulder boards.

infantry discs   Light blue plastic discs worn as a backing on Class A and B uniforms behind the enlisted men's infantry branch of service and US collar insignias. They must possess an infantry (11-series) MOS and be assigned to an infantry unit. Infantrymen assigned to armored cavalry units were also eligible. A larger disc backing the US Coat of Arms was worn on the front of the service ("saucer") cap. Discs were introduced in 1952 to improve the self-esteem of infantrymen—no other branches were authorized discs. Branch of service insignia on brass discs date back to 1910. See "infantry rope."

infantry rope   Light blue Infantry Cord, a fourragere, was worn on the right shoulder of the Class A and B uniforms by officers (not generals) and EM with an 11-series (infantry) MOS and currently assigned to an infantry unit. Introduced in 1952 with the above infantry discs.

insert   To deliver a reconnaissance team or an infantry unit into enemy territory by helicopter or watercraft. An insertion. See "extract."

Instamatic   Small, inexpensive point-and-shoot Kodak 104 Instamatic camera using 126 film. Arguably one of the most popular cameras in Vietnam.

In your face.   Originated with the practice of Marine drill instructors yelling at recruits just inches from their face. Quit intimidating. Came to mean anyone shouting at another close up. "Get outta my face!"

Iron Triangle   Key VC base area in Binh Duong Province 40km north of Saigon. Numerous offensives were launched from the area to include the final assault on Saigon. Owing to its proximity to Saigon a great deal of action was seen there.

I stepped on a mine.   Countless movies and TV shows have shown individuals stepping on an antipersonnel mine, hearing an ominous click, and saying, "I stepped on a mine." It is assumed that if he lifts his foot it will instantly detonate, so his squad either finds some implausible means to counter it or he is left to die alone. This is a complete myth. There is not nor ever has been a mine in any country's inventory that operated in such a manner, nor do any mines malfunction in this manner. Step on it and it detonates—verified by the US Army Countermine Training Support Center.

It don't mean nothin'.   Don't worry about it. No big deal. It's unimportant. Let it go.

I was there ribbons   Three ribbons all personnel deployed to Vietnam were automatically eligible for: National Defense Service Medal (covering any military service between 1961 and 1974, whether one deployed to Vietnam or not), Vietnam Service Medal (1962–75), and Vietnam Campaign Medal (awarded by RVN 1961–73).

J   JULIET

jack shit   This can be used in multiple contexts, but "jack" basically indicates nothing, disdain, or ignorance. "He doesn't know jack shit" ("He doesn't know squat"—indicating the act of shitting), "It isn't worth jack shit," "He doesn't have jack shit," or "His shit's weak." The origin of this use of "jack" is from the British where Jack was a nickname for a common poor person.

Jake No-shoulders   A snake. Obviously lacking shoulders since they want for arms/legs.

jerry can   A 5-gal fuel can carried on vehicles. Had a large screw-on cap as opposed to the water can's smaller latch-on cap. Aka "jeep can." "Jerry" is derived from WWII as the design was copied from the German 20-liter fuel can (Jerry = Germans). Aka "G.I. cans," which can be confused with garbage cans sometimes called the same. The can was actually Italian-designed before WWII. Water cans were sometimes referred to as "jerry cans" as well. Sometimes marked with MOGAS, DIESEL, or other fuels. Some cans' tops were painted red for mogas and yellow for diesel. (Plastic cans were not adopted until the 1970s.)

Jesus nut   The geared rotor retaining nut securing a helicopter blade system to the drive shaft. Aka "Jesus pin." One has faith the nut/pin will stay on and not crash, screaming, "Oh, Jesus!"

jet pilot's survival knife   Typically called an "Air Force survival knife," it was used by many soldiers. It had a 5in blade with a serrated top edge for cutting through aluminum and Plexiglas. Aka "bolt knife" owing to the large nut-shaped pommel useable as a hammer.

Jitterbugging   Dividing an AO (Area of Operations) into grid squares of several square kilometers and inserting squads and platoons by helicopter in selected squares. The subunits would search the squares and set up ambushes at night. If making contact reaction forces would be inserted and/or subunits in neighboring squares would converge on the contact. If a "dry hole" (q.v.) the subunits would be extracted and reinserted in or move by foot to another square.

Jody Calls

Cadence calls were ritualistic call-and-response "work chants" sung by troops while marching or double-timing (running) in formation and in step. The formation leader, seemingly always an NCO from the deep South, led the chant by reciting each verse and the troops repeating the lines. The name "Jody" is believed to originate with the legend of the fictitious "Joe the Grinder," a man so good at lovemaking that other men feared losing their wives to his seductive powers; the "Grinder" featured in a number of Blues songs of the time. The name "Jody" doesn't feature in the majority of Jody Calls, their focus instead being common complaints of military life: homesickness, boasts of one's unit, complaints of other units, competition, service branch, or the enemy. They serve to improve morale with a bit of levity, reinforce unit integrity, take one's mind off the rigors of double-timing, and help pass the monotony of double-timing and marching. Jody Calls move to the rhythm of the standard speed marching or running cadence (180 paces per minute, 3.4mi per hour). It helps keep soldiers dressed (aligned) and moving in step in a formation. Today many of the traditional Jodys are considered controversial and forbidden. (Jodys had some influence on contemporary rap songs from the late 1970s.) Four typical Jodys:

Ain't no use in going home	I wanna be an Airborne Ranger
Jody's got my girl and is gone	I wanna live a life of danger
I'm gonna get a three-day pass	I wanna go to Vietnam
Just to kick old Jody's ass!	I wanna kill some Viet Cong!
C-130 rolling down the stripe	Mama told Jody not to go downtown
Airborne Ranger gonna take a little trip	Marine Corps recruiters are hangin' 'round
We gonna stand up, hook up, shuffle to the door	Jody didn't listen and went anyway
We gonna jump right out, and count to four.	Now he is livin' the Marine Corps Way!

Johnson's War   The Vietnam War was blamed on President Lyndon B. Johnson (1908–73) for escalating the conflict from mid-1965 beyond what President John Kennedy envisioned by committing extensive ground combat units though 1968.

John Wayne   "Duke" (1907–79) was well known as a Western and war movie actor. Extremely patriotic and supportive of the armed forces, he performed on

USO tours in Vietnam. He made what is argumentatively the one "pro-war movie" produced, *The Green Berets* (q.v.).

John Wayne bar Thin chocolate-covered candy discs in MCI ("C-rats") B-1 units (chocolate, solid chocolate cream, coconut). The preservatives covered much of the taste. It was often rumored they were full of laxatives; they were not. Aka "John Wayne candy."

John Wayne crackers These round crackers, officially called "biscuits," came in MCI ("C-rats") contained in each meal's B-unit can—four in the B-1 and B-3 units and three in the B-2 along with a small jam can, candy disc, or beverage powder packet. The crackers were dry and somewhat tasteless. B-unit = bread-unit.

John Wayne it. Tough it out. If "Duke" can do it, you can do it, or you can at least try.

JP-4 Jet Propellant 50-50 kerosene-gasoline blend fuel used in jet and turboprop aircraft and helicopters. Smells like kerosene, colorless to straw-colored.

juicers Alcoholics, boozers, drinkers, and drunks. "Shit-faced drunk"—silly drunk. Alcoholic consumption ranged from weak 3.2 percent beer to "hard liquor" and "rotgut."

jump boots Paratrooper boots or "Corcorans"—after the original 1941 manufacturer, The Corcoran and Matterhorn Company (also made by other firms). These black leather boots had capped toes, were higher topped, and thicker soled than issue combat boots. They were purchased at an individual's expense and typically cost $50–60. They were highly spit-shined and worn with Class A and B uniforms with bloused trousers. They were usually only worn in the field or when jumping after a pair was partly worn out and no longer fit for dress wear. (See "Leg.")

jumper Paratrooper or parachutist, an airborne-qualified soldier. A unit designated "airborne" does not necessarily mean all personnel were parachute-qualified. "Why would anyone jump out of a perfectly good airplane? There is no such thing as a perfectly good airplane."

jump pay Hazardous Duty Pay. $55 a month for enlisted, $110 for officers. In order to receive jump pay one had to be assigned to an airborne unit required to make frequent exits from aircraft in flight and make at least one jump per quarter (three months). In Vietnam the tax exempt pay continued as aircraft and opportunities to jump were officially not available. Hazardous Duty Pay was also allotted to demolition specialists, divers, and aircraft carrier deck crewmen. Only two categories of Hazardous Duty Pay could be paid an individual simultaneously.

Jump School Basic Parachutist Course at Ft Benning, Georgia. Three weeks' duration, physically demanding, and required five qualifying jumps under the 4th

Student Battalion (Airborne), The Student Brigade. Some airborne units in Vietnam conducted their own jump schools to qualify volunteers. Other services' jumpers trained at Benning as well.

Jump Week Third week of the Basic Parachutist Course during which five parachute jumps are made to include one with equipment. All harassment ceases during this phase so students can concentrate. Weather cooperating, the jumps are made in three days.

jumpwings Basic Parachutist Badge, aka "novice jumpwings," "Silver Wings." Five qualifying jumps were required during the three-week Basic Parachutist Course. It was considered bad luck to polish jumpwings. The Marines and sailors were awarded the same wings for the Army-run Parachutist Course. They then had to make five additional jumps in their unit to be awarded the gold Navy and Marine Corps Parachutist Badge adopted in 1963 and formerly only worn by riggers.

jungle antenna Expedient antenna fabricated by radio operators using WD-1/TT telephone wire (q.v.) and bamboo sticks to create a pyramid-shaped array suspended from a tree limb. It increased the range of man-packed radios, but had to be stationary to operate.

jungle boots M1966 tropical combat boots adopted in 1965, a popular and utilitarian design with treated black leather bottom portion with drainage eyelets, OD nylon-reinforced canvas uppers, Vibram-type cleated soles, and quick-drying insoles. In 1966, stainless steel insoles were added to protect from punji stakes (q.v.) along with Panama mud-clearing soles, but Vibram soles were issued into 1969. In the States some commanders prohibited the wear of jungle boots while others permitted it. Aka "boonie boots."

jungle clip Small wire safety clip fitted to later models of casualty-producing grenades (frag, concussion, WP) to secure the arming lever. They could be retro-fitted by units. To arm a grenade the arming pin was pulled while holding the arming lever ("spoon," q.v.) in place. The safety clip was rotated to free the lever, allowing it to spring free to arm the grenade when thrown. The safety clip prevented the lever from springing off if the arming ring was snagged on vegetation or otherwise inadvertently pulled. If the clip was not rotated before throwing the grenade, it would not detonate and could be thrown back by the enemy.

Jungle Expert School Jungle training had been conducted in the Panama Canal Zone since 1916 followed by the formal Jungle Training School at Ft Sherman from 1953. In 1963 it became the Jungle Operations Committee of the new US Army School of the Americas, Ft Gulick. In 1968 it was redesignated the Jungle Operations Training Center (JOTC), Ft Sherman. Individuals undertook the three-week course, which increased its student load during the war. Officer and enlisted replacements en route to Vietnam sometimes attended the course. Emphasis was on jungle existence and survival. Graduates unofficially wore a US Army Southern Command patch with a Jungle Expert tab on their left chest pocket. The patch was seldom worn in Vietnam as it was rather trivial compared to their present environment. (JOTC was closed in 1999.)

jungle factory   Simplified small-scale production lines and shops set up in VC base areas and villages to manufacture crude weapons, munitions, and equipment using salvaged and local materials, especially items discarded by Free World forces. Such items lacked durability and were crude, simplistic, and typically unsafe.

jungle fatigues   Loose-fitting lightweight tropical combat uniforms were based on the 1942 paratrooper's suit and issued in 1963 in Olive Green Shade 107 Class 1 and a four-color camouflage pattern Class 2 in 1969 for special units* (dark green and brown, light green, black†). The Marines began to change over to the camouflage pattern in 1968. Owing to shortages, the Marines permitted OG and camouflage jackets and trousers to be mixed. Very practical and popular uniforms.

* Rangers, Pathfinders, scout dog, tracker dog, etc.

† Aka Engineer Research and Development Laboratory (ERDL) pattern developed in 1948.

jungle rot   Infected or ulcerated sores or venous ulcers. Tropical ulcer, an ulcerative skin lesion caused by microorganisms. Aggravated by poor blood circulation in the legs. Aka "gook sores." To the soldiers on the ground it could be any skin aliment, rash, or blistering caused by infection or prolonged exposure to dampness and skin chafing, especially on the legs, feet, underarms, and groin area. The main cause was continually damp clothing and boots and inability to maintain cleanliness. See "crotch rot."

junk on the bunk   All of a soldier's web gear and field equipment laid out on his bunk for inspection. His foot and wall lockers would be open for inspection too. See "full field layout."

K   KILO

K-44 carbine   7.62mm Soviet M1944 (ChiCom Type 53) Mosin-Nagant bolt-action carbine. Aka "red stock rifle" owing to its often reddish varnished stock. Called the "AT-44" when fitted with a grenade launcher, "AT" meaning antitank. While its short length made it easy to handle by small-statured Vietnamese in dense vegetation, its recoil was severer than the longer Mosin-Nagant M1891/30 rifle's.

Ka-Bar   The 7in blade Mk 2 fighting/utility knife was originally issued to Marines with firearms lacking bayonets. The name is said to derive from a pleased user when he reportedly endorsed the blade having "killed a bar" (bear). In Vietnam Ka-Bars were widely carried by infantrymen, scouts, engineers, and others.

khakis Light tan-colored cotton summer service Class B uniform short- and long-sleeve shirts and trousers worn by all services (sailors below E-7 did not wear khakis). Sharp looking when starched and freshly donned, but after six hours it looked like it had been slept in. Aka "suntans."

Khmer Rouge Communist Party of Kampuchea (Cambodia) (*Khmer Kror-Horm*). Aka "Red Khmers." They won the 1968–75 Cambodian Civil War and were responsible for the Cambodian genocide resulting in the death of 1.5–3 million people. Kampuchea existed from 1951 to 1999 although it had virtually dissolved by 1993.

Kick ass and take names. To shake things up, sort things out, or find out who's to blame. "Top's coming to kick ass and take names." More intimidating was, "kick ass and not bother with taking names." "I'm going to kick some ass."

Kicked in the ass. Booted in the butt. The effort taken to get someone moving, not just physically moving, but to get them motivated. To say "My butt's been kicked" is to say one is physically worn out or worked over. "He had his boot up my ass." "He jumped on my ass."

Killer Junior 105mm howitzer HE rounds with mechanical time fuses set to airburst 30 feet above ground at 50–1,000 meters and absolutely devastating to enemy attacking firebases.

killing trees Harassing and interdiction (H&I) fires fired by artillery or mortars on areas in which the enemy might be assembling or passing through. Intended to harass, disrupt, demoralize, and deny sleep. Often there was nothing in the targeted area. The US had to pay rubber plantations—most were still French-owned—$200 for each rubber tree destroyed.

kill zone Point or area on which the ambush attack force's weapons are trained to cause as many casualties as possible on the enemy force.

KILO Radio abbreviation for a KIA. Especially used by MEDEVAC helicopters.

Kiowa Bell OH-58A Kiowa observation helicopter derived from the commercial Bell 206 JetRanger. Arrived in Vietnam in 1969 to begin replacing the OH-6 "Loach" (q.v.).

KISS Keep It Simple Stupid. A self-explanatory recommendation/warning. Somewhat related to "No plan survives contact with the enemy." (The many variations of this dictum have been credited to numerous military notables, but none verified.)

Kit Carson Scouts Program for integrating VC defectors (*Hôi Chánh Viên*) or ralliers into US units, begun in 1966 by the Marines. The Army adopted the program the next year and it proved successful, with the KCs serving as scouts, pointmen, guides, and interpreters. The 9th Infantry Division called them Tiger Scouts. KCs were selected, trained, and assigned to US units, often one or two per platoon. There were trust issues, but with few exceptions they were loyal. Of the almost 7,000 KCs, 230 were KIA and 716 WIA in US service. From the end of 1970 they began to be turned over to the National Chiêu Hồi Center in Saigon. They were mass executed by the NVA after the downfall.

Kiwi The most common and popular black boot polish. The brand dates back to 1906 when introduced in Australia. Black leather replaced brown in 1958. Kiwi also produced black leather dye. Both polish and dye produced by other companies were also used.

Kiwis New Zealand Army (NZA) soldiers attached to the 1st Australian Task Force 1965–72. Aka New Zealand "V" Force. 3,890 Kiwis volunteered for Vietnam, the peak being 543 in 1969; 37 KIA and 187 WIA.

KKK *Kampuchea Khmer Krom*, a political organization of Vietnam-born Khmers (Cambodians) from the Delta region. *Krom* means "below" in reference to Cambodia. The region was Khmer controlled prior to 1700. KKK desired to gain control of the Delta and secede from RVN as an independent Khmer state after the common communist enemy was defeated. Many Cambodian companies in the Special Forces-advised CIDG were KKK.

klick Kilometer (km = 1,000 meters, 1,093 yards, 0.62 miles). Aka "K's"—"We're moving six 'K's'." Military topographic maps were overlaid with 1km gridlines for determining coordinates. Sometimes spelled "Click." There is debate over which spelling is "correct." "Click" is said to be derived from the *click* sound made when adjusting a weapon sight's range, which has nothing to do with kilometers.

Note: The US military generally used kilometers and meters to specify distances and ranges, while using inches and feet for other measurements, the exception being millimeters for certain weapons' calibers.

Kool Aid   1) Kool Aid-flavored beverage powder. Very popular, especially the pre-sweetened variety added to drinking water to cover local "exotic" tastes and the taste of halazone (q.v.) purification tablets. Pillsbury marketed a similar product, the "Funny Face" brand.
2) Killed in action, owing to it being spelled similarly to KIA.

KP Kitchen police. Soldiers detailed to work in the mess hall. On large bases they were supplemented by Vietnamese civilians. KP duty positions included servers working the serving line (only an actual cook could serve the meat), dining room orderly (DRO) cleaning and keeping the dining room in order, pots and pans man (handwashing large pots and pans), dishwasher (handwashing or operating the automatic dishwashing machine), and outside man (manning the loading dock to unload food delivery trucks, dispose of refuse, and clean garbage cans). Never spoken phonetically as "KILO-PAPA."

KP pusher Cook detailed to oversee the KPs ensuring they do their jobs—usually a natural born hard-ass harasser or sadist.

L LIMA

laager Site where a convoy would Remain Over Night (RON) (q.v.), usually a firebase or other installation. Tank and mechanized units also established laagers with the AFVs in a defensive perimeter. Sometimes spelled "lager." Derived from the German *Lager*, an encampment.

ladder lacing Combat boots were ladder laced by some individuals and if properly laced provided firmer ankle support. The cross laces could also be adjusted to different degrees of tightness and looseness in different portions of the boot front. It did take longer to lace. They were especially preferred by paratroopers, but were more commonly worn as it looked more "tactical" or for "dress" wear. They were also popular with white laces (q.v.) worn by honor and color guards (q.v.), bands, and MPs.

Lambretta Italian-made three-wheel motor scooters with a covered passenger/cargo bed and carrying 12 or more clinging passengers. They were imported in the 1950s and 1960s. Also popular were regular two-wheeled Lambrettas, Vespas (Italy), Hondas (Japan), and Peugeots (France) on which entire families might be transported. They are seen in use in Vietnam to this day.

landing mats Metallic mats or plates that locked together to provide aircraft runways, taxiways, turnaround pads, hardstands, packing areas, and helicopter pads. They were also used to build aircraft revetment walls, bunkers, roadways, and other structures and construction projects. Older Pierced Steel Planks (PSP) or "Marston matting" was 15in x 10ft and M8A1 solid planking was 17½in x 11ft 9⅗in.

landline Wire-connected field telephones, TA-1/PT and TA-312/PT. The term came to mean any telephone system including civilian.

Lark-Five LARC-V (Lighter, Amphibious, Resupply, Cargo, 5-ton) (V = 5-ton), a four-wheel boat-like amphibious cargo vehicle. Approximately 70 deployed to Vietnam. Used from 1963 to present.

Lark-LX *or* 60 LARC-LX (Lighter, Amphibious Resupply, Cargo, 60-ton), (LX = 60-ton). The wheeled carrier was employed for ship-to-shore supplies transport. It was originally designated BARC (Barge, Amphibious Resupply, Cargo) and changed to LARC in 1960. Used from 1952 to 2001.

last four Within a company/battery individuals went by their last name or initials when marking clothing and equipment. To prevent confusion if men had the same last name, the "last four" of their serial/Social Security numbers were included in the markings. This was also practiced on administrative documents.

laterite Rusty-red gravelly soil rich in iron and aluminum and widely found in hot-wet tropical areas. Troops operating in laterite soil (*terre rouge*—French) areas would find their sweat/rain-dampened uniforms, gear, hair, and skin permeated with laterite dust for a reddish cast. "Dangest unit I've ever seen. Everyone was a redhead."

LAW The 66mm M72-series Light Antitank Weapons. Sometimes misspelled "LAAW" (extra "A" said to be "Assault") or "LAWS rocket." The "S" is incorrect, apparently meaning "System." While enemy tanks were scarce, the LAW proved useful against bunkers, buildings, and suppressive fire against snipers and infantry undercover. It could knock out NVA PT-76 and T-54 tanks. Improved versions are still in use.

Lay it on me. Tell it like it is. "I'm going to lay this at your feet."

lean and mean Physically fit and aggressive. "A lean, mean fighting machine."

Leatherneck A common term for Marines. Originated from the high-necked stiff uniform collars, because of the leather liner protecting from cutlass slashes. "Jarhead" was another term for Marines because of their high collars and pre-WWI small-visored "bell crown" service caps—smaller diameter crown than other services', giving a mason jar look. "Gyrene" is a jocular reference to Marines since WWI bestowed by sailors—etymology unknown. Marines are *never* called soldiers, other than the little-used "sea soldiers." A less appreciated term was "seagoing bellhops" (q.v.).

Leatherneck Square An area just south of the Vietnamese DMZ. The corners of the square were Marine bases at Con Thien and Firebase Gio Linh in the north, Dong Ha Combat Base and Cam Lo in the south, making it about 6mi wide east to west and 9mi deep north to south. Inland from the coast.

lemon grenade Oval-shaped M26 fragmentation hand grenade. Other versions included the M26A1, M26A2,* M56,† M57,*† and M61.†

* Extremely unpopular impact-detonated versions.

† Safety clip factory-installed.

leopard camouflage Several patterns of spotted camouflage uniforms were used. The earlier US-style "duck hunter" or "frog-pattern" was worn by the CIDG (dark and medium browns, dark green, and olive drab on light green or tan backing) until the mid-1960s when tiger stripes (q.v.) were adopted. The Vietnamese called it the *quân phục da beo* or simpler *đồ da beo*. The Vietnamese National Police Field Force from 1967 used the "earth-color flower" (*hoa mâu dât*) uniform (dark and light browns, tan, and sand); ineffective in jungles. The ROK Marines used a version (dark and light brown, leaf green on grass green background).

Let's say we did and don't.   Example is a security patrol tasked with circumnavigating a firebase outside its perimeter wire. Instead, they vanished into the bush, hunkered down, and after a suitable span of time returned to base.

liberation money   This was North Vietnamese-printed currency in *dong* denominations found in NVA base areas in Cambodia, Laos, and RVN. It was to be distributed upon liberation of the South. US troops found crates of it and kept some as souvenirs, but it was monetarily worthless. It was not issued after the 1975 downfall of RVN.

Lieutenant with a map and compass.   The most dangerous thing on earth. Ask any NCO. An equally dangerous alternative is a "lieutenant with a .45."

Life expectancy of a…   One often hears such nonsensical statements as, "The life expectancy of a radio operator in Vietnam ran between five to six seconds and up to a slightly-more-optimistic thirty seconds." This has been applied to platoon leaders, squad leaders, machine gunners, medics, etc. ("bullet magnets"). Such statements are nonsense. If this was even remotely true there would have been no soldiers left in Vietnam after about a month. True, these positions drew more fire, but their life span was not in seconds, minutes, or even days. For one to say their unit was a "suicide squad" was merely boastful fatalism.

lifer   Career senior NCOs or lower rankers who declared they would make the service a career. It required at least 20 years' service to draw retirement pay and benefits. Mandatory retirement/separation age for active duty soldiers was 55 (now 62).

light colonel   Lieutenant colonel (LTC, O-5). Aka "half colonel," one rank below a "full colonel," or "short colonel." Derived from the old rank abbreviation (Lt. Col.). Lieutenant colonels commanded battalions and squadrons and were staff officers on brigade, group, and higher staffs.

Light 'em if you got 'em.   Alternative, "Smoke 'em if you got 'em." A common phrase granting permission to smoke during a break. "The smoking lamp is lit" and the "smoking lamp is out" were used by the Marines.

lighten up   Ease off *or* ease up, take it easy, cut some slack (q.v.).

light fire team   "Mission package" of one gunship and one observation helicopter for aerial fire support missions typically provided by air cavalry units. See "heavy fire team."

Like peaches and pound cake.   C-ration favorites of peach slices and broken up pound cake in a canteen cup. It means "something virtuous." Another C-rat favorite was to mix a little water with C-rat cocoa beverage powder and drizzle the thick cocoa "icing" on pound cake.

LIMA-CHARLIE Radio term for "loud and clear." "I hear/read you loud and clear." See "five-by-five." "I read you" was often used, but one does not "read" a voice transmission. "Read" was meant to be used with radio-teletype, which automatically typed the message.

LIMA-LIMA "L-L." Pronounced "El-El." Short for LLDB (*Lực Lượng Đặc Biệt*)—Vietnamese Airborne Special Forces—the counterpart of the US Special Forces. Disparagingly referred to as "Lying Little Dirty Bastards" or "Bugouts," or "Look Long Duck Back" (sort of a phonetic pronunciation). Over the radio "L-L" were referred to as XRAY rather than LIMA-LIMA to prevent the enemy from identifying the unit as CIDG, which the L-L accompanied.

line haul Long-distance combat supply convoys through contested areas (q.v.). "Line haul" referred to transportation to faraway bases as opposed to "local hauls" in-and-about military posts or local areas. Ambushes and harassing attacks were common, necessitating the use of armed and armored gun trucks (q.v.). Some transportation units awarded a semi-official LINE HAUL RVN tab in recognition of running the dangerous convoys.

Little Miss Sunbeam Club Soldiers would state they were members of the "Little Miss Sunbeam Club," if they had no wounds—a reference to the "batter-whipped" bread's promotional claim of "no holes" ensuring freshness and firmness. "Little Miss Sunbeam" was the packaging and promotional "mascot" for Sunbeam brand bread appearing in the 1950s and is still sold.

little people A then non-derogatory term for Vietnamese and other Asians. Usually it referred to friendly Vietnamese rather than the VC/NVA. Used by some units to signify Vietnamese civilians, ARVNs, or CIDG. Today it would be considered demeaning, but at the time was considered civil and respectful.

Loach Hughes OH-6A Cayuse observation helicopter adopted in 1965 and developed from the Hughes Model 500. It was introduced in Vietnam in 1968 to replace the O-1 Birddog observation aircraft and OH-13-series Sioux and OH-23G Raven observation helicopters. "Loach" is derived from LOH—Light Observation Helicopter. Sometimes misspelled "Loch." It was considered the most crash-survivable helicopter. It began to be replaced by the Bell OH-58A Kiowa in 1969 due to Bell underbidding Hughes after a legal dispute and a rebid.

Locked and loaded. The ammunition magazine/belt is loaded, a round in the chamber, and the weapon cocked and ready to fire. The command, "Lock and load" is an order to prepare to fire.

log   Logistics: supplies, maintenance, and transportation. Medical and/or personnel services are sometimes included under the logistics umbrella.

loggies   Logistical support personnel, "logisticians"—then little used. "Log" for short. Service support troops in the rear: quartermaster (supplies), ordnance (maintenance, ammunition), transportation, adjutant general (admin), and finance. Signal, engineer, and medical branches were responsible for their own specialized supplies and maintenance functions.

Long Binh Jail   MP stockade at Long Binh Army Base, 1966–73, officially US Army, Vietnam, Installation Stockade (USARVIS). Aka "LBJ," "LBJ Ranch," or "Camp LBJ." "Big Max" was the maximum security section using sun-heated CONEX (q.v.) containers as cells. Coincidentally it used President Lyndon Baines Johnson's initials.

Long Binh Junction   Long Binh Post located between Saigon and Bien Hoa Air Base. Aka "Disneyland Far East." Established in 1965 and turned over to the ARVN in 1972. It served as HQ of US Army, Vietnam (USARV), several major commands, and the main in-country logistical base. At its peak it was home to 60,000 troops. Long Binh grew to 3,500 buildings with 180mi of roads spread over an area the size of Cleveland, Ohio. It boasted 81 basketball courts, 64 volleyball courts, 12 swimming pools, eight multipurpose courts, eight softball fields, six tennis courts, five craft shops, three football fields, three weight rooms, three libraries, three service clubs, two miniature golf courses, two handball-court complexes, a running track, an archery range, a golf driving range, a skeet range, a party area, an amphitheater for movies and live shows, 40 open mess bars, a bowling alley, a go-cart track, a scheduled bus service, and running water and sewage systems. It has been compared to 82 sq mi (12mi perimeter) of the US transplanted to Vietnam. After the war it became a major industrial park.

long green line   Companies generally moved through dense vegetation and rough terrain in a single file; sometimes in two parallel files separated a short distance. The density of the vegetation, rugged terrain, and the much reduced cross-country walking rate made conventional maneuver formations impractical.

long line commo   Integrated Wide Band Communications System linking regional commands with tropospheric scatter link fixed communications sites. These were large, slightly curved antenna arrays larger than drive-in movie screens.

loose cannon   Uncontrolled or unpredictable person causing unintentional damage. Typically out of step with the CO or even the entire unit. Derived from when sailing warships' heavy cannons broke loose from their rigging and rolled about the gun deck causing immeasurable harm.

low and slow   Helicopters flying low (near treetop level) and slow while following the terrain's contour. This was an evasive measure to avoid ground fire. Aka "terrain masking."

Lower than whale shit. Someone who's pretty low. A "lowlife."

lowest bidder "I remind myself that my rifle (insert weapon, equipment, aircraft) was made by the lowest bidder." A sage fatalistic observation, but not always true.

low-quarters Black leather low-topped, laced dress shoes worn by all services.

LRRP Long Range Reconnaissance Patrol companies and detachments. Aka Long Range Patrol (LRP). Pronounced "lurp," but the units' designations should never be spelled "Lurp." On 1 February 1969 they were redesignated Ranger companies of the 75th Infantry, but continued the LRRP mission.

LRRP or LRP rats

Long Range Reconnaissance Patrol food packets were developed in 1964. Pronounced "lurp rats." They were packaged in OD foil-lined fabric pouches in 24-meal cases. The meals were freeze-dried in a plastic bag and much lighter and more compact than C-rations (MCIs). They were reconstituted with cold, tepid, or hot water (seldom could water be heated on patrol). They could be eaten dry on the move, but water had to be drunk with them. They included an accessory packet (q.v.) similar to the MCI's plus a compressed fruitcake, cereal, or tropical chocolate bar. A common complaint was the absence of cigarettes found in MCIs—one does not smoke on patrol. Opinions differ, but menu Nos. 3, 5, and 8 were popular, with 1 and 6 the least. No. 2 was good, but one had to be cautious of the stray bean failing to absorb water—this could break a tooth. (Post-war LRP rats had different menu numbering.)

No. 1—Beef hash	No. 5—Chicken stew
No. 2—Chilli con carne	No. 6—Escalloped potatoes with ham
No. 3—Spaghetti with meat sauce	No. 7—Beef stew
No. 4—Beef with rice	No. 8—Chicken with rice

LT Lieutenant. Pronounced "el-tee." "Two LT" and "One LT" referred to 2d and 1st lieutenants after their rank abbreviations, 2LT and 1LT (O-1 and O-2). The old terms "louie" and "shave tail" were seldom used.

Lyster bag A 36gal "water sterilizing canvas bag" with six spigots for filling canteens. Suspended from a tree limb or tent pole-tripod. Sometimes misspelled "Lister."

LZ Landing zone. This could be a temporary helicopter landing zone to deliver troops or it could be an LZ used as a temporary firebase. It also designated small temporary fixed-wing aircraft landing strips. LZ was sometimes used to designate a point where helicopters would extract troops, but was more properly a pickup zone (PZ, q.v.). The 1st Cavalry Division designated most of its firebases as "LZs"—LZ Bird, for example.

M MIKE

M1 pencil When a soldier was said to have "qualified with an M1 pencil,"* he had not made a qualifying number of hits, but a qualifying score had been penciled in anyway.

* M1 pencil could refer to a fictitious pencil model, but sometimes "M14 or M16 pencil" was used.

M1 thumb It is often thought the "M1 thumb" tragedy occurred when loading an 8-rd clip into the magazine well. It occurred when the rifle was unloaded and the bolt locked open for inspection. To close the bolt the edge of the palm pushed the operating handle to the rear. With the operating rod locked back the cartridge follower could be depressed with the thumb almost all the way down before the bolt was released to close it. If the operating rod was pushed back further with the follower depressed by the thumb, then the bolt would slam closed, and if insufficiently fast or clumsy, the thumb could have been caught by the bolt slamming closed. Painful, but seldom resulted in serious injury.

M10 revolver The supposed, but incorrect, military designation of the S&W .38 Special Model 10 revolver issued to aviators. Model 10 was the commercial designation recognized by the military. "M10" also designated the little-used Remington 12-gauge Model 10 riot shotgun. USAF Security Police used the S&W .38 Special Model 15 revolver and it too was mistakenly called an "M15."

M14 AR The squad automatic rifle version of the M14 was the M14 AR, modified by removing the selector lock allowing full-automatic fire and adding an M2 bipod. (The intended M15 AR with a heavier barrel never entered production to reduce costs.) See "Fourteen." The M14 AR proved to be inaccurate on full-automatic and the barrel overheated rapidly. The 20-rd magazine was inadequate for sustained fire. The Army adopted the M14E2 in 1965, redesignated the M14A1 in 1966,* with a straight-line stock, two pistol grips, and muzzle compensator, but it also performed poorly. It was theoretically replaced by the M16A1 with a M3 "clothespin bipod" (q.v.) in 1967. For all practical purposes there no longer was a squad automatic rifle.

* The Marines did not use the M14E2/A1.

M16 bong A true "bong" is a glass smoking tube filtering the smoke of various drugs (cannabis, opium) through a water pipe. In Vietnam an M16 rifle and in some instances, a 12-gauge pump shotgun was used—first unloaded. A small ball of marijuana was placed in the breech chamber, lit, and a man blew the smoke up the barrel. It emerged from the muzzle in a stream and was inhaled by a man holding the muzzle. He could also be inhaling vaporized oil in the bore.

MAC-10 Military Armament Corporation M10 compact silenced .45-cal SMG seeing limited use by SEALs. Pronounced "Mac-Ten."

Mad Bomber In 1966 assault helicopter units were authorized to fabricate expedient Mortar Aerial Delivery Systems (MADS) on Hueys. This was a wooden chute holding 20 modified 81mm mortar rounds mounted in both doors. They could be dropped on suspected VC/NVA positions, especially covering LZs. Their degree of success was variable.

Makarov Soviet 9mm *Pistolet Makarova (PM)*. Pronounced "Ma-kar-ove." Made in China as the Type 59 and North Vietnam as the K-59. All relatively scarce. It fired the 9mm Makarov, shorter and not interchangeable with the 9mm Parabellum used in US and Australian weapons.

McGuire rig This helicopter extraction system was developed by SGM Charles McGuire of Project Delta* and was first used in mid-1966. It used three 120ft ropes (aka "strings") dropped from a helicopter with web straps in which each man would secure himself after snap-linking on his rucksack. See "STABO rig," which replaced the McGuire.

* Not to be confused with today's Delta Force.

McNamara's 100,000 Project 100,000 was a Department of Defense effort initiated by Robert S. McNamara (1916–2009), Secretary of Defense (1961–68) running from October 1966 to December 1971. This was an effort to recruit at least 100,000 troops who were just below the 10–30 percentile range (Category IV) in the Armed Forces Qualification Test—those with low mental aptitude, minor physical deficiencies, slightly over or underweight, or non-English speaking. The results were mixed, with some successes, but there were discipline, inefficiency, and morale issues. The numbers conscripted and recruited are not clear, but some sources state well over 300,000. The most vehement opponents of the program were the NCOs who had to train and supervise what was aka the "Moron Corps."

McNamara Line A 1966 unrealistically conceived, barely commenced anti-infiltration barrier line, the Trace (q.v.). It was proposed to stretch across RVN south of the 17th Parallel DMZ (q.v.) and supposedly into Laos, where Free World forces were prohibited. Its proposed length was never accurately calculated. The straight line distance across Vietnam at the DMZ was approximately 45 miles. Running due west from the South Vietnamese border, it was approximately 120mi across exceedingly rugged Laos to the Thai border. The system of firebases, outposts, and aerial surveillance was to be backed by multiple barbed-wire barriers, minefields, chemical and seismic sensors, ground surveillance radar, and searchlights under Task Force 728. They would detect and interdict enemy infiltration. The numerous existing firebases would reinforce the proposed line. Such bases and supporting infrastructure would be impossible to emplace in Laos. Regardless of the excessive distances and necessary manpower and resources, construction was to commence in September 1966 and it was to be sufficiently completed across Vietnam by September 1967. The ineffectiveness of France's failed Maginot Line was ignored. The Trace was constructed in the summer of 1967 and was the only phase completed. It was estimated to require four years to fully complete. It was never addressed where the additional forces would come from to man the Laos portion or how it would be sustained.

Mad Minute An approximately one-minute period when all defensive armament on a firebase was fired: small arms, MGs, recoilless rifles, tank guns, mortars, and artillery. This served to test-fire weapons, expend outdated ammunition, build crew proficiency and morale, and demonstrated the hell that would be unleashed on an attacking enemy. Usually conducted before first light or after last light.* Many soldiers did not fire their weapon so as not to have to clean them. Some units specified a minimum number of rounds to be fired by different weapons. Accredited to 1st Battalion, 7th Cavalry in the Ia Drang Valley in fall of 1965.

* 20 minutes before sunrise and after sunset.

Mae West Influenced by the Coca-Cola bottle-shaped actress, Mae West (1893–1980; measurements 38-24-38).

1) A parachute malfunction in which suspension lines were thrown over the partly inflated canopy or part of the canopy is turned inside-out (semi-inversion), causing it to appear as a giant bra.

2) Type B-5 pneumatic life preserver vest used by aviators. When inflated the two chest flotation bladders were suggestive of a buxom woman.

mag Weapon's detachable or integral ammunition magazine. It is incorrect to call a detachable magazine a "clip."

Maggie Martha Raye (1916–94), actress, comedian, and singer who undertook numerous overseas USO tours in WWII, Korea, and Vietnam. Myth had it she was an Army Reserve Nurse Corps LTC. Actually she was only an honorary Special Forces LTC (she visited most Special Forces camps) plus an honorary Marine COL. She did in fact help treat wounded soldiers in combat conditions. She received civilian awards for her dedication to the military and is the only woman buried at the Ft Bragg Main Post Cemetery (aka "Special Forces Cemetery").

maggot Typically a reference to recruits and other lower lifeforms. "I have never seen such a sorry bunch of…." In other contexts, "That'll gag a maggot." Something pretty gross.

maggot tag   Trainees at Ft Ord, California wore a black-on-white unit tape above the black-on-OG name tape on the fatigue uniform's right chest. This identified the training company's designation* and was meant to keep trainees from different companies from mingling in an effort to control rampant meningococcal meningitis. Basic trainees were restricted to their company areas for eight weeks. It first broke out in 1962. Basic training was suspended in 1964–65, but resumed. Ft Ord meningitis outbreaks continued at reduced rates through the war. The tape was removed after BCT, but the stitch marks remained identifying one who trained at Ft Ord.

* Example: "A-4-3" = Company A, 4th Battalion, 3d Training Brigade (Basic Combat Training).

maint   Maintenance, pronounced "mate." The repair and upkeep ("preventive maintenance" [PM]) of vehicles, weapons, equipment, and materiel.

maint truck   2½-ton or 5-ton cargo trucks accompanying convoys with mechanics, tools, spare tires, parts, and a towbar. A "gun/maint truck" was additionally armed and armored for convoy escort.

Make love, not war.   A G-rated* whimsical antiwar slogan seen on buttons and posters. A variation was "Make peace, not war." X-rated versions were "Fighting for peace is like fucking for birth control," "Bombing for peace is like fucking for virginity," and the less imaginative, "Stop the War" and "Love not War." There was also "Draft beer, not boys." "Ho, ho, Ho Chi Minh, the NLF is gonna win." Such slogans were ideological dreams bolstered by sentimentality and the honest desire for world peace, but with a naive ignorance of the problem.

* The Motion Picture Association of America rating system was adopted in late 1968 and was somewhat different than today's. In this instance the rating does not refer to a movie rating.

man with a/the plan, the   More formally the operations officer (S-3) or the briefing officer knowledgeable of the upcoming operation or event. Informally, the guy with the information; one who knows what is going on. Information is power.

marker rounds   Single artillery or mortar round fired by a battery from which the following rounds will be adjusted or "walked" onto the target. White phosphorous (WP) smoke rounds might be used as they were easier to spot in dense trees and they rise above trees. Designated Targets (DELTA-TANGOs) were selected while still daylight from which to adjust fire at night.

Mark 69   AN/MRC-69(V) radio terminal set was a higher command radio relay system transported in a van aboard a 2½-ton truck. "Mark" was a name derived phonetically from "MRC" rather than a mark number designation. Aka "Freq Freak." MRC = Mobile (ground)-Radio-Communications. A lighter airmobile system was developed in Vietnam as the "AN/MRC-34 ½" mounted on a ¼-ton trailer.

MARS   Military Auxiliary Radio Station. A system of civilian volunteer ham radio operators working with the military to allow overseas service members to call home from US bases using military radios integrated with ham radios "phone patched" to residential phones. The story goes that an elderly lady mistakenly dialed a MARS station. The operator said, "MARS Station KISMA55, Airman Flyboy speaking." "Oh, I'm sorry," she said. "I dialed the wrong number. I didn't know we'd gone that far!"

Marvin the ARVN   Lighthearted nickname for ARVN soldiers—*Kinh Binh* (riflemen). It was not derogatory and recognized their plight. (Thought derived from the cartoon character, "Marvin the Martian"—short-statured, oversized helmet—who first appeared in 1948 in Bugs Bunny cartoons and received his name in the 1960s.) "Marvelous Marv the ARVN" was another "light" nickname.

mass-cas   Mass casualty situation experienced by aid stations and field hospitals during a major battle.

Master Blaster   Holder of a Master Parachutist Badge. Participated in 65 jumps to include 25 with combat equipment; four night jumps, one as a jumpmaster; five mass tactical jumps which culminated in an airborne assault problem; graduated from the Jumpmaster Course; and served in jump status with an airborne unit for a total of at least 36 months. A star and wreath was atop the jumpwings (q.v.). A Senior Parachutist or "Senior Jumper" participated in a minimum of 30 jumps to include 15 with combat equipment; two night jumps, one as jumpmaster; two mass tactical jumps which culminated in an airborne assault problem; graduated from the Jumpmaster Course; and served in jump status for a total of at least 24 months. A star topped the jumpwings.

Master Guns   Marine master gunnery sergeant (MGySgt) (E-9). Aka "Master Gunny."

MaT-49   French compact 9mm MaT-49* SMG (telescoping stock, folding magazine) used by VC/NVA. North Vietnam produced a copy, the K-43, with a longer 7.62mm barrel—same round as for the Tokarev TT-33 pistol (q.v.).

* MaT = *Manufacture Nationale d'Armes de Tull*, pronounced "Matt."

meat wagon   Ambulances, specifically the ¾-ton M43B1 ambulance for up to four litters or six to eight sitting patients and ¼-ton M718 frontline ambulance produced from 1966 and based on the M151A1 utility truck for two litters or four seated.

mech   Mechanized infantry unit mounted in M113 APCs and other full-tracked vehicles. While Vietnam was *initially* deemed poor armor terrain with little need for such units, ten mechanized infantry battalions served there along with nine M113-equipped armored cavalry squadrons.

MEDCAP Units would dispatch Medical/Civil Action Program (pronounced "med-cap") teams to provide outpatient medical and other aid to Vietnamese civilians. Besides medical and dental services they would provide veterinary and engineering aid and material. The efforts accomplished much by aiding civilians, although some wounded and ill VC were inadvertently aided. Over half of the provinces had US Military Provincial Hospital Assistance Program teams (MILPHAP—pronounced "mil-phap").

MEDEVAC Medical Evacuation referring to MEDEVAC helicopters. Often misspelled as "MEDIVAC." Pronounced "med-ee-vac." See "DUSTOFF" and "CASEVAC."

MEDEVAC bird Unarmed Army UH-1-series helicopters with litter racks for four casualties. From 1966 many were fitted with personnel rescue hoists. They carried a medic and were marked with red crosses on white square backings. The Marines used mostly UH-34 and CH-46 helicopters without red cross markings. Corpsmen were aboard dedicated helos, but others were given an "as needed" MEDEVAC tasking and would not have a corpsman aboard.

medical tag The Medical Warning Tag was a third "dog tag" (q.v.) authorized in August 1968. The red anodized tag served to alert medical personnel of allergies and other conditions in the event a patient was unconscious. (Some reconnaissance team members had name tag-style medical alerts on their uniforms—"NO PEN" [No Penicillin]—for example. Their blood group was also sometimes marked on uniforms.)

Mermite can An M1944 insulated metal container for carrying up to 5gal of food or beverages from a rear area kitchen to the field. Derived from French in WWI, *marmite* = cooking pot. Hot chow could be "Mermitted" to units in the "bush" to include helicopter delivery on resupply days. "Mermite inserts" were three separate removable 1.4gal uninsulated canisters allowing three different foods and beverages to be carried. Marines called it a "vacuum can"—"vac can."

mess kit repair unit A farcical unit indicative of any rear service support unit of little consequence. The original such unit was the Soviet 393d Field Mess-kit Repair Battalion stationed in East Germany and reported to be the cover designation of the 1292d Nuclear Weapons Storage Depot. A unit briefing book with all available intelligence had been prepared. However, the unit's existence was a gag created by US intelligence analysts.

mess tray Five-compartment light brown Melamine* thermosetting plastic resin mess tray. Older stainless steel six compartment mess trays were still in use.

* Melamine bowls, tumblers, and cups were also used.

Mickey Mouse unit   The well-meaning, good-natured, but amateurish Walt Disney cartoon character was used to personify some units as insufficiently serious or professional or in some way lacking militarily. "The 13th Ordnance is a real Mickey Mouse outfit."

Midnight Hook   A myth that some higher commanders sent a CH-47 Chinook to pick up a relieved commander and drop off his replacement in the middle of the night. He was flown to an unspecified location and never seen again. It is true that relieved commanders were removed quickly and were seldom seen by their former unit, but they were usually reassigned to another unit's staff or to an administrative or command staff in the rear.

midnight requisition   Underhanded and usually illegal means of obtaining supplies, equipment, weapons, radios, rations, building materials, spare parts, and anything else a unit needed or might have even a remote use for. This was accomplished by covertly "raiding" other units' motor pools, warehouses, and supply rooms. Sentries were posted as much to prevent midnight requisitions as VC infiltration and civilian pilferage. To hypothetically explain the concept, for every 500 M151 trucks the Army acquired it needed 1,000 side mirrors. Apparently, the Army only purchased 990 mirrors per 500 M151s. See "scrounger."

Mighty Mite   ¼-ton 4x4 M422 and M422A1 utility trucks. Aka "Mite." Poorly performing Marine jeep-type vehicles designed light enough to be sling-loaded under helicopters—the lightest cargo vehicle in the US inventory and produced from 1959 to 1962. By the time it was fielded in 1960 new helicopters could lift heavier loads, making the Mite unnecessary and M151A1 utility trucks began replacing it in the mid-1960s.

Mighty Mouse   2.75in (70mm) Folding-Fin Aerial Rockets (FFAR) launched from helicopter gunships, ground attack aircraft (prop and jet), and as target markers from observation aircraft. HE, WP, HEAT, illumination, and flechette rockets. Originally designed as unguided rockets launched from jet interceptors against bombers. Named after the Mighty Mouse cartoon character—small, but with a punch—a nickname little used in Vietnam.

MIKE boat   Monitor riverine gunboats based on the LCM(6) landing craft, aka "MON." The main gun was a 40mm Bofors forward with an 81mm direct fire mortar in the well deck. Command and control boats, aka "CCBs" or "CHARLIE boats" (q.v.), were modified monitors retaining the 40mm, but lost the 81mm. Later monitors had a turreted 105mm howitzer. Hull numbers were prefixed by "M."

MIKE Force   Mobile strIKE Force (MSF or MF). 5th Special Forces Group operated five regimental-size MSFs (2–4 battalions each), one in each CTZ plus the 5th MSF for country-wide employment. The reaction forces were manned by various indigenous CIDG ethnic groups and part of the units were parachute-qualified.

MIKE-MIKE Millimeter (mm) referring to a weapon's caliber, e.g., 40 MIKE-MIKE for 40mm.

mikes "Minutes" as used in radio-telephone communications. "We're moving out in one-five mikes." Derived from the phonetic alphabet MIKE.

million-dollar wound Wound of such severity to send one back to the States, but not seriously handicapping. Those wounded or killed in action (WIA/KIA) were bestowed the Purple Heart (PH). Established as a wound decoration in 1932, posthumous awards were not permitted until 25 April 1962.

mine-sweep An early-morning chore for firebases securing major roads was to conduct a mine-sweep to the next firebase or meet a sweep originating from the next base halfway. Accompanied by a security team and usually a gun jeep and ambulance, two engineers with AN/PRS-7 mine detectors swept the road for command-detonated* or pressure-detonated mines. Civilian traffic was held up until the sweep was completed. The mine-sweepers were usually given the rest of the day off. PRS = Portable-Radio-Detecting and Search.

* Command-detonated or remotely controlled mines today would be called improvised explosive devices (IEDs).

Mini-Arc Light A rapidly responsive combination of air strikes and artillery employed in the defense of Khe Sanh Combat Base in 1967–68. Army 175mm guns at distant firebases initiated the Mini-Arc Light with 60 rounds into one half of the designated 500m x 1,000m target block. Thirty seconds later, A-6 attack aircraft delivered 56x 500lb bombs along the block's long axis. At the same time, artillery at Khe Sanh fired 200x 105mm howitzer and 4.2in mortar rounds into the other half of the target block. The fires were coordinated to strike at the same instant. A "Micro-Arc Light" delivered approximately half the amount of ordnance in a 500m x 500m block.

mini frag Dutch-made V40 fragmentation grenade (*V40 fragmentatie handgranaat*). Aka "hootch-popper." Used by MACV-SOG and SEAL reconnaissance teams. The smallest hand grenade ever fielded. Three weighed as much as a 14oz M67 "baseball frag."

Minigun The 7.62mm M134 six-barrel, "Gatling-like" electrically operated, rotary MG mounted on attack helicopters and USAF fixed-wing gunships. They were occasionally ad hoc vehicle-mounted. The USAF version was the GAU-2/A. Rate of fire was adjustable up to 6,000 rpm—3,000–4,000 rpm was the general rate. With every fifth round a tracer, the tracer stream appeared as a solid red streak.

mini smoke XM166 white, XM167 green, XM168 red, and XM169 yellow ground smoke grenades. Used by MACV-SOG, LRRPs, and SEALs for emergency position marking. Approximately the size and appearance of an aluminum 35mm film canister.

Mini-Tet Offensive   This smaller offensive was Phase II of the February to March 1968 Tet Offensive (q.v.) which lasted from 29 April to 30 May 1968. Aka "Little Tet" or the "May Offensive." Actions were launched throughout Vietnam, but on a smaller scale than the Tet Offensive.

Missed it by *that* much.   An explanation or excuse for failing an attempt or effort. Holding up thumb and forefinger, Agent Smart declared despairingly that he "missed it by *that* much," underplaying his failure to execute his plan. A phrase made popular by Maxwell Smart, aka Agent 86 (Don Adams) in the TV comedy series, *Get Smart* (1965–70).

Mity Mite blower   The M106 riot control agent dispenser for spraying teargas (CS) powder on riotous crowds and to pump CS and smoke into tunnels and fortifications. It also blew air to flush out CS before "tunnel rats" (q.v.) entered and then blew in air while tunnel rats explored. "Mity Mite" portable insecticide blower was its commercial marketing name. Often incorrectly spelled "*Mighty* Mite."

Mk 1 eyeball   "Mark One Eyeball" refers to using unaided vision to spot something or estimate the range as opposed to binoculars, telescopes, night vision devices, radar, etc.

Mobile Guerrilla Force   MGFs were reinforced and specially trained CIDG companies conducting covert strike operations (Blackjack Operations) within enemy territory from 1966. Absorbed into the Mobile Strike Forces in 1967.

mo-fo   Motherfucker, muthafucka, mutterfoker, or simply "MF." (Some MIKE Force [q.v.] units displayed "MF" on their shoulder patches.)

MOGAS   autoMOtive GASoline. 87-octane leaded regular gasoline. Pronounced "mo-gaz." (Unleaded gasoline was not in use.)

monkey harness *or* strap   Mk II helicopter safety harness—a web harness and restraining strap worn by helicopter crew chiefs and door gunners to prevent their falling from maneuvering helicopters. Some door gunners did not use restraints, to allow them to stand on the landing skid to fire forward or to move about in the troop compartment. Nickname derived from the harness and leash used by Italian street organ grinders to restrain performing monkeys.

Monopoly money   Military Payment Certificates (MPC), Aka "funny money," "script," or "game money." They were called "Monopoly money" as the dollar and cent denomination banknotes (no coinage) were small and brightly colored. The Vietnamese called them "red dollars" as opposed to US dollars being "green dollars." Issued by the Department of Defense rather than the Department of the Treasury, they were legal tender on US installations. They were not authorized for trade with Vietnamese, nor could US dollars be used for civilian trade. Arriving Americans were to exchange dollars for MPCs or Vietnamese piastres (or "Pees," q.v.). MPCs were exchanged, however, and were a black market item. Americans could not possess American dollars in-country (weakly enforced). MPCs were used in US installations (PX/BXs, clubs, post offices, and authorized on-base Vietnamese concessionaires— barbers, tailors, etc.). MPCs were denominated in amounts of 5¢, 10¢, 25¢, 50¢, $1, $5, $10, and $20 (from 1968). The dollar bills were larger than the cent bills. When returning home there was a limit of how much could be exchanged for US dollars. MPC had no value outside of Vietnam (other than collectors). There were occasional MPC conversions; see "C-Day" and "Pees."

Montagnard bracelets　Montagnard tribesmen habitually wore metal bracelets, sometimes with simple scrollwork, but often plain. They were made from scrap metal and copper, but also hammered brass cartridge cases and from pounded and rolled Vietnamese xu or su (pronounced "sue") coins, which were worthless to them—aluminum, cupronickel, and nickel-plated steel. Legend says the bracelets were presented to Special Forces soldiers made honorary members of the tribe or clan, usually as part of a ceremony. This was true in some cases, but more commonly they were given as a sign of friendship and respect. Most bracelets worn by US troops were simply purchased as souvenirs from entrepreneurial Montagnards and Vietnamese.

More Flags　On 23 April 1964 President Johnson first publicly appealed to other countries to aid Vietnam in the escalating war in what was the "More Flags" Free World Assistance Program. He told the UK he would even take just a bagpipe band. The US considered accepting a Gurkha brigade, which the British Army was considering disbanding. The idea was cancelled for different cultural, training, and philosophical reasons, and the potential for leadership conflict plus the UK delayed their disbandment.

Mosin-Nagant　The 7.62mm Soviet M1891/30 bolt-action rifle. There was also a 3.5x telescoped sniper version. The carbine version was the M1944; see "K-44 carbine."

mosquito wings　Specialist 4 through 7 rank insignia displaying a spread-winged US Coat of Arms eagle. This term was sometimes limited to Spec 4, as Spec 5 through 7 eagles were crowned by arches to indicate the more senior grades. Also worn as a branch of service collar insignia by enlisted soldiers categorized as "branch unassigned," which included Special Forces.

motor stables　When vehicle crews performed preventive maintenance and 1st echelon maintenance (operator level), and mechanics performed 2nd echelon maintenance (company/battalion-level) on vehicles in the motor pool (truck park) or the field.

Motor-T　Marine Corps Motor Transport (MT) units.

mousetrap　A means of rigging an M18A1 Claymore antipersonnel mine with a tripwire-activated firing device. Aka "automatic ambush" (ALPHA-ALPHA) rather than as a command-detonated mine as normal. "Daisy chaining" was linking two or more Claymores with "detcord" (q.v.) to be simultaneously detonated when tripwire- or manually activated.

movement "Movement" was reported when enemy troops were discovered moving cross-country, on a road or trail, or crossing a river. "Movement in the wire" is detecting enemy penetrating or infiltrating through an installation's barbed-wire barriers.

Mule M274-series 4x4 "Mechanical Mule" ½-ton platform utility truck. The only cargo vehicle that carried more than its own weight—by 130lb. Aka "Military Mule." A "one-oh-six Mule" mounted a 106mm M40-series recoilless rifle. Built from 1956 to 1970 and used into the 1990s by the Army and Marines. It was impractical in the field in Vietnam, but used as a light utility vehicle on firebases. It could operate with a front wheel removed.

Mustang/Mustanger Marine officer who served as an enlisted man prior to commissioning through Officer Candidate School (OCS).

My grandma was slow, but she was old. Chastisement for moving or responding too slowly.

N NOVEMBER

Nam, the "The Nam" was simply South Vietnam or Republic of Vietnam (SVN or RVN). To a vet the Nam is a time, a place, and a state of mind with a tangle of memories.

nap Napalm. "Nap" was a little-used term for jellied gasoline* delivered in aerial bombs. The word Napalm is derived from aluminum salts of Naphthenic and Palmitic acids. Napalm-B (NP2) used in Vietnam was 46 percent polystyrene, 33 percent gasoline, and 21 percent benzene. A BLU-27/B firebomb was filled with 100gal of NP2 (874lb). The Dow Chemical Company manufactured Napalm-B from 1965 to 1969. Nap smelled like gasoline and a firebomb attack was sometimes called a "barbeque." The quip, "I love the smell of napalm in the morning," spoken by LTC Bill Kilgore played by Robert Duvall in *Apocalypse Now* (1979), was never actually spoken in Vietnam. Napalm was probably one of the most popular names for servicemen's pet dogs. (Napalm was internationally outlawed in 1980.)

Nathaniel Victor North Vietnamese. Little-used term often incorrectly reported to be from the phonetic alphabet, which would be "NOVEMBER-VICTOR." "Nathaniel" was used similarly to "VICTOR-CHARLIE"—"Sir Charles," to show a grudging respect. Aka "Nate," and "Gomers"—possibly derived from Gomer Pyle; see "Surprise, surprise, surprise!"

NCOIC Noncommissioned officer in charge. An NCO placed in charge of an activity, facility, vehicle, detachment of troops, work detail, etc. Temporary in nature.

Equated to "chief cook and bottle washer"—one granted authority, but with little clout. Officers too could be assigned OIC temporary duties.

NEGATIVE Radio-telephone procedural word for "no" or "none." It was commonly used in everyday speech for "no." "That's a big Negative." "Negative to that." See "ROG/ROGER."

Never volunteer for nutin'. A reminder not to do so. You would most likely regret it.

Nguyen The most common Vietnamese family name, equating to the Anglo-Saxon "Smith"; some 40 percent were so named. A general nickname for any Vietnamese. (Vietnamese naming practices call for the family name first and the given name follows it. Vietnamese living in America have mostly reversed their names to Western-style.)

Nighthawk Huey UH-1H "slicks" (q.v.) mounting an AN/VSS-3 Xenon searchlight with an AN/TVS-4 night vision device (normally tripod-mounted) and an M134 Minigun or AN/M3* MG in a side door to search for and engage enemy personnel. Targets were acquired by the night vision device, illuminated by the searchlight, and engaged with the MG.

* 50-cal AN/M3 aircraft MG had over twice as high a rate of fire as the .50-cal M2.

nine-millimeter 9mm Parabellum (aka "9mm Luger") pistol and SMG ammunition used in US and Australian special-purpose weapons. Parabellum is derived from "*Qui desiderat pacem, praeparet bellum*" (Whoever wants peace should prepare [for] war). "Parabellum" was DWM's (German ammunition firm) cable address.

Nine Rules

A business-size pocket card with the rules of conduct toward the Vietnamese people issued to all MACV personnel:

For personnel of US Military Assistance Command, Vietnam

The Vietnamese have paid a heavy price in suffering for their long fight against the communists. We military men are in Vietnam now because their government has asked us to help its soldiers and people in winning their struggle. The Viet Cong will attempt to turn the Vietnamese people against you. You can defeat them at every turn by the strength, understanding, and generosity you display with the people. Here are nine simple rules:

DISTRIBUTION—one to each member of the United States Armed Forces in Vietnam (September 1967).

1. Remember we are guests here: We make no demands and seek no special treatment.
2. Join with the people! Understand their life, use phrases from their language and honor their customs and laws.
3. Treat women with politeness and respect.
4. Make personal friends among the soldiers and common people.
5. Always give the Vietnamese the right of way.
6. Be alert to security and ready to react with your military skill.
7. Don't attract attention by loud, rude or unusual behavior.
8. Avoid separating yourself from the people by a display of wealth or privilege.
9. Above all else you are members of the US Military Forces on a difficult mission, responsible for all your official and personal actions. Reflect honor upon yourself and the United States of America.

ninety   The 90mm (3.5in) weapons included:

    1) 90mm gun on M48-series Patton main battle tanks.
    2) 90mm gun on M56 Scorpion antitank vehicles.
    3) 90mm M67 recoilless rifle seeing limited use in Vietnam.

No ammo, no brass.   This phrase had to be uttered to the range NCOIC as each man left the firing line, declaring he had not retained any live ammunition or expended cartridge cases. Some troops declared with a slurred, "No ass, no grass." Detecting it, most NCOs ignored the mocking declaration.

No Fire/No Fly Zones   These were small areas of operations designated by the HQ controlling the Tactical Area Of Responsibility (TAOR) as prohibited from firing artillery/mortars and aerial delivered ordnance into without approval—cannot engage unidentified targets of opportunity. Reconnaissance teams or other small units were conducting operations in such areas. See "Free Fire Zone."

non-chargeable leave   This was personal leave time granted for special circumstances and was not charged toward one's 30 days' annual leave. It included: 30-day leave prior to deploying to Vietnam, 30-day leave back to the States for extending in Vietnam for six months, 30-day emergency or compassionate leave for the death of an immediate family member, and convalescence leave to recover from wounds, injuries, or illness (duration dependent on medical condition).

Note: Chargeable leave is the 30 days' annual leave for all service members. Individuals could take a seven-day in-country chargeable leave in addition to R&R while in

Vietnam. Few did this or even knew it was possible. In-country R&R (q.v.) was not charged to leave time, but was a three-day pass.

noncom   Noncommissioned officer (NCO). Enlisted men in the pay grades E-4 to E-9. NCOs were sergeants and corporals.* Note Army and Marine sergeant rank titles may be dissimilar for the same pay grades.

* The Army rank of Specialist 4 (SP4), pay grade E-4, the same as a corporal, was not rated as an NCO.

non-rated men   Marines in the pay grades E-1 through E-3, below corporal, and not rated as NCOs.

North Vietnam   Democratic Republic of Vietnam (DRVN) (*Việt Nam Dân Chủ Cộng Hòa*). RVN surrendered on 30 April 1975, but was not formally absorbed into the DRVN until 2 July 1976.

North Vietnamese Army (NVA)   People's Army of Vietnam (PAVN—pronounced "pavin," *Quân Đội Nhân Dân Việt Nam*). Aka "NVA Regulars" (q.v.).

No shit?   Said when questioning someone's comment or statement, i.e., "You're kidding me." The usual affirming response was "I shit you not."

notebook   Officially a "memorandum book," a small notepad with dark green cover and ruled pages. Usually carried in left chest pocket with black or blue/black ballpoint pen or No. 2 lead pencil, the Army standard.

"No way, Jose."   "Ain't happenin'." Something that will never occur or never be authorized. The appendage "Jose" was added simply as it rhymed with "No way" and had no racial connotations.

Nung   Ethnic Chinese in North Vietnam, *Hoa Nùng*. Many evacuated to South Vietnam in 1954 to settle in the Central Highlands. They were known for their loyalty to Special Forces and served in reconnaissance projects and as bodyguards.

Nuoc mam   *Nước mắm pha* (mixed fish sauce). An important staple of the Vietnamese diet and a primary source of protein liberally doused on rice and other foods. Made from fermented fish sauce, sugar, lime juice, vinegar, and varied spices. There are numerous varieties for different foods as well as regional varieties. Nuoc mam has a strong pungent odor which many Americans found unpleasant and seemed to permeate villages.

Nuoc mam and sweat.   Describing the smell of VC/NVA in the jungle. It is true that VC/NVA were sometimes detected by the smell of nuoc mam, mainly from cooking in basecamps.

NVA Regulars   Used somewhat ominously when referring to North Vietnamese Army troops and even VC Main Force units, which were largely manned by NVA troops after 1968. American troops for the most part grudgingly respected the NVA. Vietnamese referred to them as "hard hats" (*non coi*) owing to the rigid sun helmets.

NVA tanks   The NVA used five models of ChiCom and Soviet tanks:

> 1) Soviet-made PT-76 amphibious reconnaissance tank with 76.2mm gun.
> 2) Soviet-made T-54 and T-55 medium tanks with 100mm guns.
> 3) ChiCom-made T-59, copy of T-54A with 100mm gun.
> 4) ChiCom-made T-62, improved T-59 with 85mm gun.

These tanks could be easily knocked out by US/ARVN M41A3 and M48A2/A3 tanks, 106mm RRs, and even LAWs with multiple hits.

O OSCAR

O-1 through O-6   Company grade (O-1 through O-3) and field grade (O-4 through O-6) officers' pay grade was often used in lieu of their formal rank title. "He was just promoted to Oh-Four." General officers (O-7 through O-10) were rarely referred to by their pay grade. O = Officer. See US Rank Appendices.

oak leaves   Rank insignia for major (O-4) (gold full-color, brown subdued) and lieutenant colonel (O-5) (silver full-color, black subdued).

O-Club   Officers Club. Large bases possessed an O-Club. Warrant officers could attend, but were only marginally welcome. Extremely rare for even senior NCOs to be invited, even for special occasions. NCO clubs were available for E-4 (corporals, not SP4s) to E-9s. It was equally rare for officers to be invited. Distinct officer and NCO clubs began to disappear in the 1990s.

Off the edge of the world.   A unit in the field that had moved off the map sheets it had on hand. A risky situation making it difficult to call in artillery and air support.

"Off your ass (butt, back, rack) and on your feet, out of the shade and into the sun."   A self-explanatory command. Break's over.

...of the Marine Corps   Only five Marines include this distinction in their billet titles:

Commandant of the Marine Corps   General

Assistant Commandant of the Marine Corps   Lieutenant General (General from 1968)

Chaplain of the Marine Corps   Captain (Navy)

Sergeant Major of the Marine Corps   Sergeant Major of the Marine Corps

Color Sergeant of the Marine Corps   Sergeant

oh *or* **zero dark thirty**   Really early in the morning. Between midnight (0001 Hours) and sunrise.

Oki   Okinawa Island, aka "the Rock," where the 173d Airborne Brigade and 3d Marine Division had been stationed prior to deploying to Vietnam. It remained a key support base for US Armed Forces through the war. Okinawa and the Ryukyu Islands were a US possession from 1945 to 17 June 1972 when it was returned to Japanese authority and became a prefecture of Japan (similar to a county).

Old Man, the   Commanding Officer (CO, q.v.) in company and field grade ranks. If a general officer, he was officially the Commanding General (CG). See "Six, the."

Oleo Strut, The   "G.I. coffeehouse" (q.v.) established in 1968 in Killeen, Texas outside of Ft Hood. An "oleo strut" is a pneumatic shock absorber on aircraft. The Oleo Strut coffeehouse attempted to give returning vets a "softer landing" by reducing stress, to decompress. It became an antiwar nerve center, published an underground newspaper, organized boycotts and peace marches, and established a legal aid office. It closed in 1972. Other G.I. coffee houses opened from 1968, two of the better known being the UFO (a play on USO—United Service Organization, q.v.) outside of Ft Jackson, South Carolina, The Shelter Half outside of Ft Lewis, Washington and Pentagon GI Coffeehouse, the main deployment/return bases for Vietnam. All of the coffee houses closed their doors by 1974.

One 'aw, shit…' erases a hundred Attaboys.   Do one little thing wrong and all the past good you've done is for naught. It can also mean, keep your opinions to yourself.

one-five-five   The 155mm M114A1 towed howitzer, M123A1 towed/auxiliary-propelled howitzer, M53 self-propelled gun, and M109 self-propelled howitzer. The M53 was only used by the Marines. (Prior to 1962 the M114A1 howitzer was known as the M1A1.)

one-five-one   The ¼-ton 4x4 M151-series utility truck. Aka "quarter-ton" or "jeep"—even though it was technically not a Jeep, being designed and built mostly by Ford. Some were later built by Jeep. Soldiers *never* referred to it as the "MUTT" (Military Utility Tactical Truck), its developmental program designation. The M151A1 was widely used in Vietnam and some issue made of M151A2s from 1971. Built by Ford, Jeep, and Kaiser. (Some 1950s Willys ¼-ton M38A1 Jeeps saw use in Vietnam.)

100-mile per hour tape   Basically duct or "duck" tape. It was required to remain externally adhered to helicopters at 100mph. Widely used for many types of repairs to include field gear and uniforms. The 2½in-wide 60yd rolls were Kelly (bright) green—not OD.

150-day early out   Five-Month Early Out Program. When completing a Vietnam tour, if one had five or fewer months remaining in his active duty enlistment, he was automatically discharged rather than going to the expense of reassigning him to a new unit with Permanent Change of Station (PCS) orders. Some individuals volunteered to extend one or more months in Vietnam in order to take advantage of the "five-month early out."

one-oh-five   The 105mm M101A1 and M102 towed and M108 self-propelled howitzers. Marine LVTH6 landing vehicles, howitzer also had a 105mm howitzer as did the monitor (MON) riverine gunboat. (Prior to 1962 the M101A1 howitzer was known as the M2A1.)

one-oh-six   The 106mm (4.1in) M40-series recoilless rifles mounted on M151A1C jeeps, M274 Mules, and M50 Ontos (6x 106mm). It could also be ground-mounted on a one-wheeled three-legged mounting removed from the M151. Some were retrofitted on M113A1 APCs.

one-one-three   The M113-series amphibious armored personnel carrier (APC) and support vehicles. See "ACAV" and "track." The ARVN and VC called it the "Green Dragon." (Some claim post-Vietnam that it was called the "Gavin." The M113 *never* carried this designation in Vietnam or today.)

M113-series Tracked Vehicle Variants

M106A1 4.2in mortar carrier

M113A1 armored personnel carrier

M113A1 armored cavalry assault vehicle

M114 reconnaissance vehicle (withdrawn)

M125A1 81mm mortar carrier

M132A1 flamethrower

M548 6-ton cargo carrier

M577A1 command post vehicle

XM741 20mm Vulcan antiaircraft system

XM45E1 flamethrower service vehicle

1-2-3-4 W.D.W.Y.F.W.   Antiwar protest slogan seen on buttons and posters. "One-two-three-four! We Don't Want Your Fucking War!" A G-rated variation was, "One, two, three, four! We don't know what we're fighting for!" Others were "Ho, Ho, Ho Chi Minh! The NLF is going to win!" and "Hey, Hey, LBJ, how many kids did you kill today?"

one-seven-five   The 175mm (6.8in) M107 self-propelled gun, the longest ranged (33km/20.5mi), but poor accuracy at long ranges and a slow fire rate. It was effective, however, as a long-range area fire weapon.

one-star general   Brigadier general (BG) (O-7). Aka "BG" pronounced "bee-gee." Commanded separate brigades or were assistant division commanders.

one-twenty   Soviet 120mm (4.7in) HM43 (ChiCom Type 55) mortar. Considered one of the most effective mortars in Vietnam in spite of its weight.

on the ground   In the field, someone actually on the ground where the action is and not in a firebase TOC or overhead in a helicopter. From the air, the relatively small piece of terrain on which an action is being fought looks unchallenging terrain-wise and distances short and easily and quickly traversed by boots. Actually with boots on the ground, it is much more difficult.

Ontos   Full-tracked lightly armored M50 and M50A1 antitank vehicles mounting six 106mm recoilless rifles. Pronounced "on-tose." Aka "Pig"—it was squatty and ugly. They were used by the two Marine antitank battalions as suppressive fire weapons. In Greek, *óntōs* is said to mean, "Thing," but it actually means: "truly, in reality, being."

Ooh Rah! or AHUGA!   Marine battle cry dating back to WWII. Exact origin cannot be determined and theories abound. It is said the future sergeant major of the Marine Corps, GySgt John Massaro serving in the 1st Amphibious Reconnaissance Battalion, used "AHUGA" in his cadence calls, replicating the "Dive, dive!" claxon of the special operations submarine they employed. It was picked up and spread by other NCOs and morphed into "Ooh Rah!" Besides running chants, it is a basic war cry signifying readiness, enthusiasm, and motivation—*Esprit de Corps.*

op/ops   Operation (Oper) *or* Operations. "He's out on an op." "He's the ops shop (S-3)." "He's assigned to the Ops Section." An Operation Order was an OPORD ("pronounced "Op-Ord") and an Operation Plan was an OPLAN (pronounced "Op-" or "Oh-Plan"). A FRAGO (pronounced "Frag-Oh") is a Fragmentary Order, an addition or update to an OPORD.

open door policy   Many commanders, especially at company and battalion levels, maintained an "open door policy" in which any soldier could request to see them, usually to express a grievance. Courtesy called for soldiers to let their chain-of-command (squad leader, platoon leader, etc.) know of the visit and to first see if grievances could be settled before disturbing the "old man."

Open mouth, insert boot.   Putting one's foot in his mouth. Misspeaking. Saying something out of line (q.v.) or "stupid."

ordnance   Any type of ammunition, bombs, demolitions, and certain chemical munitions. The term was used loosely to cover a wide variety of munitions, things that go boom. The fast-mover (q.v.) dove in and released all its ordnance on the tree line (q.v.). Ordnance Branch was responsible for ammunition handling, vehicle and equipment maintenance (until 1966 when changed to composite maintenance units), and Explosive Ordnance Disposal—EOD.

OSCAR-MIKE   Radio code for "on the move" meaning the unit is moving or is en route. An individual stating he is "OSCAR-MIKE" means he is doing well, feeling good.

Otter   M76 full-tracked 2½-ton amphibious cargo carrier used by the Marines.

Outhouse on a Hill   Red, white, and blue patch of the 1st Logistical Command. It had a broad circular border with an angled arrowhead inside the patch's lower right quadrant looking much like an outhouse precariously perched on a hillside.

Out of line.   Speaking out of turn or making an inappropriate statement. Originated with a soldier being "misaligned" (slightly out of place) in a unit formation. "Out of step" implies the same. Someone not on board or not going along with policy or requirements.

Outside my lane.   "That's outside of my lane." "Isn't that outside of your lane?" "Stay in your lane." The "lane" refers to designated lanes on firing ranges with corresponding firing positions and targets. The lanes were marked, but one could accidentally fire into adjacent lanes. "Mind your own business." See "Above my pay grade." (This did not originate from today's "lane training exercises.")

Outside the wire.   Everything beyond the outer perimeter barbed wire barriers surrounding a base or installation.

"Outta sight, man!"   Something incredibly good. "Hey, man! That's boss!" Really, really cool.

Outta sight, outta mind.   If the 1st sergeant can't find you he can't make work assignments. Of course once you're found…

Over and out.   Both are communications procedure words. "Over" means you have heard the message and expect a reply. "Out" means you have heard the message but are ending the conversation. One or the other is used. They are *never* used together.

Overseas Bar   Overseas Service Bar was a small embroidered gold-yellow bar on an Army Green backing worn above the right cuff of the Army Green coat. One bar represents six months' service in a combat zone. Army only.

over the beach   An amphibious assault landing by Marine units via amtracs, landing craft, and helicopters from the Special Landing Force—a one- or two-battalion force aboard an amphibious ready group as a floating reserve off the coast of Vietnam. They conducted short-term operations and raids ashore. "Over the beach logistics" is the landing of supplies and materiel ashore where no port facilities exist.

P PAPA

P-38 Four "folding hand can-openers" in small brown envelopes were issued in C-rat cases with 12 MCI meals. Better known as the "P-38," it was said to be developed for the Army in 1942, but this type of can-opener had been in use by Boy Scouts and campers since 1914. It could be strung on dog tag chains or key rings and held in helmet camouflage bands. The nickname is theorized to be derived from the Lockheed P-38 Lightning fighter (as the can-opener was as fast as a P-38), or the German Walther P.38 pistol (no relationship), or because 38 punctures opened a can—but the author knows this is not necessarily true; it can be more or less. The P-38 is exactly 38mm in length, but its design drawings were not metric. The truth is that the nickname's origin remains a mystery. P-38s have been used as screwdrivers, to clean boot cleats and fingernails, rip open care packages, strip insulated wire, cut string and tape, disassemble weapons and equipment for cleaning, and scraping, scoring, and more. (The now oft-seen larger P-51 can-openers did not appear until 1985 for the Tray or T-rations.)

paceman Soldier designated to keep the pace count to aid in estimating distance covered and assisting with navigation. It involved more than simply counting paces, the paceman had to allow for shorter paces moving uphill and in dense vegetation, longer paces downhill, and the added distance of weaving around trees, dense brush, bamboo clumps, and rough terrain. Sometimes two pacemen were designated and their count averaged. Depending on terrain a pace (roughly 30in) count averages 120–140 paces per 100 meters. Some pacemen tied a knot in a string/cord every 100 paces. Others stowed pebbles in a pocket and moved one to another pocket every 100 paces. (Montagnard scouts tied knots on strings to count the number of VC they spotted.)

pacesetter The individual designated to set the speed of movement on foot or convoy driving speed.

1) In a convoy a designated vehicle near the column's head. Not necessarily the convoy commander, as he would travel back and forth monitoring the convoy's progress. An experienced truck driver heading each convoy serial to regulate speed. A "serial" is a sub-element of a convoy march column. Typically 10–30 vehicles.

2) In a tactical movement traveling cross-country the speed varied dependent not only on desired movement rate, but terrain, vegetation, visibility, weather, and enemy situation.

3) In a small unit conducting a non-tactical foot march a designated individual at the head of the column sets the pace. It might be an officer or senior NCO.

Pacific Architects and Engineers   PAE or PA&E, Inc. is an American defense and government services contractor founded in 1955. It worked in Vietnam since 1963 providing facilities engineering support to the US Armed Forces and the CIA. Two similar major contractors were DeLong and Vinnell Corporations.

pack rat   Soldier with a tendency to accumulate and hoard useful items, to include C-ration extras. It was not considered a favorable trait owing to one's "luggage" being limited to a rucksack, duffel bag, and pockets. Some, though, collected useful items and shared with their buddies. "Pack it up" meant load it up.

Pac-Vee   Bell SK-5 air cushion vehicle (ACV—Army, PACV—Navy for Patrol ACV). A lightly armed and armored hovercraft for carrying troops and supplies in the Delta and conducting river patrols. The Army and Navy each operated three from 1966 to 1970. The VC called them *Quai Vat* (Roaring Monsters).

pajamas   American nickname for Vietnamese peasant black, white, or blue work clothes worn as daily wear. Aka "P.J.s." The Vietnamese called them white outfits (*bộ đồ trắng*) and black outfits (*bộ đồ đen*).

Palace Guard   Tongue-in-cheek title for a dedicated security unit or a field unit temporarily providing security at a major headquarters. The 5th MIKE Force headquartered in Nha Trang was referred to as the "Palace Guard," being co-located with the 5th Special Forces Group HQ. Some ARVN divisions raised a ranger-type or reconnaissance company serving primarily as a guard unit.

pallet   Wooden shipping pallets of varying sizes were wisely repurposed, being a source of quality lumber, although short in length. Pallets allowed forklifts to pick up a complete stacked load and they could be moved and loaded in trucks and cargo aircraft. The wood was used to construct small structures, furniture, shelves, tent floors, and other uses. See "speed pallet." (Consequently, Vietnam today mass produces shipping pallets and so-called "pallet furniture.")

Panama soles   Original jungle boots had Vibram-type hiking boot cleated soles. From 1966 they were made with "Panama soles," with wider cleats providing a better traction and "grip" in slick mud and helped push accumulated mud out of the cleats' groves. The Vibram soles remained in use at least into the 1970s.

paper plates   Paper plates and cups and plastic eating utensils began to be used in basecamps and firebases in 1966 in lieu of mess kits. This eliminated the need for mess kit washing lines, reduced fuel consumption, and were far more sanitary. See "wash line."

party jacket *or* **suit**   Special reconnaissance units, Special Forces, and aircrews sometimes possessed party jackets or shirts worn off duty in their team house or unit/base club. They were often made of camouflage fabric and tailor-made—not simply modified field uniforms. They typically had various colorful insignia and tabs sewn on and sometimes embroidered outlines of RVN, flags, dragons, enlarged unit insignia, or other designs on it. Being informal, they were worn with non-matching trousers or shorts and sandals or tennis shoes.

pass A pass (liberty in the Marines/Navy) may be one, two, three, or (rarely) four days (aka 24-, 48-, 72-, and 96-hour pass/liberty) and are not chargeable to leave. Weekend passes can be 48- or 72-hour depending on if it is a three-day or "payday weekend." (Today paydays are twice a month.)

patch Officially a "shoulder sleeve insignia" (SSI). An embroidered unit insignia worn on the left shoulder by separate brigades, divisions, higher commands, and various agencies and organizations. See "pocket patch." (The Marines ceased wearing shoulder patches [aka "battle blazes"] in 1948.)

Pathet Lao Lao Nation, the Lao Communist Party; a generic name for Laotian communists, 1955–72. They never fully controlled Laos until 1975 and then under North Vietnamese domination. They were absorbed into the Lao People's Democratic Republic. Aka "Lao People's Party."

patrol base Small temporary position from which a platoon or company dispatched reconnaissance patrols and then moved on to search other areas. A patrol base was compared to a miniskirt as being temporary, providing minimal concealment, and defendable for a short time.

patrol cap Officially the "cap, field, cotton, wind resistant, poplin, M1951." An OD visored cap with internal ear flaps. Aka "Ranger cap." Little worn in Vietnam. When it was the lining and ear flaps were cut out. See "Ridgeway cap."

Patton tank M48A2, M48A2C, and M48A3 main battle tanks used by the Army and Marines, over 600 deployed plus 379 to RVN. Mounted a 90mm gun. Aka "Elephant" or "Big Boy"—both little used. The Marines also used the M67A2 Patton flamethrower tank. Named after GEN George H. Patton (1885–1945). (Phased out in the mid-1990s.)

PAX Abbreviation for aircraft passengers. Pronounced "packs." Sometimes referred to PAX aboard ground vehicles and watercraft.

payday loan Payday was the last Friday of the month and in the States usually resulted in a "payday weekend" with time off from Friday afternoon to Sunday night. See "pass." Loan practices varied. Payday loans were from one serviceman to another. One example was the minimum interest was $5 no matter how small the loan (if under $5). If over $5 it could be twice the loan amount—loaned $10; with interest it was $20. Others loaned on a more reasonable basis, e.g., loaned $20 and were paid back $25. Of course buddies would loan each other cash with no interest.

payday pussy   Visit to a prostitute on the end of month payday.

Peacenik   Early protesters opposing the Vietnam War, the term coined in 1962. They tended to live a Bohemian or countercultural lifestyle closer to the earlier Beatnik* style, which had not yet dissolved, and supplemented by the Hippies (q.v.). A lesser used term was "Vietniks."

* The "Beat Generation" existed from c.1950 to the early 1960s. The term "Beatnik" originated in 1958—aka "Nogoodniks." "*Nik*" is derived from a Russian term relating to a person associated with a group, belief, concept, or function. It approximately corresponds to the suffix "-er" or "-ist."

peace sign   The sign for "V" for Victory using the first and second fingers in a "V" shape originated in WWII (dit-dit-dit-dah in Morse Code). It saw very limited use in Vietnam as a victory sign. President Nixon frequently used it as a victory sign. Troops in Vietnam more and more frequently used it as a peace sign. Some senior officers thought they were seeing WWII-reminiscent victory signs. It was picked up by antiwar protesters in the States and given palm-out.

Peace Symbol   What became the "peace symbol" claimed a number of origins. One was in 1958 by British artist Gerald Holtom for the Campaign for Nuclear Disarmament. It superimposed the semaphore flag letters "N" and "D." Not copyrighted or trademarked, the symbol spread to other disarmament and antiwar movements during the 1960s. Those opposing the peace movement wrongly declared it was a symbol for the death of man and a Nazi symbol. Likewise some members of peace movements made equally false declarations of the origins and meanings of the symbol's elements. It was in fact used by the German Army as a vehicle identification symbol of 3. Panzer-Division from 1941 to 1944. It was not a German runic symbol, however. By the late 1960s it was readily accepted as a peace movement and antiwar symbol and worn by some service members on necklaces, wrist bands, posters, and marked on helmet covers and other objects.

Pees   American name for South Vietnamese piastres, aka "Ps." In 1953 Indochina issued as its official currency (*đồng tiền*) what were officially known as the *dong*, but popularly known as the *piastre* (frequently spelled as "piaster"). In 1966 the Bank of Vietnam (*Ngân-Hàng Việt-Nam*) issued new currency with which most G.I.s were familiar. Additional currency and coin denominations were issued through the war years.

Banknotes: 20, 50, 100, 200, and 500 *piastres* or *dong*.

Coins: 10, 20, and 50 *xu* or *su* (pronounced "sue"). They were near valueless and so little used that Vietnamese had to check to see what denomination they were.

The official exchange rate in 1969 was US $1 was worth 115$ VN (115 Pees). A 100 P note was simply equated to a dollar and a 500 P note to $5.

Pen Double-E Olympus PEN EE 35mm single lens reflex (SLR), half-frame compact camera issued through military intelligence and Special Forces channels. Introduced in 1961, it was compact, reliable, and simple to operate. "PEN" appears to have no specific meaning.

penflare gun M186 personal signal kit was issued with three red and two each white and green flares while the M185 had seven red flares. The A/P255-5A personal distress signal set was issued with seven red flares better designed to penetrate overhead foliage. They were used by ground elements to mark their location at night for aircraft. They were also in aircrew survival vests. It was advised never to fire a penflare toward a helicopter as it might be mistaken as tracer fire and fire returned. The penflare projectors were small tube-like devices, looking like a fountain pen, with an internal firing mechanism and cocking/firing release. The flare cartridge screwed into the projector's muzzle.

penny-nickel-nickel "1-5-5," radio slang for 155mm howitzers.

Pentagon Far East Military Assistance Command, Vietnam (MACV) headquartered in Saigon 1962–73; first in Cholon and from 1966 on Tan Son Nhut Airport. Aka "Disneyland Far East."

people Generalized group of soldiers or Marines—"warm bodies." "You people better listen up!" "Get your people moving!" "I need some warm bodies. You five men, half ya come with me."

people-sniffer The XM2 olfactonic* personnel detector (aka E63) was a 1967 man-packed sweat odor-detection device with an intake tube mounted under the barrel of an M16A1 rifle. Issues included its oversensitivity as it would detect the sweat of its users and it made a "ticka-ticka-ticka" sound. The airborne XM3 was helicopter-mounted and could more effectively detect sweat, urine, and campfire smoke plus truck exhaust. The enemy did manage to adopt some marginal means to counter it.

* Olfactonic or olfactory—relating to the sense of smell.

perimeter wire "The wire" (q.v.) or "barrier wire." The belt or belts of barbed wire surrounding a base or installation—"obstacle belt." It could range from a single coil of concertina up to half a dozen barriers and fences of varied design, width, and height. Interspaced through the barriers could be Claymore mines (q.v.), trip flares (q.v.), booby-trapped grenades, and tanglefoot (q.v.).

pests and vermin Annoyances included venomous snakes, centipedes, scorpions, spiders, mosquitos, bees, wasps, ants, water and land leeches, rats, mice, bats, roaches, flies, ticks, fleas, and mortars. Many carried diseases or bit or stung. Rats and bats could be rabid.

Phantom Blooper   This elusive, marauding grenadier is reputed to have been a turncoat US Marine who threw in with the VC. He is said to have operated in 1967–68 in I CTZ of northern RVN. Even after this period he was still reported in even more distant parts of Vietnam conducting numerous harassing attacks on US bases and fabled to possess uncanny accuracy with his M79. Just how accurate one can be firing blind from a couple of hundred meters into a blacked-out firebase at night is questionable. Firebases were so densely packed that some random rounds would invariably hit something. These were hit-and-run attacks in which a few rounds would be rapidly fired indiscriminately and the "Phantom Blooper" vanished before return fire was offered. Most likely "he" was actually different local VC guerrillas undertaking solo pestering attacks. There is no solid evidence that an American "Phantom Blooper" plagued firebases.

PHILCAG-V   "Phil-cag-vee." The Philippines was represented by the Philippine Civic Action Group-Vietnam, 1966–69 with 2,000 troops including a security battalion. Total Filipino contribution was 4,000 personnel suffering 9 KIA and 64 WIA.

pickets   U-shaped OD-painted steel barbed-wire picket posts (2, 3, 5, and 8ft). Besides erecting barbed-wire obstacles, they were used for various construction and fabrication projects.

pictomaps   Full-color aerial photo 1:25,000 scale map sheets overprinted with terrain contour lines, gridlines, and standard map symbols indicating manmade features. The terrain, vegetation, and manmade features, especially roads, trails, bridges, towns, etc. were more up to date than 1:50,000 topographic maps (see "funny papers").

Pigs   Military Police (MP), the same derogatory term as used for Stateside civilian police. Mainly used by Black deserters.

pile-on   Once an enemy force was detected and fixed or its movement direction determined, friendly forces would "pile-on" it, inserting pursuit and blocking forces and committing air and artillery support.

pill bottles   Some soldiers carried brown (amber) or clear plastic pill bottles with white plastic snap-on caps. (Child-proof caps were introduced in 1968, but not seen in the military.) The bottle might hold an assortment of aspirin (aka acetylsalicylic acid [ASA] tabs), Darvon (q.v.), salt tabs, chloroquine-primaquine and Dapsone anti-malaria pills, Lomotil (loperamide) anti-diarrhea pills, and sometimes codeine (opioid analgesic).

pineapple grenade   Mk 2A1 fragmentation hand grenade. This WWII grenade saw use early in Vietnam. Called a "pineapple" owing to its oval shape, the segmented scale-like skin similar to the grenade's segmentations (for a better grip, not for fragmentation). Prior to 1943 they were painted yellow rather than OD, further contributing to their "pineapple" nickname.

pin-on and sew-on insignia Officer and enlisted collar rank insignia, officer branch of service insignia, and specialty skill badges were provided in two styles—cloth sew-on and metal pin-on. Both types were available in full-color and subdued. The Marines did not use sew-on insignia. Full-color sew-on insignia used white in lieu of the silver and gold-yellow for gold metal. Enlisted full-color collar rank insignia were gold and subdued were matt black. Officers' silver metal rank insignia were matt black while the two gold insignia (2LT and MAJ) were brown instead of the full-color gold. Marine enlisted and officer pin-on rank insignia were the same colors as the Army's.

Pipsy-4 *or* -5 AN/PPS-4 or -5 ground surveillance radars. Transported by ¼-ton truck, but could be man-packed a short distance. PPS = Manportable-Radar-Surveillance.

piss and punk Bread and water ration served in Marine/Navy brigs (q.v.). Monotonous, but prisoners were given all they wanted and received regular meals every four days.

piss house Unannounced urine tests for drug consumption. Aka "golden flow." Yes, a medic had to watch. It was not until August 1970 that all returning troops were drug tested prior to departing. If tested positive they were removed from the Freedom Bird (q.v.) manifest to depart later after "detox." This was necessary due to increased use of heroin over marijuana.

piss marks Urine marks on the ground, usually alongside trails, indicating the enemy were present. Other indications were boot and Ho Chi Minh sandal (q.v.) prints on trails, scuff marks on rocks, flattened areas on the ground where men slept, faint rub marks on tree trunks caused by hammock cords, and banana leaves with rice grains (in which rice balls were wrapped).

piss tube Urinal tube on bases lacking a sewage system, which meant most were without. A 4in-diameter pipe or 81mm mortar plastic ammunition shipping tube with the bottom cut out and set at an angle to protrude a couple of feet from a gravel-filled hole. They could be located by following the distinct odor of ammonia and lime powder dusted to hold down flies. Aka "rocket launcher" as it was an angled tube imbedded in the ground.

platoon commander The official term was "platoon leader," but commander was often used. An infantry rifle platoon leader was an entry-level position for 2nd lieutenants and typically would serve in the position for six months before assuming support platoon or service positions at battalion and higher levels.

pocket CS grenade   The small XM58 CS pocket hand grenade saw limited use by MACV-SOG and LRRPs. The burning-type tear gas (CS)-filled grenade was used to flush out bunkers and small structures and for breaking contact.

pocket patches   Embroidered unit insignia sewn on a shirt pocket or plastic-covered and suspended by a hanger from a chest pocket button. Unofficial (q.v.), but locally authorized to identify a company or battalion-size or other small units—"morale or novelty patches." Especially popular in aviation units, but worn by others in base areas. US advisors wore the shoulder patch of the ARVN unit they advised on their left pocket along with other uniform distinctions.

poc time   Afternoon break from lunch for up to two hours during the hot part of the day, "siesta time." "Poc" or "pok" is not a Vietnamese term, possibly Korean; its etymology undetermined. Vietnamese *giac ngu trua* (noon nap).

pogey bait   Candy, snacks, and other goodies purchased from the "geedunk bar" (ship's canteen or snack bar). A Marine term.

pogey rope   Fourragere indicating a French unit award. This was a colored, braided shoulder cord worn on the left shoulder of service uniforms. "Pogey rope" specifically referred to the red and green *croix de guerre 14-18 fourragères* (Cross of War 1914–18) representing receiving two citations. They had been awarded to the 5th and 6th* Marines while assigned to the 4th Infantry Brigade (Marine) of the Army's 2d Division 1917–19. Units of the 82d and 101st Airborne Divisions were awarded numerous French and Dutch fourrageres in WWII.

* The 6th Marines did not serve in Vietnam.

pogue   Originally a Marine recruit, but came to include HQ and rear service personnel. Said to be an acronym for "Personnel Other than Grunts" or "Person Of Greater Use Elsewhere." Not true; it was never an acronym, but its origins are uncertain.

pointman   Lead man in a patrol or small unit in a tactical movement formation "running point." He was alert for signs of the enemy and booby-traps. The duty was rotated—"Take the point"—but selected proven soldiers with a keen eye were detailed when the opportunity for contact was high.

police call   A maneuver in which a unit lined up along one side of the company (or other designated unit area), "assumed the position" (q.v.), and moved in a loose line formation through the area "picking up anything that didn't grow there" (q.v.), to be deposited in the dumpster or garbage cans ("G.I. cans").

Police up the brass.   Informal order to pick up all empty cartridge cases and ammunition residue (q.v.) at shooting range firing positions and turn them in for reuse/disposal.

poncho hooch   Tent-like shelter made from one to four ponchos. No matter how it was rigged, it leaked. Aka "poncho tent," "poncho shelter." Pitched over static APCs and tank turrets as sunshades.

poncho liner   Officially "liner, wet weather, poncho." A lightweight "quilt" with a thin layer of polyester batting between two layers of thinner camouflage pattern nylon. It was an effective blanket helping retain body heat even when wet. They have been used to make "party jackets" (q.v.) or jacket liners. (Today it is known as a "Woobie," a security blanket, but that nickname did not emerge until the 1983 movie *Mr. Mom*.)

poncho raft   Expedient raft or float made of one or two ponchos with one or two soldier's packs, web gear, boots, helmets, and clothing bundled into a flotation device. Ponchos could also be wrapped around a bundle of small limbs and brush as a flotation device—"brushwood float."

Poop, dope, scoop, scuttlebutt   This could be factual news, rumors, or BS. If factual it might be "the word." *Poop from the Group*—an example newsletter title.

pop smoke   To ignite a colored smoke grenade to identify a unit's position to aircraft. To the Vietnamese, "pop-smoke" was a noun, a "smoke hand grenade." When igniting a smoke grenade to mark a unit's location, the ground force did not tell the helicopter what color the smoke was, only that they were popping smoke. The aircraft would identify the color he saw and that was confirmed by the ground unit. This prevented the enemy from popping the same color of smoke in different locations to confuse the aircraft.

pop-up   Three types of small handheld, ground, rocket-projected colored flares and smoke signals. Contained in a handheld tube launching pyrotechnic signals:

      1) Star cluster projecting five freefalling flares—green, red, or white.
      2) One-star parachute suspended flare—green, red, or white.
      3) Single smoke canister parachute signal—green, red, or yellow.

porta-bridge   The M113A1 marginal terrain vehicle carried a scissors-type 30ft folding bridge for mechanized infantry and armored cavalry units.

post   1) A place of duty, "His post is in the orderly room." A guard post.
      2) A "post" is any military installation or garrison, a "fort" being a permanent post and a "camp" being a temporary installation, although most are permanent.

pot   M1 steel helmet with liner, aka "steel pot," "tin pot," "piss pot," and "brain dome or bucket." The steel shell was just that and the web and leather suspension system was integral to the separate phenolic resin-impregnated rigid canvas liner—often called "plastic" or "fiberglass." The helmet could be used for a seat, heating water, washbowl, or bailing out foxholes. It was seldom used as such owing to the difficulty and time involved in de-rigging the shell from the liner and camouflage cover. See "helmet cover graffiti" and "helmet litter." (For "pot" related to marijuana, see "grass.")

POW Prisoner of War. ("PW" was used prior to the Vietnam War.)

POW bracelet A commemorative bracelet engraved with the rank, name, and loss date of an American serviceman captured or missing during the Vietnam War (aka POW/MIA bracelet). Created in May 1970 by the Voices in Vital America (VIVA) student group so American POW/MIAs in SEA were not forgotten. Wearers wore the bracelets, not taking them off until the named serviceman returned or his remains recovered.

prepaid mailer Prepaid Kodak film processing mailers were purchased in PX/BXs. The exposed film cartridge/roll was mailed to California or Hawaii and the developed photos were returned to you or forwarded to your home address. The reasonable purchase price covered processing and both ways postage.

prep fires Preparatory, referring to artillery, mortar, and aerial fires (bombing, strafing) placed on a target area such as a suspected enemy position to be assaulted or a landing zone in advance of the airmobile assault force arriving. "They're prepping the LZ now." "The hill's been prepped." It may be called "softening."

Prick-6 AN/PRC-6 handheld "walkie-talkie" FM radio used by squad and platoon leaders. Owing to its 6.5lb weight, awkward handling, and short range it was little used. Intra-platoon radio communications was seldom necessary. Aka "banana radio," owing to its shape.

Prick-10, -25, -77 AN/PRC-10, -25, and -77 backpack FM radios. Aka "Ten," "Twenty-Five," or "Seventy-Seventy." PRC = Portable-Radio-Communications. They weighed over 25lb with battery and accessories. A myth said the AN/PRC-77 had a longer range than the AN/PRC-25, but the only differences were that the "77" could accept the little used TSEC/KY-38 NESTOR voice encryption system and used fewer vacuum tubes.

Principal Staff "J," "G," or "S" staff officers assigned to a unit. "S Staff" were assigned to battalions, squadrons, groups, regiments, and brigades. They did not possess a chief of staff. The "G Staff" was assigned to divisions and higher commands and overseen by a chief of staff (CoS). "J Staff" indicated Joint service high commands. Formally, G Staff officers are referred to as, i.e., "Deputy Chief of Staff, G-4." The term "S-2," for example, could identify the intelligence officer himself or the staff section supporting him, i.e., S-2 Section or "S-2 Shop." The order of numbers was adopted from the French system in WWI.

G/S-1 = Administration/Personnel
G/S-2 = Intelligence/Security
G/S-3 = Operations/Training
G/S-4 = Logistics
G-5 = Plans or Civil Affairs (Military Government) if assigned.

prisoner snatch　Small-scale ambush or raid with the objective of apprehending a prisoner for intelligence purposes. Extremely challenging and difficult to execute. Aka "snatch and grab" or "POW snatch."

projo　Projectile, specifically artillery, mortar, recoilless rifle, tank gun, etc. rounds. The part of a munition that is sent downrange. Pronounced "pro-joe." A small arms cartridge (under 15mm .59-cal) may be said to have a projectile, but is more correctly a bullet.

pronto　Spanish for "fast." "Do it pronto!" Get it done fast or now. Nothing to do with Vietnam, other than a widely used adverb.

Pro Pay　Special Proficiency Pay (SP). Three levels of additional bonus pay could be awarded to enlisted men taking a once a year MOS test. The tests were not required in Vietnam, but company COs could award SP to men highly proficient in their duties. (MOS tests and SP Pay were eliminated after the war with the implementation of new evaluation procedures.)

Psyops　Psychological operations or PSYOPS—pronounced "sigh-ops" or "sai-aaps." Military information and propaganda operations directed against the enemy. "Winning Hearts and Minds" (q.v.). To show Free World forces in a favorable light and VC/NVA in a factually negative light.

PTSD　The term "Post Traumatic Stress Disorder" was *not* used during the Vietnam War and did not appear until 1980 in the American Psychiatric Association's *Diagnostic and Statistical Manual of Mental Disorders.* Chronic, i.e., persistent and long-lasting, "PTSD" did not come into common use until the mid-1980s. During the war the terms "combat fatigue, exhaustion, and stress" were used along with the non-clinical "flaky." In Vietnam there were an estimated 12 mental breakdown cases per 1,000 troops. In WWII there were 101 cases per 1,000 and 37 per 1,000 in Korea. This may not sound like many, but they were concentrated in combat units and the disorder might manifest itself years later.

pukes　Jerks, slobs, dirtballs. "Y'all just a bunch of pukes." See "maggot." Aka "shit bag" or "shit bird."

pull rank To remind lower-ranking soldiers of one's more exulted rank when it came to disagreements, trivial duties, privileges—"rank has its privileges."

Pull up stakes. Originated with the horse cavalry when picket line stakes were pulled up to depart. In modern use it indicated tent stakes being pulled up for a unit to depart. It means "pack up and let's go."

punji stakes The modern concept of embedded wooden stakes originated in the Indian Punjab Region. The sharpened wooden or bamboo stakes were used in scores of manners as obstacles and booby-traps. Barbed steel spikes were also used. Spoiled meat or feces were sometimes smeared on stakes to cause infection. They might be concealed in vegetation, hidden in punji stake pits, planted in stream crossings, etc. They reinforced wire barriers and were planted in moats around South Vietnamese outposts and defended villages. They were a significant enough problem for anti-stake soles to be installed in jungle boots (q.v.).

pup tent Two-piece shelter tent shared by two men with each carrying a buttoned together "shelter half," one three-section tent pole, guy line, and five tent stakes. Little used except in secure areas for temporary shelter owing to the "two sandbags by sunset" rule (q.v.).

push As in, "What's your push?" or "My push is…" "Any station this push"—an open call usually in an emergency. Radio frequency. Radio frequencies were graduated in megahertz (MHz) at half MHz intervals: 101.0 MHz, 101.5 MHz, 102.0 MHz. Aka "freq" (q.v.) for frequency. The term derived from models of AN/VRC-12, -42, -43, and -44 radios used in AFVs with push-buttons to select preselected frequencies rather than dials, which were difficult to manipulate in a jolting tank.

pussy cutoff date PCOD was a calculated date from which one was DEROSing (q.v.)—returning home. To prevent contracting a venereal disease before departing for home, sex was avoided for typically 10–14 days, allowing time to detect and treat VD (q.v.). Some took antibiotic pills (e.g., tetracycline) before and/or after sex—called "no sweat pills."

Puzzle Palace Headquarters of the Department of Defense, the Pentagon is in Arlington County, Virginia, but its mailing address was: 1400 Defense Pentagon, Washington, DC 20301. Aka "The Building," "Fort Fumble," or "Great White Puzzle Palace." The term "the Pentagon" also refers directly to the Department of Defense overseeing the Departments of Army, Air Force, and Navy.

PX commando Individual who purchased unearned/unauthorized badges, decorations, and other insignia to adorn his uniform. See "Wannabes and Stolen Valor."

pyro Wide range of pyrotechnic devices and munitions for signaling, marking, and illumination, including colored flares and smoke devices. Pronounced "pie-row." This included low-explosive training devices: grenade, artillery, and booby trap simulators. The M80 firecracker was actually an Army small arms fire simulator.

PZ Pick-up zone. A site where troops were picked up by helicopters at their base or a point in the field from which to be extracted.

Q QUEBEC

QM Sales A Quartermaster Clothing Sales Store was found on Stateside Army posts to sell uniforms, insignia, and individual equipment items to soldiers at cost (lower costing than PX/BX). (QM Sales was later absorbed into the PX/BX system.)

quad-fifty M45F four-gun mount with .50-cal M2 MGs, aka "quad." The power-operated mount was on an M55 two-wheel trailer. The mounts were removed from the trailers and fitted on 2½-ton M35-series cargo trucks for improved mobility and the ability to fire on the move. The guns and mount could also be helicoptered into firebases. The "quad-fifty" term also referred to the combined gun system and truck. Employed for firebase defense and convoy escort.

quarter-ton trailer ¼-ton M416 two-wheel amphibious cargo trailer* towed by a ¼-ton utility truck. Amphibious in that it floated with a full load when towed through water. Filled with water and ice, it chilled floating cases of beer for unit parties and barbeques.

* The M100 trailer was an earlier version.

Quick Kill Quick-reaction training technique taught from 1967 to 1972 using Daisy BB guns (.177-cal) with sights removed and a longer adult stock. The "point and shoot" instinctive shooting technique involved a shooter and thrower who flipped 3.5in and 2.5in metal discs 2–4 meters vertically. Both men wore plastic goggles. It did not take long for the shooter to consistently hit the discs. This was valuable training as jungle engagement ranges were often less than 20 meters and targets visible for mere seconds. Daisy sold sets commercially from 1968 to 1970 as Quick Skill to minimize the aggressive connotations.

Quonset hut Dating from 1941, these prefab corrugated steel arched buildings were common on Stateside Marine bases and used for all manner of purposes in Vietnam. They were built of corrugated steel with a semicircular cross-section ranging in size from 20ft x 40ft to 40ft x 100ft. They saw limited use by the Army.

R ROMEO

rabbits Used by Blacks to describe White soldiers. Self-segregated Black barracks displayed signs: "No rabbits allowed." "This area for blacks and blacks only." Other terms were "Whitey," "honkie" (also spelled "honky," "honkey"), "cracker," "redneck," "hillbilly," and "White trash." (The same terms were used by Whites to describe disadvantaged/poor/low-life Whites.)

radar tower   Usually a low timber tower emplaced on many firebases mounting an AN/PPS-4 or -5 or AN/TPS-33 ground surveillance radar to detect enemy movement in the vicinity of the base. The AN/MPQ-4 counterbattery radar was emplaced on some bases to detect incoming rockets and mortars. The enemy would determine the sector covered by the radar and attack the firebase from another direction. Canvas tarps were sometimes hung around the radar to screen its orientation.

RA, US, ER, NG   Regular Army, Conscripts*, Enlisted Reserve, National Guard, respectively. Service number prefixes. Entering a mess hall in Basic one shouted his category with a number as three men at a time ran through the door, "One RA!" "Two ER!" "Three NG!"—or whatever they were in whatever order. ERs and NGs were demeaned as they were going home after AIT. The drill sergeant might yell, "ERs and NGs grab your left tit and shout it out!"

* "US" was assigned to conscripts as they were part of the Army of the United States, an administrative catagory. It has been inactive since the suspension of the draft in 1973.

raggedy assed   Slovenly. Grungy, funky, poorly uniformed, filthy and well-worn uniforms and equipment. "He's one raggedy assed marine."

railroad tracks   Double-bar captain's rank insignia (O-3). The two bars appear as railroad crossties and the two small links as rails (silver full-color, black subdued).

Rambo   To set the record straight, John J. Rambo (rank never revealed), a Vietnam Special Forces veteran (never depicted wearing a beret), debuted in the novel *First Blood* in 1972 as US troops were withdrawing. The movie by the same title was released in 1982. While popular today, "Rambo" was *not* used to describe tough, gung ho, marginally deranged soldiers during the war.

Ranger buddies   Two-man "buddy teams" were specified in the Ranger Course to watch out and cover each other, being especially alert for cold or hot weather injury symptoms. Some units made this a practice in Vietnam and in others natural friendships developed between two or three men to become informal buddy teams. Typically FNGs (q.v.) were paired with an experienced man to learn the ropes. The partnership may or may not have lasted. In rifle platoons men were teamed in pairs, carrying between them one or two ponchos, a poncho liner, an air mattress, and an e-tool to dig a foxhole and share guard duty; one on and one off—"50 percent alert."

Ranger School   Officially the Ranger Course, a demanding eight-week combat leadership course for officers and E-4s up. "Ranger" might be appended to anything demanding, tough, or gung ho. Motto: "Rangers Lead the Way!"

ratfuck Taking the best of the available courses of action and leaving the less desirable for others. A Marine term.

Ration Card The MACV Ration Card (MACV Form 333) limiting what and how many commodity items could be purchased from PX/BXs during a tour. It varied over time and was actually generous. The 1966 issue generously allowed: two still cameras, movie camera, slide projector, movie projector, three radios, record player, tuner amplifier, three tape recorders, two watches, typewriter, electric fan, and TV set. The 1969 card added a refrigerator. Beer, liquor, and wine purchases were also marked on this three-section folding card. The main reason for the card was to prevent service members from purchasing additional goods and selling them on the black market to Vietnamese. Most soldiers purchased few of these items.

rat killing Rats carrying diseases were troublesome pests on bases, which they quickly infested. The Army provided rattraps and BB guns for rodent eradication. 12-gauge shotshells were sometimes reloaded with rice for safe shooting. Vietnamese kids would be paid a piastre to bring in rat tails as proof of kill for "rodent control measures." See "pests and vermin."

rat patrol A gun jeep (q.v.) or the jeep-equipped battalion reconnaissance platoon. The term came from the WWII TV series *The Rat Patrol* (1966–68), depicting a machine-gun-armed jeep-mounted reconnaissance team in North Africa.

rat-rig Radioteletype (RATT or RTTY) set. The ¾-ton truck-mounted AN/GRC-46 RATT was the most widely used model.

razor wire High tensile strength spring steel with integral tab-like razor-sharp barbs in concertina coils (q.v.). Aka "razor tape," "barbed tape," or "German wire." Developed in West Germany in the early 1960s. Extremely sharp and tough, being difficult to cut with standard wire cutters.

real world The world outside of Vietnam, particularly the United States, Home, the States. The militarized designation was CONUS—the Continental United States, the "Lower 48."

reckless rifle Any recoilless rifle (RR): 57mm M18A1, 75mm M20A1, 90mm M67, and 106mm M40-series. Most ComBloc recoilless weapons (57mm, 73mm, 75mm, 82mm, 107mm) were properly called "recoilless guns" as most were smooth-bored and not rifled as they fired fin-stabilized rather than spin-stabilized rounds. The VC/NVA referred to them as *Dai-bac Khong Ziat (DKZ)*.

recon Reconnaissance. Describes the mission, a unit, or the action of reconnoitering (scouting)—"recon the objective." The Commonwealth term, "recce," was rarely used by the US. A "visual recon" was conducted from the air or using aerial photos. A "map recon" examined the area, route, objective, etc. using the information available on map sheets.

Recondo   Contraction for RECONnaissance commanDO, a two-week "mini-Ranger course" concentrating on patrolling skills. The MACV Recondo School was operated from 1966 to 1970 by Special Forces' Project Delta. Stateside Recondo schools were conducted, notably by the 82d and 101st Airborne Divisions.

recon gloves   Black leather service gloves with the OD wool insert liners removed and the tips of the fingers cut off at approximately the second joints (first joint of the thumb). This protected the hands from thorns, cuts, abrasions, and tree ants, but the exposed fingers allowed for the more effective operation of weapons, tuning radios, eating, etc.

recycle   An individual failing a key part of training could be "recycled" to retake remedial training and retested. For example, an individual failing rifle range qualification would complete Basic and be reassigned to another training company undertaking marksmanship training and then qualify to graduate. (Modern recycling of aluminum, other metals, glass, and plastic was virtually unknown until the growth of the environmental movement in the early 1970s. Paper was being recycled.)

Red Ball Express   During WWII the Red Ball Express signified trucks carrying priority cargo to the frontlines in France. In Vietnam labels with a red disc and marked in white identified high-priority repair parts shipped from Stateside depots to Vietnam in the shortest possible time starting in late 1965.

Red Berets   ARVN airborne units wore a rose (bright) red beret (*bere do tuoi*). Also referred to ARVN Ranger units wearing maroon berets (*bere nau*).

Red Hat   Parachute riggers wore red baseball caps identifying them in marshalling and rigging areas. Quartermaster Corps riggers packed and repaired parachutes and "air items" as well as rigged cargo and heavy equipment for parachute drops.

Red Haze   AN/UAS-4 or -14 infrared sensor system aboard OV-1C/D Mohawk aircraft capable of detecting vehicle engine heat, campfires, etc. and recording the readings on film.

Red Leg   Artilleryman. Derived from the red seam stripes formally worn on blue trousers. Some artillery officers unofficially wore red socks rather than regulation black with Class A and B uniforms. See "gun bunnies."

red line   Paved highway was indicated on a map by a red line. Term used in radio traffic. Aka "Red Ball" loosely after the World War II Red Ball Express priority resupply convoys (q.v.).

Reds, Whites, Blues, Pinks, and Purples   Air cavalry troops (company-sized) possessed three platoons informally identified by colors: "Reds or Guns"—gunship platoon (red being the artillery branch color); "Whites or Scouts"—scout platoon (white being one of the cavalry guidon colors); and "Blues"—aero-rifle platoon and its lift section (blue is the infantry color). The "Pinks" were pairs of Guns ("Reds") and Scouts ("Whites") operating together. Some units employed "Purples," a gunship ("Red") and Huey with a squad of aero-riflemen ("Blue"). The helicopters of these elements might be described by their platoon colors: "white, red, or blue birds." (See "heavy and light fire teams.")

red smoke   Standard signal using an M18 red smoke grenade to signify contact with the enemy or warning of danger such as alerting an approaching aircraft of ground fire. Vehicles in convoys popped red smoke to let other vehicles know they were receiving fire. Red "pop-up" flares were used at night. See "smoke."

reefer   7½-ton M349 refrigerated two-wheel semi-trailer towed by 5-ton truck-tractor.

Regular Army   Full-time active duty component of the US Army as opposed to the Reserve Components: Army Reserve and Army National Guard. Enlisted men volunteering for the Army were classified as Regular Army (RA). RA officers were commissioned at West Point (q.v.).

REMF   Rear Echelon Motherfuckers. Pronounced "rimph." "Rear Echelon Military Forces" in polite company. Rear service support personnel who never left bases. Usually anyone at brigade level and higher echelons. A "Saigon warrior" was a soldier based in the Saigon area. There are different interpretations as to at what level one was considered a REMF. One scale defined REMFs as those getting "three hots a day and/or had a roof over their head at night." Approximately one in ten soldiers in Vietnam were combat troops, but again this varied widely depending on interpretation. To a grunt "busting brush," a REMF was the lowest form of life; the higher the echelon the lower in esteem they were held.

repple depple   Replacement depot; referred to the 22d (Cam Ranh Bay) and 90th (Long Binh) Replacement battalions, which processed incoming personnel. Pronounced "rep-pel dep-pel." It also referred to the divisional and separate brigade combat training centers required by GEN Westmoreland in 1967. They were operated by the divisional replacement detachments to provide two weeks' tactical and acclimatization training, aka "charm school." They were generally given a catchy name relating to the unit.

Reserves, the   Each of the armed forces' branches possess Reserve forces consisting of Reserve units and individual Reservists to be called to active duty in event of war or other national emergency. USAR, USAFR, USMCR, USNR, and USCGR. Thirty-five USAR detachments and companies deployed to Vietnam.

Rest and Recuperation   Incorrectly aka "rest and recreation" or "rest and relaxation." Service members were allowed one out-of-country R&R during a tour and another if extending six months plus a shorter in-country R&R. This was non-chargeable leave, i.e., not counted against the standard four weeks' annual leave. The duration of R&R was five days for most destinations. Due to their greater distance, seven-day leaves were permitted for R&R in Hawaii and Australia. Bangkok was reportedly the most popular for single G.I.s and Hawaii most popular with married G.I.s planning to holiday with spouses. Pan American World Airways was exclusively contracted to airlift the troops. Aka "Intoxication and Intercourse" (I&I), "Rest and Wreckage," "Rape and Pillage," or "Rape and Run." The R&R centers closed between 1970 and 1972. Below are the R&R destinations and the required parenthesized months served in-country for eligibility:

Bangkok, Thailand (3)	Penang, Malaysia (6)
Hong Kong (3)	Singapore (3)
Honolulu, Hawaii (6)	Sydney, Australia (10)
Kuala Lumpur, Malaysia (6)*	Taipei, Taiwan (3)†
Manila, Philippines (3)	Tokyo, Japan (6½)

* Kuala Lumpur closed July 1969 due to declining use.

† Republic of China (aka "Nationalist China," "Formosa").

re-sup Resupply. Pronounced as spelled. Logistics resupply of a unit in the field via helicopter (aka "log bird") or cargo parachute drop. Every three days most units in the field received a "light re-sup" by helicopter, delivering mainly rations, batteries, and water. A "major re-sup" was received on the sixth day, usually a rest day. Rations, batteries, ammunition, water, replacement uniforms, mail, "DX'ed" (q.v.) equipment, etc. was received. It was also a taxi service for replacements, those returning from R&R and picked up for R&R, and vets completing their tour. Aka "light log day" and "heavy log day."

re-up Reenlist, to sign up for another tour of duty—"re-upping." The Marines call it "shipping over."

rice paddies Rice paddies are found throughout Vietnam on the flatlands and on terraced hillsides. Vietnam is one of the most productive rice cultivating regions of the world and the Mekong Delta is the heart of the rice bowl. During the war, though, much of the arable land could not be cultivated and from 1965 rice was imported from the US and elsewhere. Production did increase gradually through the war and drastically after the war. In Vietnamese culture rice is considered a "gift from God" as "white gold." It has been said, "A grain of rice is worth a drop of blood." Rice (*cơm*) is essential to the Vietnamese diet as all three daily meals are with "rice and something else." Eating something without rice is not a meal, but a snack.

Rice paddies were the bane of infantrymen. They covered wide areas, having to be crossed while exposed to enemy observation and fire. When dry they were rock hard and dusty. There were often numerous ankle-twisting dried water buffalo hoof holes. When flooded, they were up to a foot deep of water afloat with fertilizing human and animal waste. There could be several inches of mud to drag the feet. Crossing a paddy atop the grid of 1–2ft-high dykes when flooded channeled the troops into kill zones and booby-traps. Paddies did provide good assault LZs being clear of obstacles and the choppers could land next to dense vegetation along the paddy's perimeter.

ricky-tick "Get it done ricky-tick." Do it now, do it fast. A Marine phrase. Derived from Rudyard Kipling's 1894 story of a speedy, agile cobra-hunting mongoose in India, "Rikki-Tikki-Tavi."

Ridgway cap Modified M1951 "patrol cap" (q.v.) with a "coffee can" or pillbox-style stiffened sidewall and flattop crown. Many officers did not like the "slovenly style" of the patrol cap. The stiffened and blocked commercial version could be purchased in PXs. They were optionally purchased from 1953 and approved by GEN Matthew B. Ridgway (1895–1993). Impractical in the field as it had a distinctive silhouette and could not be folded and carried in a pocket nor packed in a duffle bag. Definitely intended for "garrison" wear. Aka "Castro cap," as it was a signature headgear of the Cuban prime minister, *El Comandante* Fidel Castro. Replaced by the "baseball cap" (q.v.) in 1962.

riding shotgun Detailed to ride along as an assistant driver on line-haul truck convoys for escort duty.

right-angle flashlight MX-991/U flashlight. The standard handheld flashlight. Aka "Fulton flashlight" after the principal manufacturer. MX-993/U was a similar, less used, straight flashlight.

Right on. You're right, dead center, you got that right, I agree.

righteous Something good, justified, well done.

right-seater "Aircraft commanders" in helicopters sit in the right seat, while fixed-wing aircraft commanders sit in the left. Informally known as "pilots," while "co-pilots" ("left-seaters") were actually designated "pilots."

rip-stop Cotton twill fabric with a ¼in grid pattern of reinforcing threads that reduces ripping if torn. Used in jungle fatigue fabric from 1968 and a light nylon version was used in later poncho liners.

riverine Military river patrol, security, and combat operations. The Mobile Riverine Force was a joint Army and Navy task force operating in the Delta from 1966 to 1972. See "Brown Water Navy."

river patrol boat Navy-operated 31ft Patrol Boat, River (PBR) employed for river patrols mainly in the Mekong Delta (q.v.). Standard armament: three .50-cal MGs, one each M60 MG, and 40mm automatic grenade launcher. Approximately 190 deployed to Vietnam.

RMK-LBJ It was rumored Claudia A. "Lady Bird" Johnson (1912–2007), the first lady (1963–69), was an owner of RMK-<u>BRJ</u>, its actual name,* not "LBJ." It was a consortium of firms contracted for construction and logistics work for the US, 1962–72. Lady Bird was also rumored to own or have an interest in a sandbag or wooden shipping pallet factory and encouraged the war's continuation for her financial benefit. She was additionally accused of owning merchant ships transporting supplies to Vietnam, offshore power-generating ships, and probably much more. All totally untrue.

* Raymond International and Morrison-Knudson and Brown & Root and J. A. Jones.

rockers Inverted arches below point-up rank chevrons identifying "hard-stripe" NCOs E-6 through E-9. E-6: one rocker, E-7: two rockers, E-8 and Army E-9: three rockers, USMC E-9: four rockers.

rocket belt A band of terrain outside of bases and installations from which ChiCom 107mm, 122mm, and 140mm rockets were fired at the base—two concentric rings indicating the rockets' minimum and maximum effective ranges—8,000 and 12,000 yards. The first such rockets were fired in Vietnam in February 1967.

rock 'n roll While Rock and Roll music was in its heyday, in this instance it meant setting an M16 rifle on full-automatic fire, for which it was actually ill-suited owing to overheating. The term was not used as much as depicted in movies. Full-auto was also inaccurate and for this reason was called "pray and spray" in hopes the target, seen or unseen, might be hit. Most of the shots went high.

ROE Rules of engagement. Pronounced "R-O-E," not "roe." ROE in Vietnam is a sensitive and complex topic and can only be briefly discussed here. ROE differed over time and area. Changes were made for military and political reasons at different levels. It could vary in adjacent unit areas of operation (AO), districts (sub-sectors), and provinces (sectors). Specific examples include: no fire into built-up areas (towns and villages) unless positively receiving fire from an identified area and its source, no damage to infrastructure, no fire at or close to unarmed civilians, no indirect fire on targets near civilians, cannot return fire unless fired on and then only when the enemy was positively identified and in close contact. Sniper and mortar fire and indirect fire was not considered identifiable enemy fire. There were also temporary restrictions such as Christmas ceasefires. Ground assaults in urban areas known to shelter enemy forces generally had to be preceded by loud-speaker warnings and leaflet drops. Only flat-trajectory weapons (rifles, MGs, grenades, and recoilless rifles) could be used in civilian-populated areas, and then only if there was a specific, identifiable target. The ROE for the employment of air support, fighter-bombers, or helicopter gunships were even more restrictive. There were situations too in which there were restrictions on artillery fire, for example, owing to shortages. During the period of US withdrawals units were cautioned not to initiate engagements. See "Free Fire Zone" and "No Fire/No Fly Zones."

ROG/ROGER ROG was short for ROGER, used as a pro-word for "Received and understood" in radio-telephone conversations as well as informally. Also simply means "yes." "That's a big ROG" = "That's a big yes." "ROGER that" = "I understand/I agree." Prior to 1956, ROGER was also the phonetic alphabet word for "R" to result in confusion because of its dual meanings. From 1956, ROMEO was used for "R." AFFIRMATIVE for "yes" was also used. See "NEGATIVE."

Note: The phrase "ROGER WILCO" is procedurally incorrect, as it is redundant with respect to the intent to say "received."

ROKs Republic of Korea (South Korea). A general term for South Korean troops, pronounced "Rocks," under the ROK Forces Vietnam Field Command. Sign spotted near a South Korean drop zone—"Lookout for falling ROKs." The ROK presence in Vietnam was from 1964 to 1973 with a total of 320,000 troops deployed. ROKs were often said to be highly aggressive and took no nonsense from the Vietnamese and harassed them. Others reported they limited combat operations to reduce casualties. The Korean Army and Marines lost 5,099 KIA/MIA and 10,962 WIA. Main ROK units were the Capital Division, 9th Infantry Division, 2d Marine Corps Brigade, and 100th Logistical Command.

Rolex (Switzerland) and Seiko (Japan) watches Just about everybody had one. Bulova, Elgin, Benrus, and other brands were sold in PX/BXs. Often worn inside the wrist rather than on the top of the wrist to better protect from bumps. In bases some secured the coupled band under a jungle fatigue shirt pocket flap.

ROMEO Informally a radio. ROMEO is the phonetic alphabet for "R." "The ROMEO's dead. It needs a fresh 'bat' (battery)."

Rome plow "Rome plow" refers to the Rome Plow Company of Rome, Georgia. They were heavy-duty dozer blades affixed with a spike-like "stinger" on the left end to first split a tree, then back off and push it over. The massive blades were mounted on Caterpillar D7E and D6B and Allis Chalmers HD-16M bulldozers. Engineer land-clearing companies escorted by mechanized infantry and tanks clear-cut forested areas beginning in 1968. This prevented the enemy from conducting close ambushes and allowed crossing enemy to be detected and engaged. It also denied the enemy concealed camps and bunkers, which were destroyed by land-clearing units. There were three types of "cuts": 500m wide "road cuts" along both sides of highways; "area cuts" were large swaths cleared to keep areas under surveillance and reduce infiltration; and "tactical cuts" around the perimeters of firebases, installations, and towns. As a noun "a romeplow" signified the bulldozer as well as the flattened path created by Rome plows and tanks. Aka "tank-bust" (q.v.).

RON Remain Over Night. A unit's nighttime position in the field. Pronounced "Ron." As a verb, pronounced "We're going to R-O-N at this location." Aka "night defensive position" (NDP).

ropes Loose hanging seam threads on uniforms. Aka "Irish pennant." Not recommended to pull them off as the stitching thread may unravel. Clip or burn off with a cigarette.

ROTC Reserve Officer Training Corps. Pronounced "Rot-See" although usually spoken as "R-O-T-C." There were two programs. High school Junior ROTC (JROTC) offered basic military instruction, but upon joining the Army provided no rank or pay benefits. Completing the four-year college Senior ROTC (SROTC) program resulted in a Reserve commission in the Army or other branches of service followed by a four-year active duty and two-year Reserve obligation. Future Marines attended Navy ROTC (Marine Option). It was compulsory in most state-sponsored colleges for male students to undertake Military Studies their first two years, which gave them no military credit unless they completed the second two years. An alternative for Marines was the college-based Platoon Leader Course (PLC). ROTC was the largest source of Army commissioned officers, followed by OCS and then West Point. Campus SROTC armories were sometimes a target of antiwar protests.

rotor-head Army aviators, specifically helicopter pilots and crewmen. Army aviation units began arriving in Vietnam in 1961. Then there was no Army Aviation Branch until created in 1983. Aviators and units were assigned throughout the Army and included: infantry, armor, artillery, transportation, medical, and military intelligence flying units.

round eye Caucasian, a white man. A "round eye woman" was a much discussed near mythical creature.

round file Paperwork discarded, or "round-filed," in a wastebasket; especially applied to requests for leave and other favorable personal actions. Aka "circular filing system" and "File 13." "I'll be sure to file it in File 13," i.e., throw it away.

RPD The 7.62mm RPD (ChiCom Type 56) belt-fed light MG firing AK-47 ammunition. RPD = *Ruchnoy Pulemyot Degtyaryova* (Degtyaryov handheld MG).

RPG "Rocket Propelled Grenade." Actually the Soviet designation meant *Reakeivnoi Protivotankovii Geanatomet* (hand antitank grenade launcher). RPGs launched recoilless projectiles, not rockets. The RPG-2 was an early simplistic model, while the improved RPG-7 was introduced in Vietnam in late 1967. The VC/NVA called the RPG-2 the B-40 and the RPG-7 the B-41, the "B" meaning *Badoka* (bazooka). The ChiCom versions were the Type 56 and Type 69,* respectively.

* The ChiCom Type 69 was not used in RVN.

RPG range boosters Soviet PG-2 and PG-7 shaped-charge (antitank) projectiles for RPG-2 and -7 launchers were sometimes turned into intelligence with "range boosters or extenders" fitted to the tailboom. These were nothing more than standard tubular propellant charges which screwed onto the end of the tailboom. Many soldiers did not realize the propellant changes were separate from the projectile and attached before firing.

RPG screen An 8ft-high section of chain-link fence (hurricane fence) erected on barbered wire pickets (q.v.) 2–12ft in front of perimeter bunkers and AFVs parked in defensive positions. Closer than 4ft was less effective. The screens prevented the RPG and other sharped-charge projectiles from detonating by damaging its fuse system or breaking up the projectile, or causing it to pre-detonate. The screen could be rolled up and carried on the front of AFVs.

RTO Radio Telephone Operator. Each field officer was accompanied by an "R-T-O" carrying a backpack AN/PRC-10, -25, or -77 radio. There was very little telephone-operating involved. These radios weighed over 25lb plus spare batteries and accessories. The Marines called them "radiomen," or officially, "field radio operators." There were two methods of employing RTOs. Some only carried the radio while the officer did all the talking. Other RTOs did all the talking, relaying what his officer said and repeating what the officer/RTO on the other end said. On bases RTOs doubled as officers' drivers. "RTO" was one of the Army's more used abbreviations, but was only listed in the AR 25-52, *Authorized Abbreviations, Brevity Codes, and Acronyms* as "Rail Transport Officer."

rubber "In the rubber" means operating within a rubber plantation. Rubber trees were planted in orderly rows with a dirt road grid network, and if under tended cultivation, devoid of undergrowth. The overlapping treetops prevented helicopters hovering over a plantation from seeing anything on the ground.

rubber bitch A pneumatic mattress, aka "air mattress." Useful in the field to allow a man to sleep more comfortably some inches off the ground, avoiding creepy-crawlies and flooding rainwater. They could also be used to float casualties and equipment across streams and aid heavily loaded individuals to cross.

rubbers Condoms were sometimes fastened over rifle muzzles to keep out mud and water. They did not have to be removed before firing. They also kept cigarettes and matches dry. A supposed dread was that water leeches could enter the penis, causing some men to habitually wear condoms—the threat and practice are a myth. See "blousing rubbers."

ruck Rucksack, a large backpack with two or three external pockets and metal pack frame. Included the lightweight rucksack, tropical rucksack, ARVN rucksack, and CIDG rucksack (latter lacked a frame). "Put on your fuckin' ruck." "Ruck up."

rucksack flop Plopping on the ground for a break with the rucksack positioned to support the sitting grunt. Preferably the ruck would rest against a tree.

Ruff-Puffs   Derived from the initials RF/PF. Collective term for Vietnamese Regional (*Dia Phuong Quan*), and Popular Forces (*Nghia Quan*) provincial ("state") and local village defense forces, respectively. Often they are addressed as if they were a single organization or interchangeable.

Rumor Control   The source of all rumors, which by definition cannot be controlled. The most accurate information source until after the event occurs.

Rung Sat Special Zone (*Đặc khu Rừng Sác*)   A military area in the Sác Forest (*Rừng Sác*—Salty Forest) through which the Lòng Tàu shipping channel to Saigon flowed. It was incorrectly known as the "Forest of Assassins," being a misinterpretation of *Sác* (Salty) to mean *Sát* (Assassin).

S   SIERRA

saddle blanket patch   The shoulder patch of the 1st Cavalry Division (Airmobile), which was twice as large as other patches, said to be so large so it could be seen better in dust raised by horses. The patch was cavalry gold-yellow, with a black diagonal bar, and a black horse's head unfairly said to represent "The horse they never rode,* the line they never crossed, and the color tells you why," which is far from an accurate description of the division.

* The division was horse cavalry from 1921 until dismounted in 1943 and had since served as infantry in the Pacific, Japan, Korea, and Vietnam. It was converted to airmobile in 1965. Another myth was that it had dishonored itself in WWII and remained overseas from 1943 (except for three months in 1965) until returning to the States in 1971.

Saddle up.   "Gear up." The order to don rucksacks and be ready to move out. Also to mount or load onto vehicles and depart. "Hat up" and "Let's hat out of here" saw some use—sort of put on your hat and say goodbye.

sage green   Light gray-green used in most Air Force flying uniforms and equipment. Sometimes Sage Green Shade 509 items were issued to Army aviators as substitutes.

Saigon cowboys   Cowboys were young Vietnamese smalltime street hoods and found in other cities as well. Pronounced "KOboy." Many were unfit for military service, possessed student deferments, were draft dodgers or deserters, or social rebels. Many were sons of middle and upper class families and draft exempted. ARVN and police made sweeps pressganging them into the military. VC elements in cities sometimes blended into the street gangs. They typically wore sunglasses, sports shirts, and tight bellbottoms. Most had motorbikes. They dealt in drugs, the black market, gambling, and snatching valuables from pedestrians. Many harassed prostitutes catering to Americans shouting, "O.K. ten dollar" or "O.K. Sahlem"

("Salem," general name for cigarettes), accusing them of selling themselves cheaply. Others simply wanted to party, drink, and chase girls themselves.

Saigon taxi   Typically French-made blue-and-white-painted Renault 4CV compact cars (CV = *cheval-valeur* = horsepower). Looked like a miniature 1939 Ford. Many owners of motor scooters, cyclos (q.v.), Lambrettas (q.v.), etc. would transport servicemen for a minimal fee.

Saigon tea and tea girls

"You buy me dink G.I. You hansome boi. Me so horny I love you beaucoup long time."

A glass of actual weak tea, Kool Aid, Coca Cola, or some other carbonated drink and even that was watered down. It was non-alcoholic, but the tea girls would have customers believe otherwise. The girls' glasses were smaller, sometimes much smaller than the customers' glasses so they could drink it quicker and entice customers to buy them another. A drink was typically US $1 or $2 (100 or 200 piastres).

Bars and tea-drinking girls were not limited to Saigon, but found in any city. Young, attractive girls were hired to pretend to date or be interested in the G.I. clientele and would visit their table, flirt, chat them up if they knew enough English, urge them to buy them drinks, and make whatever promises the clientele desired. They used common American girl names (or "Kim") and usually bore different aliases at different bars. They would periodically excuse themselves and temporarily work another customer or two out of sight of the table. If two to four hostesses were at one table working drinking buddies, at least one of the girls would always remain at the table to keep the customers from leaving or attracting other girls—they were competitive. If they got their customer drunk enough they might ask for small gifts or cigarettes—to sell on the black market. Most hostesses did not drink alcohol or smoke themselves. The goal was to keep the customers there as long as possible to buy themselves and the girls more drinks. The girls got a percentage of the drinks they sold, with the bartenders keeping tab. They wore long straight hair and traditional áo dài dresses or American pop "big hair" hairstyles or "go-go" girl outfits with micro-minis and spike heels. Some were actually prostitutes, legitimate waitresses and barmaids, or strippers and dancers and may have worked several jobs in different establishments on different nights.

Most of the girls were relatively good honest girls and while they would take all of one's money, seldom was there any malice. Most G.I.s knew the game and played along, knowing what was going on. It was simply a diversion and a chance for female companionship. Green G.I.s could be scammed, but most quickly learned the score. Many of the girls were married, or had Vietnamese or American boyfriends and actually made a good living. Off-duty American MPs and Vietnamese MPs (QC) patrolled the bar districts and knew the girls. After hours and off duty they could sit with the girls, visiting and getting drinks (including Saigon tea) at a discount.

Salt and Pepper   There were repeated reports of what was thought to be a pair of Black and White American defectors, possibly Marines. Some suggested they might be French, but there is no evidence. They were dubbed a "Salt and Pepper VC armed propaganda team." The reports emerged through the war and mostly in eastern I CTZ but were reported elsewhere. They were mainly reported by aircraft, and the distance allowed no clear identity of two men dodging through vegetation. In some instances patrols were inserted to intercept them. Other reports said they were seen accompanying NVA troops in firefights. No clear or confirmed identification was ever made nor was their ethnicity determined. In all probability they were a myth.

salt tabs   Sodium chloride white 1-gram tablets taken with at least a quarter canteen cup of water for excessive salt loss. They were withdrawn from use in the late 1970s as sufficient salt intake occurred with issue field rations. "Sports drinks" and commercial bottled water did not exist at the time.

Salute Report   SALUTE Report was an aide-mémoire for the intelligence report format. A simple report made to higher HQs when necessary.

S—Size of enemy force.

A—Activities of enemy and direction.

L—Location with grid coordinates.

U—Unit identification and uniform.

T—Time and date of sighting.

E—Equipment and weapons.

sa-maj   Little-used term for sergeant major (SGM) and command sergeant major (CSM) (both E-9) and especially frowned on by sergeants major. The Army's modern sergeant major originated in 1958. The position of Sergeant Major of the Army (SMA) was created on 4 July 1966, but did not receive a unique rank insignia until 1979. On 28 May 1968 an additional E-9 rank was approved, command sergeant major as the CSM of battalions/squadrons and higher echelon units serving as the senior advisor on enlisted affairs. SMG held staff NCO positions at division and up. Within the Marine Corps sergeant major was reinstated in 1954. The Sergeant Major of the Marine Corps (SgtMajMarCor) was established in 1957.

sandbag   Filled 4.75in x 10in x 19in tan and green fabric sandbags weighed 40–75lb depending on the soil and its moisture content. Average weight with dry sand was 65 pounds.

14in x 26in greenish-gray polypropylene ("plastic") sandbags were introduced early in the war and lasted longer in the harsh climate.

sand-bagging   Goofing off. Implying one was lying around useless.

sandbag rucksack   Rucksack with at least a 35lb sandbag, frequently heavier, for physical fitness and acclimatization training.

Sandbags, barbed wire, and Lambrettas.*   The three most commonly seen things in Vietnam.

* The Italian-designed Lambretta, q.v., three-wheel motor scooter was one of the most common private motor vehicles.

S&P   Stake and Platform. A flatbed 12-ton M127 four-wheel cargo semi-trailer. "Stake" referred to the vertical posts installed to support removable side panels. Aka "stake bed trailer."

sappers   Sappers or reconnaissance-commandos were the VC/NVA Special Attack Corps (*Bo Tu Linh Dac Công*). A little used term was "zapper"—a play on "sapper" and "zap"—to kill. "Sapper" was a European term for assault engineers who dug "saps"—approach trenches when attacking fortresses. They were comprised of hand-picked militarily proficient and politically reliable troops. The quality of training ranged from minimal to quite advanced. They were trained to infiltrate through barbed wire barriers, clearing paths for follow-on assault troops, entering the base, and swiftly attacking key targets with satchel charges and grenades, what they called "going for the guts." In effect they were the VC/NVA's precision artillery. They were an alternative to mass assaults, resulting in heavy personnel and equipment losses. They also conducted reconnaissance and security patrols, gathered intelligence, laid booby-traps, kept Free World installations under surveillance, and made maps of targeted objectives. They were noted for detailed reconnaissance, precise planning and coordination, realistic rehearsals, surprise, and extremely violent rapid action once initiating an attack.

saucer cap   Visored service cap. Aka "bus driver" or "flying saucer cap." Worn by all services of the appropriate colors with dress and service uniforms with the exception of airborne (garrison cap) and Special Forces (green beret).

sawed-off M79   Reconnaissance teams used shortened 40mm M79 grenade launchers as break-contact weapons firing multiple rounds into the enemy force at short ranges. Between 2in and 3.5in of the muzzle was cut off, with the front and rear sights removed and the stock cut off to reduce the overall length by 13–14 inches. Aka "shorty" or "cut-down M79."

Say again, over.   Say what you just said again as I did not understand. One never says "Repeat." Repeat is reserved only to request follow-on artillery, mortar, or air strikes on the previous target. "Hit it again."

scabby sheep   Nickname for the US press corps according to President Diem and his aides. *Báo-Chí* was the official term for "press," what would be called the "media" today.

Scorpion   The 90mm M56 self-propelled full-tracked antitank vehicle also called the "SPAT" (self-propelled antitank—pronounced "Spat"). Unpopular as the crew was completely exposed to fire, vulnerable to mines, and had no armor other than the small gun shield. Used by the 173d Airborne Brigade in 1965–66 and replaced by M113A1 ACAVs.

scrounger   A skill possessed by one of the most essential, valuable, and maligned members of a unit. Scrounging is an art requiring skills in communications, negotiations, patience, ability to show empathy, gaining trust, sucking up, bull-shitting, lying, and closing the deal. See "midnight acquisition."

scuttlebutt   Marine/Navy rumors and gossip. A scuttlebutt is a ship's water cask or modern-day water fountain.

Seabag   Marine/Navy equivalent of the Army duffle bag for stowing clothing and other belongings. Duffle and sea bags were service members' "baggage."

Seabees   Derived from the abbreviation "CB"—Construction Battalions. Navy construction engineer personnel performing a wide variety of construction tasks and supporting shore parties. "As busy as worker bees." CBs performed construction work for all services.

seagoing bellhops   Little-used name for Marines, owing to their dress uniforms and Marine ships detachments in which some served as the ship captain's orderly. A misconception is that the Marine Corps, the "Corps," was a component of the Navy. The Corps was a separate branch of service from the Navy and assigned to the Department of the Navy alongside the Navy.

SEA hut   Southeast Asia hut. A simple one-or two-story wood and corrugated metal hutment for quartering troops on larger bases. It was high-ceilinged to allow heat to rise, with large mosquito screen window panels allowing air circulation, lift-up window covers to close against blowing rain, and built off the ground to prevent heavy rain flooding and keep out pests. Sides and ends were sometimes sandbagged approximately halfway up the walls.

search and destroy   An offensive operation deploying a number of different-sized units in specified areas of operation (AO). Initiated by the ARVN in 1964. The goal was to first tie down the enemy in the area then saturate it with patrols to search out enemy elements and caches plus destroy infrastructure and pro-VC villages—"Zippo missions" (q.v.). Once the area was cleared of enemy forces, Free World forces withdrew and the enemy reoccupied the area. The media made much of the aggressive name for the strategy, endangering civilians, and that it was only a short-term solution. In order to downplay the destructiveness of the operations in April 1968 GEN Westmoreland ordered them renamed "reconnaissance-in-force," "search and secure," or "search and clear." "Clear and hold" missions emerged later in an effort to clear the enemy from the area and insert security forces to hold towns and villages. This tied down a great many troops and was only of limited success. Some ARVN units were accused of conducting "search and avoid" operations in which they dodged enemy contact.

security clearances   There are three levels of security clearances: TOP SECRET (TS), SECRET (S), and CONFIDENTIAL (C). For Official Use Only (FOUO) is not a security classification, but are documents which may not be appropriate for public release. All officers had at least a SECRET, but were cleared for TOP SECRET if necessary. A wide range of enlisted specialties were assigned clearances as duties required.

sergeants   The Army and the Marines practice different means of addressing sergeants (NCOs).

Army—Sergeants, staff sergeants, sergeants 1st class, platoon sergeants, and master sergeants were addressed simply as "Sergeant." First sergeants were "First Sergeant," and both grades of sergeants major were "Sergeant Major."

Marines—All ranks are addressed by their full rank title.

Note: "Sarge" is only used in the Army under informal circumstances or when indirectly addressed. The term is particularly frowned on in the Marines.

serial number   Actually the "service number" (S/N) assigned to every armed forces member. From 1 January 1968 Social Security Account Numbers (SSAN or SSN) replaced S/Ns on orders and were embossed on dog tags (q.v.) by July 1969. (At the time there were no "identity theft" problems.)

serum albumin   Human serum albumin blood-volume expander. It helped maintain blood pressure in severely hemorrhaging casualties. This set was carried by medics and reconnaissance teams to replace blood in hemorrhaging casualties by drawing water from the body. The beer can-sized key-and-strip opened can held a 100ml bottle of serum albumin, IV needles, and IV surgical tubing.

service magazines   Each service distributed monthly magazines for information, professional education, and morale. Listed are those intended for enlisted personnel and junior officers. Not included are branch magazines and professional journals.

> *Stars and Stripes (Pacific)*—all services, five days a week newspaper
>
> *Army Digest,* renamed *Soldiers Magazine* in June 1971—Army
>
> *Gung Ho Magazine*—Marine Corps
>
> *All Hands Magazine*—Navy
>
> *Airman Magazine*—Air Force
>
> *PS, The Preventive Maintenance Monthly*—Army

The *Army, Navy,* and *Air Force Times* were three independently and commercially published twice-a-month newspapers. (*Marine Corps Times* was not established until 1999.)

782 gear   "Seven-eighty-two gear." Marine term for individual web gear, so called after Navy and Marine Corps Form 782, "Quartermaster Receipt for Individual Equipment," which one signed for his gear. Aka "deuce gear."

seven-six-two   The 7.62mm (.308-cal) cartridges for M14 rifles and M60, M73 and Mk 21 (Navy) MGs. Aka "seven-sixty-two," "seven point six-two," "7.62mm NATO." The four ComBloc 7.62mm (.311-cal) rounds were *not* interchangeable with the 7.62mm NATO, an oft heard myth. (Prior to 1954, during its development, the 7.62mm NATO was known as the .30-cal T65E3.)

seventy-five   1) 75mm (2.95in) M20A1 recoilless rifle used by the ARVN and VC/NVA, which also used the ChiCom 75mm Types 53 and 56, copies of the US M20. The Type 56 fired a fin-stabilized HEAT round, which the Type 53 could not.
2) 75mm gun mounted on the M24 Chaffee light tank used by the ARVN until 1965.

seventy-five pack   The 75mm M116 pack howitzer used early in the war by the ARVN. Prior to 1962 it was known as the M1A1 pack howitzer. It was designed to be broken down into seven components for pack mule carriage or parachute drop. Phased out by 1964. (Often used as salute guns on Stateside posts as the M120 salute howitzer modified to accept blank cartridges only.)

seventy-six   The 76mm (2.99in) gun mounted on the M41A3 Walker Bulldog (q.v.) light tank employed by the ARVN from 1965. The NVA's Soviet-made PT-76 amphibious light tank had a 76.2mm gun, slightly inferior to the US 76mm.

Sgt. Rock   Tough hardcore soldier (not necessarily attributed only to NCOs) either in jest or seriously. Derived from the fictional central character Sgt. Franklin

"Frank" John Rock, in the *G.I. Combat* comic book series from 1952 to 1988 (422 issues). Rock himself debuted in 1959 (#82). The series title was changed to *Sgt. Rock* in 1977.

Shackle Code   Simple alpha-numeric substitution brevity code for transmitting grid coordinates and other numbers. This was a ten-letter word with no repeated letters. For example:

B L A C K N I G H T

1 2 3 4 5 6 7 8 9 0

To transmit the grid coordinate 294685, the sender would say:

Sender: "Ready to Copy? Over."

Receiver: "ROGER. Over."

Sender: "I shackle, LIMA, HOTEL, CHARLIE, NOVEMBER, GOLF, KILO. How copy? Over."

Receiver: "I copy, LIMA, HOTEL, CHARLIE, NOVEMBER, GOLF, KILO. Over."

Sender: "Good copy. Out."

Shade 51   1940s and 1950s Olive Drab Shade No. 51, a dark chocolate brown, was an officer's service uniform color. Even though Shade 51 was an obsolete color, it sometimes referred to Black soldiers.

shades   Sunglasses, often called by a brand name, "Ray Bans." They were discouraged in the field as it might make it difficult to detect the enemy in jungle shadows and hidden in vegetation. Depending on light conditions and shadows they were said to hamper the detection of tripwires. The attitude was that wearing sunglasses one was trying to be "cool" or "hip." Most officers frowned on their wear.

Shadow Government   The VC was represented by its political arm, the National Liberation Front (NLF). The "VC Infrastructure" was a political and administrative system established at local levels overlaying the South Vietnamese Government. US and ARVN forces expended much effort to destroy the VC Infrastructure. A key weapon was the Provincial Reconnaissance Unit (PRU—pronounced "Proo"), a covert operation under the CIA's Phoenix Program (1965–72). In 1969 the VC established the Provisional Revolutionary Government of the Republic of South Vietnam to represent the VC in international diplomacy, i.e., Paris Peace Talks. Its intent was to pursue a "People's War" and make it a viable part of the new Vietnam. Instead, the North Vietnamese marginalized the lingering VC remnants, ensuring much of it was wiped out during the 1968 Tet Offensive, and took over the control of South Vietnam themselves in 1975.

shag ass   Book 'em. Hook 'em. Haul ass. Turn-tail. Takeoff. Run like hell, beat feet, hat it, split, get a move on. I'm outta here.

Shake 'n Bake*   Graduate of the Army Noncommissioned Officer Candidate Course (NCOCC) conducted at Ft Benning, Georgia, from August 1967. NCO shortages were severe owing to casualties, medical disqualification, need for NCOs in units outside of Vietnam, trainers, retirement, and the 25-month Stateside assignment between Vietnam tours. Qualified volunteers completing 16 weeks' Basic and AIT undertook 12 weeks' intense leadership training followed by 9 weeks of OJT as a drill corporal in a Basic or AIT training company. NCO Candidates (NCOCs) were promoted to corporal, but did not wear chevrons. Some attended Jump School. Graduates were promoted to SGT and assigned to NCO slots in Vietnam, usually after "shadowing" an existing squad leader for a time. They were often criticized as being inexperienced, with arrogant attitudes. The latter may have been due to their experience as drill corporals, and their "drill sergeant" mentality directed toward subordinates may have carried over. There were hard feelings too that inexperienced E-5s were taking over as squad leaders while there were more experienced E-4s in the platoons, some filling squad leader positions. Career NCOs were jealous, having taken 4–6 years to earn their stripes and the Shake 'n Bakes were sergeants after ten months. 20,068 NCOCs graduated (1,003 KIA) and the course closed out in March 1972. The Armor and Artillery branches formed similar courses for another 6,000 NCOs.

* Betty Crocker's Shake 'n Bake of 1965 was a flavored bread crumb-style coating for chicken and pork. The product is applied by placing raw meat pieces in a bag containing the crumbs, closing the bag, and shaking so the crumbs adhere. The crumb-coated meat is then oven-baked. A lesser used term was Jell-O's "Whip 'n Chill," an instant mousse-style dessert.

Sheridan   M551 Armored Reconnaissance/Airborne Assault Vehicle (AR/AAV), a parachute-droppable "light tank" used by armored cavalry units for reconnaissance and security missions. It was frowned upon to call it a "tank" in an effort to prevent a false sense of security because of its thin aluminum armor and unrealistic expectations of its capabilities. Regardless, it was commonly called a "tank," even in official documents. It was armed with a 152mm (5.9in) gun/launcher. Besides caseless HEAT and flechette gun projectiles, it could launch MGM-51 Shillelagh antitank wire-guided missiles, but these were not used in Vietnam. Introduced in 1969 to replace M113A1 ACAVs that had replaced M48 tanks in most armored cavalry units in Vietnam. Sheridans were highly vulnerable to mines and RPGs and never faced enemy tanks. Named after GEN Philip Sheridan (1831–88), a proponent of fast-moving cavalry operations.

Shit a brick.   The ol' man's going to shit a brick over this." "Top's shitting a brick sideways." "He's having a kitten." A pain in the ass.

shit-burning detail   Latrine or head burnout detail or "crap detail." Outhouse-like latrines, with one to three holes ("one to three-holers" and "six-holers"), were provided catchment containers ("shit barrels") made from half a 55gal steel drum. These were inserted in an opening in the latrine's back under the seats, which may have had actual toilet seats or simply holes in a plank. The barrels were carried by two men to a burn area, usually close behind the latrine. Two or three gallons of diesel or other fuel was poured in, the contents stirred with a board, and lit. Shit-burning detail was considered a distasteful duty—or in some instances, punishment—but was undertaken once a day. Often Vietnamese employees on larger bases performed the duty. Black smoke columns rising from bases led new arrivals to think it was under enemy fire. Repugnant as it was, it was more sanitary than digging pits and setting a latrine over it. Once filled with waste the pit was back-filled and a new pit dug. The buried waste would saturate the surrounding ground when it rained. (There were no "porta-potty" chemical toilets pumped out by contractors as today's practice.)

Shit don't stink.   "He thinks his shit doesn't stink." Someone with an inordinately high opinion of himself.

Shit for brains.   Stupid or foolish. A shithead. "He's got shit for brains."

shithole   It might be a latrine, but more likely it described any other dump; a filthy or sorry place. "That bar's a shithole." "Firebase (enter name) is a shithole." See "shitter."

Shithook   CH-47A/B/C Chinook cargo helicopters. Aka "Hook." While named after the Chinook Indian nation as are most other Army helicopters, Chinook also represents the Chinook winds—wet, warm coastal winds in the US Pacific Northwest. The aircraft's twin-rotors generated strong winds, and passengers experienced hot exhaust-blast when loading and unloading. The inclusion of "hook" refers to the large cargo hook for lifting external sling loads.

shit list   A notepad or mental list of men unfortunate enough to have made the drill sergeant's/instructor's, 1st sergeant's, or sergeant major's list of those responsible or guilty of transgressions, infractions, and violations, real or imagined.

shit pot load   Indicative of a filled chamber pot; a whole lot of something. "I just got in a shit pot load of radio batteries." "You're in a shit pot load of trouble, pal."

shitter   An outhouse-like latrine; a latrine (bathroom) in general. Aka "shithouse," "shithole," "crapper," "the John," or "the can." In the Marines/Navy it was a "head"—an open-pit latrine. On a base aka "washroom," with toilets, washbasins, and showers.

shop   Informal term for an office and/or work area, e.g., S-3 Shop, Intel Shop, Commo Shop, Maint Shop, etc.

short time   One-time short-term sex act provided by a prostitute, a "quickie."

Short-timer

A soldier was considered "short" when nearing the end of his tour, usually when within a month of finishing. Many units pulled men out of the field in their final 2–4 weeks; not necessarily a hard and fast rule. "I'm so short I can do a PLF off a dime." To understand this paratrooper's comment one must know that a PLF (parachute landing fall—q.v.) was practiced by jumping off a 3ft platform into a sawdust pit and executing the PLF roll. To be so short to able to use a dime for the jump platform meant one was indeed "short."

"_____ **days and a wakeup.**" Insert number of days remaining in Vietnam with the "wakeup" being the day of departure. The newly arriving optimistic soldier could say, "364 days and a wakeup." "Three days and a wakeup and I'm going on R&R."

Short-timer calendar. Many men had a pictographic calendar of a woman's nude body suggestively posed (most common), a helmet (sometimes perched on a pair of boots), map of Vietnam, Snoopy (cartoon character), or a Boeing 707 airliner ("Freedom Bird"—q.v.). It was divided into either 30, 100, or 365 numbered day segments. They would be penciled or grease pencil-colored in counting off the remaining days.

Short-timer stick. With one or two months of his tour remaining some men marked or notched a stick with the requisite number of notches. He would cut off one notch a day until only a stub remained. Less widespread than calendars.

shorty carbine The .30-cal M2 carbine with its barrel cut off just forward of the forearm and the butt stock sawn off, leaving a pistol grip. A last resort personal defense weapon. Its rapid overheating, excessive muzzle blast, and highly inaccurate fire (no front sight) made it a "spray and prey" (q.v.) weapon. Aka "cut-down carbine" or "sawn-off carbine." M14 rifles and M60 MGs were occasionally cut down, but experienced the same problems.

Shot out. Actually "Shot. Out." but altered to a single phrase, practically a single word, "Shot-out." An artillery fire direction center's (FDC) radio message to the unit requesting fire support that the first round or volley has been fired—"On the way." See "Splash. Out."

showdown inspection Clothing and individual equipment inspection in which troops assembled in an extended formation (double-arm interval) and dumped out their duffle bags and stacked their uniforms. The supply sergeant calls off each item and it is held up as squad leaders confirm each item's presence. They are also inspected for condition and replaced if necessary. Aka "shakedown inspection."

shrapnel Common, but incorrect term for "fragmentation" caused by grenades, mortar shells, recoilless rifles, artillery projectiles, tank guns, rockets, aerial bombs, and other high-explosive casualty-producing munitions. "Secondary fragmentation" was gravel, rocks, rubble, wood splinters, etc. kicked up by the explosion. (Actual shrapnel are metallic balls filling a HE projectile with a time-delay fuse to achieve an airburst and shower troops on the ground with shrapnel. Named after the British officer who invented the projectile. Actual shrapnel projectiles were phased out by WWII.)

shrinking bird disease The myth of this disease was perpetrated by the VC as a propaganda tool accusing Americans of purposely spreading it through prostitutes. The penis is said to recede into the body. It is a delusional disorder, but symptoms are indicative of other actual illnesses.

sick call Morning sick call took place on firebases and other installations at the aid station or dispensary. The Marines used the terms aid station and sickbay. A "sick call commando" or "sickbay commando" describes a perpetual malingerer.

Since Christ was a corporal… Since time immemorial, this is the way it's always been. (In no way meant as sacrilegious.) "He's been in the Army since Christ was a corporal."

SITREP Situation Report. Pronounced "sit-rep." A periodic report describing the current situation or any recent developments and situation during the specified time period. Formats varied between HQs.

Six, the "The Six" identified the unit CO (q.v.) when appended to the unit's radio call sign and in conversation. The CO's M151 jeep bumper number was always HQ-6. "Six" was also used in informal call signs, e.g., "DANGER SIX" or "THUNDER SIX." Six was used as One through Four were used by the principal staff officers (S-/G-1 to S-/G-4) and Five by the XO.

6-month extension An individual could extend his tour for six additional months (or shorter periods). He would actually spend only five months in Vietnam with each extension—so called "early outs." Such an extension allowed him a non-chargeable* 30-day leave back to the States. A second six-month extension rated an additional R&R. From late 1969 married individuals extending their tour six months were required to provide a letter from their wife agreeing to the extension, which, if she approved, might make him wonder what her motivation was. Many infantrymen with less than 6–12 months' service remaining after returning from Vietnam were assigned to the 197th Infantry Brigade (Separate) at Ft Benning, Georgia, while paratroopers went to the 82d Airborne Division at Ft Bragg, North Carolina. Two six-month extensions reached the restricted tour length to no more than 24 consecutive months. Some individuals did remain longer. A 25-month break was required between involuntary tours.

* Non-chargeable (q.v.) leave did not count from one's regular 30 days' annual leave.

6x6   The 2½-ton and 5-ton trucks and truck-tractors with six powered wheels for improved cross-country mobility. Aka "six-by." They can be switched to power only the rear four wheels to reduce fuel consumption. The rear four wheels had dual tires.

sixty   1) 7.62mm M60 MG. Aka "the Pig," as some considered it ugly. "Number 60" was the Vietnamese term. The Australians called it the "GPMG" (General Purpose Machine Gun), a term seldom used by the US until after the Vietnam War. The unknowing or a mind-slip called it a ".60-caliber." That does not necessarily mean a "faker."
   2) 60mm (2.36in) M2 and M19 mortars. The 60mm was obsolete in the Army, but used by the Marines, ARVN, CIDG, and Vietnamese security forces.

sixty-one   ChiCom 60mm Type 31 and Type 63 mortars—modified copies of the US M2 mortar. They were called "61mm" in intelligence documents as that was the true bore diameter. It was assumed that the ChiCom ammunition was not interchangeable with the American, but both rounds were actually 60mm and interchangeable regardless of rumors saying otherwise.

Skipper   Informally a captain (O-3) in the Marines, specifically a company/battery CO. "The Skipper's on deck" ("The CO's present," or less formally, "The Ol' Man's showed up.")

SKS   Soviet 7.62mm SKS (ChiCom Type 56) semi-automatic carbine. Not to be confused with the ChiCom Type 56 assault rifle—the AK-47. SKS = *Samozaryadniy Karabib sistemi Simonova* (Simonov self-loading carbine). When the AK-47 replaced the SKS in the NVA in 1967, the carbines were reissued to the VC.

sky pilot   Chaplain. Aka "Padre" and "Holy Joe." Chaplains' position and rank were shown, for example, "Chaplain (CPT) Matthew" and addressed as "Chaplain Matthew." (Navy chaplains minister to the Marine Corps and Coast Guard.)

sleeping sweater   Tricot sleeping shirt, long-sleeved, two-button opening. Mainly used in the cooler northern mountains.

slick   UH-1-series Huey helicopter with only door-mounted MGs as opposed to gunship versions with side-mounted rocket pods, skid-mounted dual MGs, and chin-mounted automatic grenade launchers. Aka "school bus," as "slicks" only transported troops and supplies.

slick-sleeve private Army private E-1 or E-2 as they wore no rank insignia. Aka "buck private." On 28 May 1968 the Army privates E-2 (PV2) received a single chevron previously worn by privates first class (PFC) E-3. At the same time PFCs received a chevron with a rocker. "Slick-sleeve" then indicated only PV1s.* In the Marines an E-2 is a PFC and an E-3 is a lance corporal (LCpl). (In today's Army "slick-sleeve" means any soldier without a "combat patch" [q.v.] on their right shoulder, signifying they never deployed to Afghanistan or Iran.)

* It was first proposed PV2s be redesignated PFCs and existing PFCs be redesignated "lance corporals" as was Marine practice, but this was rejected as "corporals" were considered NCO leaders.

slop chute Marine enlisted recreation center, a beerhall. (A slop chute was the small ramp on a ship's stern from which garbage was discharged.)

smart ass/dumb ass "Smart ass" or "wise ass" was generally a smart aleck, while a "dumb ass" was, well, not very smart, a screw up. The phrases beg to ask, "Would you rather be called a 'smart ass' or a 'dumb ass'?"

smoke M18 colored smoke hand grenades available in red, yellow, violet, and green. Red meant a unit was ambushed, denoted danger, or warned away approaching aircraft. Yellow and violet were mainly "popped" to mark ground unit locations. Green was little used in the vibrant green landscape. Green could be used in dried vegetation. It was found that green dispersed swarming bees. Aviators often identified smoke colors using Pillsbury-brand powdered drink mix (similar to Kool-Aid) "Funny Face" marketing colors to delude the enemy monitoring radios: Rootin'-Tootin' Raspberry or Choo Choo Cherry (red), Lefty Lemon (yellow), Goofy Grape (violet), and Loud-Mouth Lime (green). (The white smoke grenade was the AN-M8. It was used for smoke screening and target marking, but not for signaling as it was confused as a marked target or simply as a fire.) See "red smoke."

Smoke 'em if you got 'em. Permission to light up a cigarette during a break. The Navy and Marine equivalent is, "The smoking lamp is lit." "The smoking lamp is out" means to extinguish all "smoking materials."

smokes Cigarettes. Aka "coffin nails." Refers to regular cigarettes, not marijuana. Australians called them "smacks." One-third of doctors at this time believed cigarettes caused cancer.

Smokey Bear hat The OD wool felt campaign hat with a Montana peak worn by Marine drill instructors since 1958 (originally adopted in 1912) and Army drill sergeants (M1911 hat) from 1964. DIs and DSs were known as "Smokey Bears." In the Marines the hats were aka "campaign covers" or "lemon squeezers," the latter having a similar appearance with the Montana peak. Marine shooting teams also wore it from 1961. Air Force military training instructors adopted the campaign hat in 1967. (Army female DSs did not wear distinctive headgear until 1972 when an Australian bush hat style was authorized. Marine female DIs could not wear campaign hats until 1996.)

SNAFU Situation Normal, All Fucked Up. Day-to-day routine. More of the same. Things aren't going right, as usual.

snake-eaters Specifically refers to Special Forces owing to survival training, but also applied to LRRPs, Rangers, and other special reconnaissance units.

Snakeye The 250lb Mk 81 and 500lb Mk 82 general purpose bombs when fitted with Mk 14 Tail Retarding Devices replacing the fin assembly were designated the "Snakeye." Aka "snake." The TRD slowed the bomb's descent, allowing the low-flying fighter-bomber to clear the impact area before it detonated. Playing the dice game Craps, a snake eyes thrown with a pair of one dots was good fortune.

sneak and peek The tactics of Special Forces, LRRPs, Rangers, and other reconnaissance units (aka "sneaky-peeks") of infiltrating into enemy territory, observing and reporting intelligence information, and exfiltrating from the area without the enemy realizing they had been there.

sneakers The common name for what were aka tennis, gym, and athletic shoes among other terms. Low black or white canvas laced shoes with flat, non-slip rubber soles. Today's common term of "running shoes" was little used. (Jogging did not become widely popular until the 1970s.)

sniper rifles Accurized rifles fitted with telescopic sights and selected rifled barrels for long-range precision marksmanship. These may have been especially selected and modified standard rifles or advanced purpose-built rifles.

US: .30-cal M1C and M1D, 7.62mm XM21 (redesignated M21 in 1975), .30-cal Winchester Model 70 (Marines), 7.62mm Remington M40 (Marines).

Australia: 7.62mm Parker-Hale Model 82.

VC/NVA: 7.62mm Mosin-Nagant M1891/30, Dragunov SVD (very scarce).

snipers True snipers were armed with better than average telescoped rifles and trained in long-range shooting, observation, target detection, camouflage, and advanced fieldcraft. An overused term; for example, one or two skirmishers or stay-behind riflemen were all too frequently called "snipers" for taking random shots at friendly forces.

Snoopy Snoopy was the good-natured beagle in the *Peanuts* cartoon strip (1950–2000; re-prints still published). He often mused about life and certain aspects of war via his daydreams as a WWI flying ace. While the cartoon avoided controversy in general and Vietnam especially, Snoopy was appropriated by servicemen as the happy-go-lucky WWI ace to express their own feelings about the war.

Snuffy   Grunt, Joe Tentpeg, boonie rat, troop, or trooper (not used by the Marines). Basically E-1 through E-4.

soda girls   Vietnamese girls from local villages selling sodas, ice, snacks, and souvenirs to passing convoys and troops on the road. They often had children with them to demonstrate that they were neither hostile nor the VC were waiting. Aka "coka girl." Few were prostitutes as often assumed. See "Saigon tea girl"—not the same.

solacium payment   Small death gratuity and property damages paid to families of Vietnamese accidentally killed by Free World forces whether combat or non-combat related.

SOP   Standard Operating Procedures. A unit-generated document outlining operational, logistical, and administrative procedures. As commanders' and staff's preferences changed with experience and the ever-evolving tactics, terrain, climate, and enemy situation, few units actually possessed an applicable, up-to-date SOP. When asked to see a unit's SOP by higher ups, the usual answer was, "It's undergoing revision."

Sopwith Camel   General term for "low and slow" fixed-wing observation aircraft, implying an outdated "flimsy" airplane. Perhaps influenced by Snoopy, the WWI flying acc and his doghouse-like Sopwith Camel fighter.

Sorry about that.   An understated admission to a mistake. A phrase popularized by Maxwell Smart, aka Agent 86, in the TV series, *Get Smart* (1965–70).

SOS   Shit on a shingle. Aka "stuff on a shingle." Chipped beef (ground beef or hamburger) and creamed gravy on toast served for breakfast. An unpopular alternative was cubed Spam and gravy.

Soul Alley   Trink Minh Street, Khank Hoi District south of Tan Son Nhut Airbase in Saigon, aka "Soul City," aka "100-Pee Alley."* An estimated 100–300 Black deserters resided there, often living with a Vietnamese family or girlfriend. MP raids accomplished little. The area was off limits, but numerous Black soldiers spent evenings or weekends there to return to their nearby bases. Whites were expected to stay out. A source of income was selling drugs and stolen military property on the black market. Others helped run bars, cafes, and "mama san shops" (q.v.). With the general American withdrawal in 1972 many surrendered. Some remained and it was found that most had bought their way out of RVN by the final evacuation in 1975. See "Black Power."

* "100-Pee Alley" referred to the early-on cost of a short-time sex session, 100 piastres.

Sound off like ya gotta pair!   Meaning one had better shout it out with enthusiasm. See "I can't hear you!"

Sounds like a personal problem.   Common response to a complaint or gripe. "It's not my problem." "Why are you telling me?" "Deal with it."

South Vietnam   "The Nam." The Republic of Vietnam (RVN) or *Việt Nam Cộng Hòa* established on 26 October 1955 from the Cochinchina and southern Annam regions severed from the former French Indochina. The RVN ceased to exist and was absorbed by the Democratic Republic of Vietnam (North Vietnam) on 2 July 1976. However, it ceased to exist as a *de facto* state when the North Vietnamese seized Saigon on 30 April 1975.

spam can   Key-and-strip-opened metal ammunition boxes for .30 carbine, 12-gauge shotgun, .30-cal M1 rifle clipped ammunition, and rifle grenade launching cartridges.

Spec 4, 5, 6, and 7   Specialist 4, 5, 6, and 7 (SP4 to SP7). Specialists rated just below the sergeant rank ("hard striper," q.v.) of the same pay grade; e.g., a Spec 4 was outranked by a corporal with both being pay grade E-4. Specialists had no leadership responsibilities other than minimal supervision of immediate subordinates.

Spec 8 and 9   There is much debate if the ranks of SP8 and 9 existed. They were authorized, but no T/O&E positions were assigned these ranks. It was determined that any E-8 or E-9 position required supervision of personnel. They were cancelled in May 1968 without anyone ever assigned to them, regardless of some claiming to have seen someone in the rank.

speed pallet   USAF HCU-6/E air cargo master pallets (aka "463L speed pallets") measured 88in x 108in and four wooden pallets or nine 55gal drums could be lashed to them. The metal pallets with a layer of balsa wood sandwiched between aluminum sheets with connectors for nylon tie-down straps and cargo nets. They could be loaded into the tailgate door of transport aircraft and would fit in the cargo bed of 2½- and 5-ton trucks and tractor-trailers and larger helicopters. Pallets were often reused in the construction of structures and fortifications. See "pallets."

spider hole   A VC/NVA concealed one-man foxhole with a liftable camouflaged cover or lid made of thatch-like lattice of sticks, bamboo, vines, and leaves. Excavated soil was usually removed and hidden.

Spin Code   The Separation Process Number (SPN) found in Box 11.c. (Reason and Authority) on the *Certificate of Release or Discharge from Active Duty* (DD Form 214) as a two-digit number and a letter or a three-digit number. Removed in 1974 owing to unfavorable accusations made on some individuals. Veterans discharged prior to May 1974 still had SPN codes on their military records and could request they be removed. While most spin codes were considered derogatory, some were favorable or merely administrative notations. Spin code examples:

SPN 202   Expiration of term of enlistment
SPN 220   Marriage, female only
SPN 256   Homosexual, acceptance of discharge in lieu of board action
SPN 258   Unfitness, multiple reasons
SPN 263   Bed wetter
SPN 411   Overseas returnee
SPN 41A   Apathy, lack of interest
SPN 41E   Obesity
SPN 46C   Apathy/Obesity
SPN 463   Paranoid personality

Complete list of approximately 250 SPN codes: http://www.utvet.com/SPNnumeric2012.html

The spirit of the bayonet...   is to kill! A concept taught in Basic as a means of instilling agility, aggressiveness, and self-confidence. The will to meet and destroy the enemy in hand-to-hand combat is the "spirit of the bayonet." Directed at the enemy, it was the demoralizing fear of the bayonet—cold steel.

spit-shine   Spit-shining black leather boots or low-quarter shoes using warmed boot polish and water or saliva to achieve a high sheen, a learned technique. Derived from "spit and polish."

spit-shine party   An informal small group barracks party spit-shinning footwear and BS'ing, usually while indulging in beer, soft drinks, and munchies. Materials included shoe polish and leather dye, lighters/matches, boot polish brushes, worn-out toothbrushes, and old tee-shirts and boot socks for polishing rags.

Splash out.   Actually "Splash. Out." (two one-word sentences), but altered to a single phrase, almost a single word, "Splash-out." An artillery fire direction center's (FDC) radio message to the unit requesting fire support informing them that the first round or volley will impact within seconds—"On the way." See "Shot out."

spoon   1) Demeaning nickname for cooks.
2) Stripper clip adapter. A metal bracket-like device that enabled a charging clip to be fitted on a magazine's mouth allowing clipped cartridges to be stripped into the magazine for M1/M2 carbines, M14 rifles, and M16-series rifles.
3) Hand grenade arming lever. A metal lever held while the arming pin was pulled and when thrown flew off, activating the grenade's delay fuse.
4) C-rat spoon. A white plastic spoon in a plastic sleeve issued in each MCI. Many soldiers habitually carried one in a pocket or helmet camo band.

Spot Report   SPOTREP. Pronounced "spot-rep." Reported as events occur, describing the current situation. Formats varied between HQs. See "ZULU Report."

spotting rifle   The .50-cal* M8C spotting rifle mounted on 106mm M40-series recoilless rifles. It fired a red tracer bullet with an incendiary charge, creating a flash and white smoke puff on impact. It allowed the gunner to estimate range and adjust aim prior to firing the "full-bore" 106mm round. It was occasionally used for "sniping" as was the 106mm itself to suppress snipers. The Marine's M50 Ontos antitank vehicles (q.v.) with six 106mm RRs had spotting rifles on four of the RRs.

* The special cartridge was 22mm shorter than the regular .50-cal MG cartridge.

spotting scope   Small tripod-mounted 20x M49 observation telescope. Used by artillery forward observers and sniper spotters.

squad radio   Some use was made of the AN/PRC-6 walkie-talkie handheld radio (q.v.), but it was too heavy and bulky. It was replaced by the AN/PRT-4 and AN/PRR-9 "helmet radio" (q.v.). Squad radios were for communication between the platoon leader and sergeant and the squad leaders. They could not talk to the company CO or other platoons.

squared away   Everything in order, shipshape (also used by the Army). A squared away individual "had his shit (or stuff) together." Orderly and organized.

squashed bug   The wreath-bearing and arrow-clutching spread-winged eagle insignia of the warrant officer collar and cap insignia.

squids   Other services' nickname for sailors. Aka "anchor-clankers," "swabbies." Coast Guardsmen are "Coasties."

STABO rig   STAbilized BOdy extraction harness designed by Special Forces MAJ Robert Stevens, CPT John Knabb, and SFC Clifford Roberts, pronounced "stay-bow." The web harness replaced the suspenders on web gear sets. It allowed reconnaissance team members to attach themselves with snaplinks (q.v.) to extraction ropes lowered by helicopters when cleared PZs were not available. It replaced the McGuire rig (q.v.).

stack arms   The command to "stack arms" was when three rifles' stacking swivels were latched together and stood in a tripod-like arrangement when arms were not needed for field activities—"stacking arms." Derived from the double J-shaped hook-like device fitted below the muzzle of M1, M1903, and earlier rifles. "Grab 'em by the stacking swivel and shake 'em" means getting someone's attention; to do something to make them notice you. Physically equates to grabbing someone by the throat. When a soldier was said to have "stacked arms" it implied he had given up, quit trying, was finished.

staff rats   Officers and EM assigned to unit staffs.

Stand in the door!   The second to the last of the eight parachute jump commands, the final being "Go!" when the jump light switched from red to green (paratroopers could not be color blind). "Stand in the door!" came to mean one is focused, committed, and ready to go.

starlightscope   AN/PVS-1 and -2 first-generation night vision sights and the slightly smaller AN/PVS-3 second generation.* They could be mounted on M14 and M16 rifles, M60 and M2 (.50-cal) MGs, and 90mm M67 recoilless rifles. The larger AN/TVS-2 was used on the .50-cal M2 MG and 106mm recoilless rifle. "Starlight" referred to the ambient light sources intensified by the scope: starlight, moonlight, sky glow, and nearby artificial light sources, including illumination flares. Their vision range was 300–400 meters with 4x magnification. PVS = Portable-Visual-Detecting.

* The AN/PVS-3 was aka "miniscope" or "miniaturized starlightscope."

state flags   It was common for individual state flags to be flown from AFVs and other vehicles' radio antennas. It was usually representative of the vehicle commander's home state or perhaps two or more of the crew were from that state. According to Army Regulations, state flags were only to be displayed if all 50 state and territorial flags were flown together in the order of admission to the Union. Complaints were few, even when the Confederate ("The South will rise again") or Jolly Roger pirate skull and crossbones flags were displayed.

steam and cream   Steam bath and blowjob offered by some whorehouses. ("Or was that a blow bath and steam job?" as hazily remembered by more than one drunken soldier.)

steel drums   55gal steel drums were widely used to transport fuel and other petroleum products and materials. May have had a sealed top with bungholes in the top and side or had a clamp-on removable top lid. Earth-filled drums were used for field fortifications and they were used as non-potable water barrels. With the ends cut out and welded together they were used as culverts. Drums cut in half crossways were used as latrine barrels (see "shit burning detail"). Drums cut in half lengthwise with angle iron or barbed wire picket legs welded on were used to hold cleaning solvents for weapons or modified as charcoal barbeque grills with the drum's other half hinged as a top and an expanded steel mesh grill added. The ends could be cut out of a drum, it cut height-wise, and flattened into a sheet metal panel to revet (shore-up) trenches and revetment walls.

sterile uniform   Uniforms worn by cross-border reconnaissance teams operating outside of South Vietnam. They cannot be attributed to the US by manufacture, style, camouflage pattern, markings, and insignia. The same applies to weapons and web gear. Mistakenly, many believe a "sterile uniform" merely means a US uniform devoid of insignia.

stick   Paratroopers loaded in a jump aircraft or passengers loaded in a helicopter. Aka a "chalk" because stick numbers were sometimes chalk-marked on helmets.

Stick it where the sun don't shine.   "Your proposal, recommendation, idea, etc. sucks and you can shove it up your ass" or "where the sun doesn't shine."

stoned   Doped up or wasted on drugs, usually marijuana, but any drug. A "stoner," one who does drugs and may be more in a perpetual stoned state than not. The Department of Defense reported that 51 percent of troops had smoked marijuana, 31 percent had used psychedelics (LSD, mescaline, psilocybin mushrooms), and 28 percent had taken hard drugs (cocaine, heroin).

Stoner 63   The 5.56mm Mk 23 Mod 0 rifle unsuccessfully field tested in Vietnam by the Marines and SEALs. It could be converted to a carbine or light MG. It was plagued with reliability problems, however. Designed by Eugene Stoner, inventor of the M16.

STRAC   Acronym for an elite, sharp, ready to go, perfectly uniformed soldier. Derived from STRAC (Strategic Army Corps—XVIII Airborne Corps) at Ft Bragg, North Carolina, a worldwide rapid reaction force. Soldiers assigned to STRAC were expected to be highly proficient and impeccably uniformed. Referred to highly motivated or "hardcore" individuals. Pronounced "strack." The acronym provided the Corps' motto, "Skilled, Tough, Ready Around the Clock."

straight leg   A non-paratrooper/non-jumper. Paratroopers wore their service uniform trousers bloused into jump boots. Non-jumpers wore low-quarter shoes with "straight" trousers legs. Aka simply "legs."

straphanger   An individual hitching a ride in a transport or helicopter. Originally, a non-crewmember without a seat and clinging to a cargo strap. Came to mean an extra man catching a ride in any vehicle.

Strategic Hamlet Program   Between 1952 and 1954 the French established a number of protected villages in an effort to separate the population from the communist Viet Minh and protected by local security forces (RF/PF). The Agroville Program was a forerunner of the only slightly more effective Strategic Hamlet Program. "Agroville" was derived from "centers of agglomeration," meaning to collect, to mass. The similar South Vietnamese government Strategic Hamlet Program (*Ấp Chiến lược*) was attempted in 1960, first to separate the families of known VC from the insurgents. Later, villages were relocated to concentrate and protect civilians from the VC and are still known as "agrovilles." The system proved extremely unpopular as it separated farmers from ancestral lands, an important aspect of their lives. The subsequent New Life Hamlets (*Ấp Tan Sinh*) program also failed and was canceled in 1963.

striker   Term for the indigenous members of the Special Forces-advised Civilian Irregular Defense Group (CIDG) Camp and Mobile Strike Forces. "CIDG."

Pronounced "sidge." The CIDG were not part of the ARVN, but civilian employees paid, trained, uniformed, armed, and equipped by the US government, but under Vietnamese Special Forces (LLDB) command, subject to civil law, and advised by US Special Forces. While the term was never used, they were essentially mercenaries.

strip alert   A small unit, usually a platoon or company, sometimes a battalion, on alert as an airmobile reaction/reinforcement force. The unit located at an airstrip or pickup zone (PZ) and was ready for immediate pick-up by helicopter to be inserted in support of an engaged unit or block or pursue withdrawing enemy. Fighter-bombers could be on strip alert for on-call air strikes.

stripper clip   Loading or charging clip; a metal strip holding cartridges to be loaded into small-arms internal or detachable box magazines. The M16A1 rifle and M1/M2 carbine used 10-rd clips and the M14 rifle used a 5-round. See "spoon." The SKS carbine and AK-47 rifle used a 10-rd clip and the M1944 carbine a 5-round. The M1 rifle's 8-rd *en bloc* "loading clip" is *not* a charging clip. The M1's clip was necessary to load and operate the rifle with the cartridges loaded in the clip. Without the clip the rifle did not function.

stripes   Army and Marine point-up chevrons identifying enlisted ranks. Army and Marine "stripes" included point-up chevrons and curved arches ("rockers"). USAF chevrons with a star were blunt-pointed down.

strobe light   The SDU-5/E distress light marker issued in aviator survival vests and used by ground elements to mark their location for aircraft at night. The flashing light (1-second intervals) would not cause night blindness. It was provided a blue-filtered flash guard to stop it being seen from the ground and to mute the flash, preventing it from being misidentified as a weapon's muzzle flash. Visible up to 3mi without flash guard.

subdued insignia   Embroidered sewn-on and metal pin-on insignia for wear on field uniforms and introduced in 1967 for use in Vietnam and Stateside the next year. Included rank, branch of service, specialty badges, and unit patches. Depending on the insignia design, embroidered insignia were usually black on OD. Metal insignia were all black. For the few insignia requiring a third color (including 2LT and MAJ insignia) light brown was used. The 1st Infantry and 101st Airborne divisions tended to wear full-color patches on their field uniforms, but other insignia were subdued. The Marines wore only subdued metal pin-on collar rank insignia, no embroidered.

sucking chest wound.   A serious penetrating wound puncturing a lung and can cause it to collapse or fill with blood. Nature's way of telling you to slow down. Sarcastic, but makes a point.

Suck it up.   Deal with it. Grin and bear it. Eat the pain, including a sucking chest wound.

Sundays or Sundries Pack?

Common distortion of "sundries pack" (SP)—Ration Supplement, Sundries Pack. (From a retailer's standpoint "sundries" represent miscellaneous small merchandise items.) The SP was a 36lb carton containing tobacco, toiletry, confectionary, and stationery supplies—daily use items for troops when PX/BXs were not available. A platoon might receive one every two or three weeks or one per 100 men weekly, often less frequently, depending on availably, tactical situation, and unit SOPs. They were seldom distributed on operations as so much would be discarded and scavenged by the VC/NVA. SP contents included:

10 cartons cigarettes (x10 packs each)
2 cartons book matches (x50 books each)
4 packages chewing tobacco
3 packages pipe tobacco
2 packages cigars (x5 each)
1 package pipe cleaners (mainly weapons cleaning)
2 packages lighter flints*
20 bars bath soap
5 bars laundry soap
5 tubes toothpaste
4 toothbrushes (worn out ones for weapons cleaning)
3 cartons safety razor blades (x10 blades each)

2 safety razors
3 cans pressurized shaving cream (10oz)
1 box Charms candy (x24 pieces)
1 box Jujyfruits candy (x24 pieces)
1 box Chuckles candy (x24 pieces)
1 box Lifesaver candy (x20 rolls)
1 box candy-coated chocolate (x24 pieces)
1 box tropical chocolate bars (x24 bars)
1 box Chiclets chewing gum (x100 packets)
4 pair bootlaces
3 sewing kits
6 stationery tablets
6 packets envelopes
5 ballpoint pens

* No lighter fluid was provided for safety reasons.

Super Gaggle   Flight of 8–16 CH-46A helos escorted by 12 A-4 fighter-bombers and 4 UH-1E gunships to deliver supplies to hilltop positions around Khe Sanh, 1968.

Sur-prise, sur-prise, sur-prise!   "You/I didn't see that coming." A catchphrase frequently spoken by Jim Nabors (1930–2017) as the not too bright PFC Gomer Pyle on *The Andy Griffith Show* (1962–64) and *Gomer Pyle, U.S.M.C.* (1964–69) TV sitcoms, but set in the pre-war Marine Corps.*

* *Gomer Pyle*, while filmed during the war, avoided any mention of Vietnam and actors wore no Vietnam service decorations.

survival ax   Type IV survival kit ax. A cross between a cleaver, machete, and hatchet issued in Army aviator survival kits.

survival radio   Pocket-sized air-to-ground emergency radios, aka emergency locator transmitters (ELTs), used by air crewmen and reconnaissance teams for emergency contact with helicopters: ACR/RT-10 ("Arc-10"), AN/URC-64 ("Erk-64"), and AN/PRC-90 ("Prick-90").

survival or recon vest   USAF SRU-21/P individual survival kit, vest type (also used by Army aviators). Special reconnaissance personnel modified vests for carrying combat accoutrements.

survival rifle   Ithaca M6 aircrew survival weapon, an over-and-under shotgun/rifle in USAF survival kits. Upper barrel was .22 Hornet and the lower .410 shotshell.

swapping artillery tubes   Most artillery battalions were armed with three batteries of common caliber pieces, with two exceptions. Divisional general support battalions* possessed three batteries of 155mm howitzers and a single 8in howitzer battery. 8in and 175mm battalions possessed three batteries of one caliber or the other, but in Vietnam from early 1969, 8in and 175mm battalions became dual-roled, as they could switch from one caliber to the other in about two hours as pre-planned fire missions required. Two M578 recovery vehicle cranes were required. The self-propelled full-tracked mounts for both weapons were the same.

* The division's three 105mm battalions were direct support battalions.

Swedish K   Swedish-made Carl Gustaf* 9mm m/45b SMG used by MACV-SOG as it could not be traced to the US. Aka "K-gun" or "SK." The "K" was derived from *Kulsprutepistol (Kpist.)*, Swedish for "machine pistol." Some were fitted with silencers. Replaced by the 5.56mm XM177E2 (CAR-15, q.v.) SMG in 1967 after Sweden refused further arms sales to the US in 1966 in protest of the Vietnam War.

* *Carl Gustafs Stads Gevärsfaktori*, Eskilstuna, Sweden.

Swift boat   Navy-operated 50ft Patrol Craft, Fast (PCF); changed to Patrol Craft, Inshore in August 1968 with no change in classification code. Employed for inshore and river patrols armed with an 81mm direct-fire mortar and three .50-cal MGs. Approximately 100 deployed to Vietnam.

syrette   Small morphine dose in a tiny superglue-like injector tube.

T   TANGO

3.2 beer   "G.I. beer," sold in PX/BXs, commissaries, and on-post clubs was 3.2 percent alcohol by weight (4 percent by volume). It was rumored one could not get drunk on "three-point-two," but that is a myth. Drinking five 3.2 percent "brews" would be equivalent to three regular 6 percent beers.

360 defense   Refers to 360 degrees in a circle. A "three-sixty-perimeter." An all-around defense when halted day or night. If engaged while moving, an immediate all-around defense was established regardless of the direction the fire came from. There is no such thing as a frontline. The frontline was the direction you were looking in and was 18in wide.

Tabasco sauce   Red Capsicum pepper hot sauce made by the Macilhenny Company of Avery Island, Louisiana. It was highly popular for dashing on C-rat entrees to enliven the blandness. Available in 2 and 5oz glass bottles and commonly included in "care packages" (q.v.). See "C-ration cookbook." (From 1990 ⅛oz bottles were included in MREs.)

tabs (insignia)   Embroidered arched tabs worn over the unit shoulder sleeve insignia. The only authorized tabs were:

Airborne—Worn by all personnel assigned to airborne units whether parachute-qualified or not. The tab identified the unit as airborne, not individuals. Tabs were white-on-blue or gold-yellow-on-black.

Ranger—Worn by graduates of the Ranger Course on left shoulder (above Airborne tab if worn). The gold-yellow-on-black tab identified Ranger-qualified individuals, not units.

LRRP and Ranger units—These units wore a wide variety of unofficial tabs and scrolls.

(There were no Special Forces, Sapper, Mountain, or Advisor tabs as today.)

TAC Officer/NCO   Tactical And Counseling Officer or NCO—collectively called "Tacs." A junior officer or experienced NCO assigned drill sergeant type duties over the students in schools and training courses, OCS and NCOCC, for example. Pronounced "tack."

TA-50 gear   Army term for individual web gear, so called after Common Table of Allowances 50-900, *Individual Clothing and Equipment*, the document specifying the allocation of individual gear.

tail-end Charlie   Last man in a file/column of troops or a patrol. He is to frequently check for enemy activity behind the unit/patrol and ensure no personnel are separated or equipment is left behind during halts. In a patrol the second-in-command usually brought up the rear. Aka "tail gunner." Originated in WWII, referring to the last aircraft in a bomber formation.

Take a hike.   Leave. Get lost. Scram. Antagonistically it means, "Go away and stop bothering me." "Make like a tree and leave." It can also mean to go and cool off. "Let's take a walk," meaning let's have a talk, possibly behind the barracks.

Take him behind the barracks. A method by which some NCOs "counseled" or settled a problem with one of their men or between two NCOs. Basically it was meant to knock some sense into one's head.

Takes a licking and keeps on ticking. A piece of equipment suffering abuse and still functioning. From a series of Timex wristwatch radio and TV commercials in the 1950s and '60s. The commercials demonstrated the watches' durability, shock resistance, and waterproofing after "torture testing" by TV celebrities. A piece of equipment that is "G.I. proof"—hard to break or incorrectly operate (q.v.).

tanglefoot Irregularly placed "low-wire entanglement" of single barbed wire strands strung between short pickets 9–30in off the ground. Placed between barbed wire belts to trip charging attackers and hamper low-crawling infiltrators.

TANGO boat Armored Troop Carrier (ATC) employed by the Mobile Riverine Force to transport a rifle platoon. They were converted 56ft Landing Craft, Mechanized Mk 6 Mod 1 (aka LCM(6) or "MIKE boat") with a covered troop compartment and enlarged superstructure mounting armament. Later marks had a helo landing pad over the troop compartment—"world's smallest aircraft carriers." The LCM(6) served as a basis for other riverine craft conversions. "TANGO" because of the "T" = "Troop boat" prefixing the hull number.

tank According to reporters any big full-tracked armored vehicle was a "tank," including APCs, self-propelled artillery, amtracs, armored recovery vehicles, etc. Three Army and two Maine tank battalions served in Vietnam. Tanks were also assigned to the nine armored cavalry squadrons.

tank-bust The approximately 12ft-wide trail of crushed vegetation made by tanks and APCs through the jungle. The tangle of crushed brush, limbs, and trunks was extremely difficult to follow or cross on foot, especially when new growth further entangled it. See "Rome plow."

tanker boots Unofficial all-leather combat boots worn by some tankers and AFV crewmen. They lacked laces, eyelets, and sole nails to prevent burns through heat transfer. Some aviators wore them for the same reasons. The boot was secured by a leather strap wrapped three times around the ankles and uppers and fastened by a buckle. Non-tankers claimed tanker boots were necessary as tankers were "unable to tie their shoes."

tanker-clanker Tank crewman or "tanker," because of the noisy treads. Aka "tread-head."

taping *or* double magazines Two detachable magazines were sometimes taped together using 100mph or electrical tape so they could be changed rapidly. Mainly done with the M16 rifle, M2 carbine, XM177 SMG, and M3 SMG. A drawback was the extra weight could strain the magazine release spring, causing mis-feeds. For this reason it was seldom done with the heavy M14 rifle and BAR magazines.

TARFU Things Are Really Fucked Up. Pronounced "tar-fu." ("Murphy's Laws of Combat" emerged *after* Vietnam.)

tarmac Mixture of crushed rock or gravel and tar used to surface roads and airfield runways. Tarmac is short for tarmacadam.

task truck Cargo trucks and truck-tractors (semi-trailers) for hauling cargo in line haul convoys; as opposed to the convoy's gun trucks, maintenance trucks, and other support trucks.

TC Tank or Track Commander. "Track commanders" commanded full-tracked vehicles other than tanks. A TC could rank from a sergeant to a captain.

teargas CS, its identification code for ortho-cholorobenzalmalomonitril) irritant agent. It was actually a micro fine powder that when burning created a vapor, irritating the eyes, nostrils, mouth, lungs, and sweat-damp areas (mainly underarms and crotch). It was delivered in hand grenades, cluster bombs, mortar and artillery shells, and rockets plus powder spread by aerial sprayers and handheld blowers. Besides direct use against personnel and inside tunnels and other structures, it was sprayed in enemy occupied areas such as bases, trail routes, and abandoned Free World firebases to prevent scavenging. CS in itself is not fatal. It can cause complications in those having respiratory problems and in enclosed spaces it displaces oxygen, possibly causing suffocation. CS exposure can be neutralized within 20 minutes by flushing with water and facing into the breeze. CN (phenacyl chloride) was an earlier irritant agent replaced by CS. CN munitions were used until expended in Vietnam. CS is more resistant to water.

teargas mask The M28 (XM28E4) mask was a light, compact gasmask offering protection only from riot control agents introduced in 1968 and obsolete in 1977. The heavier, bulkier M17/M17A1 gasmasks (q.v.) protected from most nerve, blister, blood, and choking agents plus CS. Aka "riot gasmask" or "CS gasmask."

teargas projector E8 riot control agent launcher was a beer case-sized device with 16 launcher tubes, each holding four 35mm CS cartridges. When pulling the lanyard 64 cartridges were launched and CS commenced streaming to saturate a 40m x 125–175m area at up to 250m range.

television war Vietnam was the first conflict to be widely televised and seen on the evening news. "Television brought the brutality of war into the comfort of the living room. Vietnam was lost in the living rooms of America—not on the battlefields of Vietnam," wrote Marshall McLuhan (1911–80, Canadian), *Montreal Gazette*, 16 May 1975. He was not the first though to observe the phenomena, having become apparent in 1965 when combat troops arrived in country.

Tell me what you want done, but don't tell me how. Special Forces credo. Other SF precepts were, "Everyone pitches in regardless of rank" and "If you see something needing fixing, fix it…unless it really needs a specialist." *De Oppresso Liber*—Liberate the Oppressed.

temporary buildings All Stateside Army posts possessed at least some temporary wood-frame one- and two-story buildings built in the 1940s. There were scores of floor plans for all necessary building uses. They were intended to be used for only ten or so years. Some were still in use well into the 2000s. Each was assigned a building number prefaced by "T." Similar temporary buildings were built on major bases in Vietnam, but were even more simplified and modified for the tropics.

10 percent There's always 10 percent of the troops who don't get the word, don't understand what was said, forgot it, or don't care. It is manageable, unless one of them is in the chain-of-command.

10 pounds of shit in a 5-pound bag. Trying to do too much, overdoing it, overextending. "The Ol' Man's trying to put 10 pounds of shit in a 5-pound bag." An informal confirmation when ordered to do something, "Ten-pounds full, sir." We'll get it done no matter what.

Tet holiday "Tet" is short for *Tết Nguyên Đán* (Feast of the First Morning of the First Day), the Vietnamese New Year, with the date falling in February or January using the Lunar calendar. It also celebrates the arrival of spring and is called the *Hội xuân* (Spring Festival). It is a rest period for rubber tree harvesting.

Tet Offensive The Tet Offensive, launched during the Vietnamese New Year on 30 January 1968, known to the VC/NVA as *Tổng Tiến công và Nổi dậy Tết Mậu Thân 1968* (The General Offensive and Uprising of Tet Mau Than 1968). The VC/NVA committed virtually all their resources to the offensive in an effort to gain control of key political and military objectives. They attacked over 100 cities and towns and their adjacent military installations to cause a general uprising of the South Vietnamese people. Such an uprising never occurred. It was a brutal and lengthy fight. The main Phase 1 offensive lasted through the end of March; it was followed by Phase 2 or the Mini Tet (q.v.), which lasted into May, and Phase 3, into September. It was an operational victory for the Free World forces; the VC units were virtually destroyed and heavy losses suffered by the NVA. It was a political and strategic victory for North Vietnam in spite of its staggering losses, especially since the news media declared it a defeat for the Free World.

Thai Citizen of the Republic of Thailand. Thailand lost 351 KIA and 1,358 WIA from its three major units: Royal Thai Army Regiment (1967–68), Royal Thai Army Expeditionary Division (1969–71), and Royal Thai Army Volunteer Force (reinforced brigade) (1971–72).

That shovel (insert any implement) fits your hands too. "Why are you telling me to do it when you're perfectly capable?"

There are three ways to do anything. The right way, the wrong way, and the Army way. Meaning, it may not always make sense, but it works…usually.

There is no such thing as a stupid question. An almost obligatory statement following, "Any questions?" at the summation of a briefing or lecture. Supposedly a means of encouraging participation and gaining clarity. The reality, of course, is that there really is such a thing as a stupid question.

"There's no doubt in my military mind…" that this or that is/isn't going to happen or go/not go in the direction or manner I hoped.

thermite grenade The AN-M14 incendiary hand grenade is actually thermate (TH3) filled, not thermite. Mainly used to destroy equipment and prevent its capture/use. Three were carried in tanks to destroy the main gun, radio, and engine. TH3 is a more effective compound than thermite and burns at 4,330°F.

thirty-cal 1) Browning .30-cal M1919A4/A6 light tripod-mounted and M37 tank/aircraft MGs. The M1919A6 also had a bipod and shoulder stock. Aka "thirty." "Number 30," the Vietnamese term.
2) Any .30-cal rifle, BAR, MG, and other weapons. Usually weapons were chambered for the ".30-06" cartridge. The "06" derived from its year of adoption—.30-cal M1906. The .30 Carbine round was much shorter than the .30-06.

3d Herd Any 3d Battalion, e.g., 3d Battalion, 508th Infantry referred to themselves as such.

thirty-eight Several models of .38 Special revolvers were used, to include the S&W Model 10 and Colt Police Positive. Aviators used the Model 10 along with riverine craft crewmen. Investigators and others requiring easily concealed weapons carried snub-nose Police Positives. USAF Security Police used the S&W Model 15. Aviators used revolvers as crashes often caused hand/arm injuries. Automatic pistols were difficult to operate and reload one-handed while revolvers were not.

Thirty-Three 33 Beer, *Ba Muoi Ba* or *Bière 33*. A locally produced rice beer popular with many Americans. It is still produced in the Democratic Republic of Vietnam and became available in the US market in 1994 as "333."

Thompson .45-cal M1928A1, M1, and M1A1 SMGs. Aka "Tommy gun" (little used term). Thompsons were used by some ARVN units.

Three bags full. I'll do anything you order. "Yes, sir! Three bags full!" Everything's done, finished, or we'll do it as ordered. Originated from the unmilitary eighteenth-century French nursey rhyme, "Baa, Baa, Black Sheep."

Three hots and dry socks. There was little more a grunt could gratefully expect than dry socks (which can be inferred as a dry place to sleep) and three hot meals a day, even if just heated C-rats.

three-point-five The 3.5in (89mm) M20A1B1 rocket launcher. Aka "bazooka." Replaced by the M72 LAW and 90mm M67 recoilless rifle and declared obsolete in 1970.

three-quarter-ton The ¾-ton 4x4 M37B1 cargo truck. Produced by Dodge from 1951 to 1968. Occasionally called a "weapons carrier." Various types of communications-electronic shelters could be mounted.

three-star general Lieutenant general (LTG) (O-9). Corps/field force CG.

three-striper Sergeant E-5 owing to three point-up chevrons. Aka "buck sergeant."

through and through Bullet or fragment wound that exited the body (T&T). This did not necessarily indicate a "clean wound." Organs, major blood vessels, and bones could still have been hit.

thumbs up Thumbs-up gesture had long been in use as an approval sign or to signal readiness as was the OK sign, "We're good to go" or "well done." (The high-five gesture did not exist until 1977.)

Thunder Road National Route 13 (*QL 13*) running north from Saigon to the Cambodian border. FSBs protecting the highway at approximately 10km intervals were designated Thunder I through X and collectively referred to as "the Thunders." Thunder Road was derived from the 1958 movie with the same name about moonshine runners. Another Thunder Road was QL 1, running from near the south tip of RVN, through Saigon, near the coast to the DMZ, and in theory, into North Vietnam and through Hanoi to the Chinese border.

tie-ties Short cords, sometimes with small clips, to secure clothing to clotheslines rather than clothespins. Aka "clothes stops." Marines.

Tiger Beer *Bière Larue* in French. A local beer not as popular as "33." Aka "Tiger Piss."

Tigerland The 3d Infantry Advanced Individual Training Brigade, North Ft Polk ("Ft Puke"), Louisiana. It included the Army's largest Vietnamese mock village at Tiger Ridge. Reputed to be the toughest of the Army's six infantry training centers.

tigerstripes "Tigers" were four-color (black, medium green and brown, tan or pale green) camouflage uniforms used by Special Forces, CIDG, special reconnaissance units, and the Vietnamese Marines ("sea wave pattern"). They were fabricated in Japan, Korea, and Thailand under US contact and were seen in a wide variety of shades and patterns. *Quân phục rằn ri* or simply *đồ rằn ri*. The Vietnamese Marines called their version the *cọp biển* (sea tiger), *hoa biển* (sea flower), or *sóng biển* (sea waves).

tiger ~~tails~~ tales   While there were actual attacks, sightings, and killings of tigers (*con hổ*) stalking units, incidents were extremely rare, but much was made of it in lore. It is known tigers, pigs, and other animals fed on abandoned bodies.

time in service/time in grade   To be promoted to higher rank or attend specific courses one was required to have reached specific amounts of time in the previous rank or have the requisite amount of time in service. To attend some courses one had to have a specified period of time remaining in the service; e.g., one had to have 18 months remaining after completing SF training.

Tipsy-33   AN/TPS-33 ground surveillance radar. Transportable-Portable-Surveillance. Transported by ¾-ton cargo truck or Mechanical Mule.

T/O&E   Table of Organization and Equipment. Pronounced "tee-oh-and-ee." The authorization document specifying a unit's internal structure, number of personnel by rank and MOS, vehicles, weapons, and other equipment.

toe-popper   M14 anti-personnel mine. A small plastic landmine undetectable by magnetic mine detectors. The small shaped-charge would mangle a foot. Only the firing pin and primer were metal. To simplify mine clearance and because the VC/NVA had no mine detectors, a steel washer was glued on the bottom of late production M14s. 2.2in diameter and 1.5in high. The VC/NVA called it a *đạp lôi* (step-mine).

Tokarev   The 7.62mm Soviet TT-33 (ChiCom Type 51) pistol. Pronounced "To-ka-rev." Carried by VC/NVA leaders as much as a sign of office as for self-defense. It lacks a safety. An underpowered handgun, but a desirable souvenir.

Tonkin Gulf Yacht Club   A tongue-in-cheek nickname coined in 1961 for Seventh US Fleet elements operating off the coast of Vietnam. Task Force 77 supported operations ashore with air strikes, reconnaissance, gunfire support, and other missions. Yankee Station was an operating area off of South Vietnam and south of North Vietnamese waters. Dixie Station was off of South Vietnam.

tooth to tail ratio   A unit's "tail" is the service support elements with the "gear in the rear" (q.v.) or "rear echelon," and the "tooth" is the combat elements. There are all sorts of comparisons in this ratio, from ridiculously small to ludicrously large depending on what units and echelons were counted.

top sergeant   Army and Marine company/battery/troop first sergeants (E-8)—both a rank title and duty position—the senior NCO in company-size units. Aka "top kick," "top sergeant," "first shirt," or simply "Top." (USAF 1st sergeants were appointments, not a rank, and could be an E-7, E-8, or E-9 depending on the unit's size.) 1st sergeants regardless of service displayed a diamond device (lozenge) on their chevrons.

TOT Time-On-Target. Pronounced "tee-oh-tee." A devastating pre-planned artillery barrage calculated for all of the rounds fired by different units from different ranges to detonate on or over the target at the same instant.

Tough shit (TS) Tough luck. Hard luck. Too bad. Tough titty. (TS is also the abbreviation for a TOP SECRET security classification.)

tour books Most divisions and separate brigades produced a "year book" style, large format hardback "coffee table" book covering the period of the unit's Vietnam tour. Typically they included brief historical sketches of major actions, abridged subordinate units' historical sketches, photos and biographies of key commanders and staffs, accompanied by numerous photographs.

TOW BGM-71 Tube-launched, Optically tracked, Wire-guided antitank missile introduced in Vietnam in 1972 during the Easter Offensive. Pronounced "tow," not "T-O-W." It saw limited use being launched from UH-1B attack helicopters and M151A2C TOW trucks fitted with M220 TOW launchers. It possessed a 152mm (5.9-in) HEAT warhead.

tower The 6–20ft-high guard towers positioned around permanent bases and airfields, providing extended surveillance coverage. The tower platform was fortified similar to a bunker and they were usually built over a ground bunker housing relief personnel. These were fighting positions and usually MG-armed. See "radar tower."

Tower Week The second week of the Basic Parachutist Course, named so because of jumps made from 34ft and 250ft jump training towers at Ft Benning, Georgia. After exiting from the 34ft tower and sliding to the ground on a slanted 200ft cable with a trolley wheel assembly, they were known as "trolley troopers." The 250ft tower was a free parachute drop under a pre-inflated canopy. See "Ground Week" and "Jump Week."

Trace, The In the summer of 1967 Marine engineers and Seabees cleared a 500m wide "Cleared Trace" from Con Thien along the south edge of the DMZ northeastward to Gio Linh and then southeast to Combat Base Alpha 1 Charlie, 5km inland from the coast. This was the first phase of constructing the ill-conceived McNamara Line (q.v.). The Trace was approximately 20km in length.

track Meaning any full-tracked vehicle, but specifically an M113A1 armored personnel carrier and its many variants.

trainee An Army recruit undertaking Basic Combat Training (BCT) or Advance Individual Training (AIT). Soldiers attending specialty schools and courses were "students."

Trainfire Automated rifle marksmanship qualification course introduced in 1957 with mechanically operated "pop-up knock-down" silhouette targets that rose and fell on electronic commands from a control tower. The terrain was partly brush and tree-covered and the partially concealed targets were irregularly set from 50 to 350m at 50m intervals. Vietnam was described as offering "live pop-up shoot 'em back targets."

trip-flare M49A1 surface trip-flare. A tripwire-activated magnesium flare attached to trees, stakes, or barbed wire pickets. Ignited, it illuminated a 300m radius and warned of enemy presence. Manuals of the era depicted only the obsolete M49 trip-flare of a much different design than the M49A1, leading to some confusion when arming them.

tripwire Tripwire-activated booby-traps, trip-flares, and certain mines were used by both sides. This could be very fine, stout string or cord, single-strand field telephone wire, or monofilament fishing line. Army issue tripwires were issued in green and sand colors.

trophies War trophies were permitted to be taken home, such as enemy uniforms, insignia, pith helmets, individual web gear and related equipment, flags (most souvenir flags were fake), publications/documents of no intelligence value,* and minor personal-type items after being cleared by the S-2. Montagnard crossbows were popular, but the bolts (arrows) could not be taken home for fear they were poison-tipped.

* NVA "occupation money" and surrender leaflets, for example.

trophy ears Collecting ears from the enemy dead for body count claim verification was supposedly practiced by some Free World units.* Such claims are unsubstantiated. Some indigenous units had practiced it.

* It was supposedly the right ears only that were turned in.

trophy firearms One captured trophy weapon could be taken home after being cleared by the S-2. Only bolt-action or semi-automatic rifles and handguns were permitted—no full-automatic or explosive-projecting weapons and no US-made* or Free World forces' weapons, which were returned to allies. No, the armed forces did not let an individual take home his issue weapon as often claimed. No ammunition could be taken home. Most common trophies were the Mosin-Nagant M1944 and SKS carbines, and TT-33 pistol. A DD Form 603 *Registration of War Trophy Firearms* had to be completed with the weapon's description. See "trophies."

* Two US-made exceptions were M1903A3 Springfield bolt-action rifles and M1 carbines with four-digit serial numbers, both of which were given to Montagnard tribesmen by Special Forces early on.

truck-tractor The 5-ton M52 or 2½-ton M48 and M275 towing trucks (aka "prime-mover") for semi-trailers. Very few 2½-ton tractors were used.

TS Card The "Tough Shit Card" or Ticket was handed out by some chaplains in an effort to ease a soldier's personal problems in an attempt at levity. Aka "Tough Stuff Card" or "Sympathy Chit." They typically showed a caricature of a G.I. in sorrow, some printed words of wit, sympathy, or advice, and small squares along the edges. A chaplain would punch or mark out a square each visit. A typical printed statement was: "This sympathy card entitles the bearer to one half-hour of crying (or beefing) in my crying room. Open all hours. Tell your troubles to the chaplain." More words of wisdom or advice or appropriate quotes may have been printed on the back.

tube A general term for an artillery ("arty") "piece." Batteries had four (175mm, 8in) or six (105mm, 155mm*) tubes, whether howitzers (short barrels) or guns (long barrels—only 175mm were guns). "Guns" was also a general term for artillery pieces, whether officially guns or howitzers.

* Some 105mm and 155mm battalions organized a fourth provisional (temporary) Battery D for use in certain situations, giving them two five-tube and two four-tube batteries.

Tu Do Street An avenue in southeast Saigon lined with bars (half seemingly named Play Boy Club), cafes, and cheap hotels; a popular hangout for G.I.s where anything or anyone could be bought. Tu Do (Freedom Street) prior to 1955 was known as Catinat Street. In 1975 after the North Vietnamese expunged the decadent bourgeoisie and all American influences, it was renamed Dong Khoi Street (General Insurrection).

tunnel rat Especially selected and trained combat engineer, infantry, and chemical warfare specialist volunteers who entered enemy tunnel and cave networks to explore them, recover equipment and materials, and destroy them with demolitions. They were of necessity short, slender, and non-claustrophobic. Aka "Mole Patrol" (little used). Their tongue-in-cheek Latin slogan was *Non Gratus Anus Rodentum* (Not worth a rat's ass).

tunnel weapons A variety of weapons were used by tunnel rats. The use of weapons in such enclosed spaces was avoided if at all possible. Even high-grade hearing protection was inadequate. The weapons were for last resort protection and had to be compact; .45-cal M1911A1 and .38 Special revolvers were the most widely used because of availability. 12-gauge pump shotguns with under 20in barrels and shortened M2 carbines were also used. Snub-nosed .38 Special and .41-cal revolvers with special suppressed cartridges were tested. Silenced .22-cal pistols saw some use. Overall, seldom were suppressed pistols available. Revolvers cannot be effectively suppressed.

Twenty MIKE-MIKE Any 20mm automatic gun mounted in certain helicopters, jet fighters, and riverine craft.

two-by-twos   Cloth 2-inch-square patches for cleaning weapons, mainly for .45-cal, .30-cal, and 7.62mm weapons. They were cut in halves or quarters for 5.56mm weapons. Aka "rifle cleaning patches," "bore patches," or "swabs." Issue 5.56mm patches were 1 ⅛ inches square.

two-niner-two   RC-292 ground plane antenna that could extend the range of AN/PRC-25 and -77 and other FM tactical radios. Required to be erected on a pole with guy lines and could not be used on the move.

201 File   DA Form 201, *The Military Personnel Records Jacket United States Army*, is a file jacket containing a variety of personal files and reports, the Official Military Personnel File (OMPF). The other armed services had their own equivalents, e.g., Form 201 *Military Personnel Records Jacket United States Marine Corps*. The "201" contained administrative, pay, training, awards, efficiency reports, and other personnel documents. Contrary to popular belief, as seen in movies and TV, 201 files cannot be acquired within hours by the police and they do not include narrative information about what a badass the suspect is.

201 File on his chest.   Describes a soldier wearing his full array of ribbons, badges, and other insignia. All authorized decorations and skill badges were listed in his 201 File.

two-oh-three   The 40mm M203 grenade launcher mounted under the barrel on M16A1 rifles. It was field-tested in Vietnam in 1969 and soon adopted, but was not fielded in until 1971.

Two sandbags by sunset.   The requirement that all soldiers in newly established firebases had to be protected from mortar fire by two layers of overhead sandbags by nightfall.

two-star general   Major general (MG) (O-8). Commanded divisions and a wide variety of higher commands and organizations.

two-striper   A corporal (E-4) identified by two point-up chevrons. "Corps" (a rarely used term) were rated as NCOs while Spec 4s of the same pay grade were not. There were very few corporal positions in the Army. Within a division the only corporals were Pathfinders and assistant gunners in artillery crews. Sergeants (E-5) reduced one pay grade were often demoted to corporals rather than Spec 4s as they retained their sergeant duty position. In the Marines, corporals were fire team leaders in rifle squads and squad (crew) leaders in MG, mortar, and bazooka crews.

two-step snake   The many-banded krait and the green bamboo viper were reputed to be so venomous that their bite would kill someone before he took two steps. A "subspecies" was the "three-step snake" for the more optimistic or "cigarette snake." If one was bitten, he might as well sit in the shade and have a cigarette before expiring. Vipers delivered little venom and kraits and cobras were scarce. About 30 of Vietnam's 140 snake species are venomous. The arboreal white-lipped bamboo viper was the most common venomous snake bite, but was never lethal. Only 25–50 US military personnel received snakebites a year with few necessitating intensive therapy. Water buffaloes were more dangerous.

TWs Tropical worsted wool. Army tan uniform. Tan (Shade 61) was a slightly darker shade than khaki (Shade 1). There were two types of TW uniforms, both privately purchased for optional wear—one similar to the khaki summer uniform and the other of the same cut as the Army Green Class A uniform, the TW Class A being eliminated in 1969. TWs were not worn in formation.

U UNIFORM

Ugly Americans A term describing unfavorable American attributes—typically an arrogant, hard-charging, take-charge attitude and apathy and unawareness of host nation customs and sensitivities. From the movie *The Ugly American* (1963). "Americans" in Vietnamese = *Người mỹ*. American soldier = *Lính Mỹ*. *Mẽo* literally means "musty," anything unpleasant. Describing Americans it roughly means "yank" or "yankee" along the lines of the Spanish *gringo*. *Mày sẽ chết, thằng Mẽo thúi tha* = You will die, yankee bastard man. *Mũi lõ* = sharp nose, disparaging description similar to "round eye" or "slant eye." *Bọn mũi lõ* = group or gang of westerners (Americans).

Umpteenth Infantry or other unit. A general reference to a fictitious unit. "So this skinny LT from the Umpteenth Arty showed up and…" Also, "I checked my watch the umpteenth time," meaning he had done so often. ("Ump[ty]" came from a verbalization of a Morse code dash.)

unass To quickly dismount or disembark a vehicle or aircraft, to get off or out, or to leave. "Unass this truck." "Unass" represents getting one's butt up from where he's seated.

Uncle Ho Nickname for Hồ Chí Minh, his pseudonym, born Nguyễn Sinh Cung (1890–1969). Chairman and First Secretary of the Workers' Party of Vietnam and the spiritual leader of North Vietnam and the communist revolution. Saigon was renamed Ho Chi Minh City (*Thành phố Hồ Chí Minh*) in his memory on 2 July 1976.

Uncle Sam Ain't Released Me Yet The explanation of the meaning of the "U.S. ARMY" tape worn over the left pocket on field uniforms. Gold-yellow-on-black, black-on-OG from 1966, first in Vietnam and then Army-wide in 1968. Marines claimed ARMY meant "Ain't Ready for Marines Yet." Of course the Army said U.S.M.C. meant "Uncle Sam's Misguided Children" or "United States Medical Corps." Both services referred to the Air Force as the "Air Farce" with "9 to 5 jobs."

Note: The "U.S. ARMY" and name tapes originated in 1953 owing to negotiations with North Korea on uniforms and individual identification during the peace talks.

underground balloon battalion A frivolous designation of a fictitious unit—a uniquely specialized unit or, more commonly, an insignificant unit. Another example is a "mess kit repair company" (q.v.).

"Un-fuck-ing believable." Meaning this is pretty difficult to accept.

unofficial Referring to unofficial insignia and uniform items "locally authorized" or at least tolerated. Sometimes called "semi-official," a tolerated or locally accepted practice. "Semi-official" was sometimes declared a "non-word"—reasoning something was either official or it wasn't.

unsat Unsatisfactory no-go. A deficiency in need of correcting, such as a uniform gig or a fouled up squad training exercise. "Unfuck this fuck up."

"Up shit creek without a paddle." A problem without a solution. Bad luck. It implies the only thing to paddle with is your hands—you're going to get your hands dirty—shitty end of the stick or the worst of options. Abridged variant was "Up the creek or river," without mention of the paddle, it being so obvious.

Urgent MEDEVAC casualty code meaning possible loss of life or limb within 2–4 hours.

USELESS A pun on the State Department's United States Information Service (USIS). It provided public information services, radio and TV broadcasting—including Voice of America*, and libraries and information centers in foreign countries. Its efforts in Vietnam seemed to have little effect.

* VOA is a US government-funded and owned multimedia agency serving as the government's official institution for non-military broadcasting to foreign audiences to influence public opinion.

USO United Service Organizations, Inc. is a non-profit organization comprising several civilian aid services partnered with the Department of Defense. Their mission is to entertain service members in the States and overseas via traveling entertainment troupes and operating service (rest) centers, a "home away from home," mainly at major airports. The entertainment troupes ranged from contacted locals to high-profile celebrities, often performing at bases in combat zones.

utilities Olive green field and work uniform—a term used by the Marines. The Army used "fatigues" (q.v.). "Camo utilities" with the introduction of the four-color camouflage "jungles" in 1968. Owing to periodic shortages of specific camo utility uniform items it was authorized to mix camo and OG components.

V VICTOR

V-100 Cadillac Gage XM706E1/M706 Commando four-wheel amphibious armored patrol and escort vehicle mainly used by the US Army MPs, USAF security police, and ARVN. Aka "the Duck," "the V." V-100 was the commercial designation, by which it was widely known. Introduced to the ARVN in 1963 and US forces in 1967.

VA Not the "Veterans Administration," but every airbase, airfield, and airstrip in South Vietnam was assigned an alpha-numeric code. Tan Son Nhut Air Base was VA3-1. "VA" = country and airfield, "3" = corps area (1–4), and "1" = individual airfield with one to three digits 1–300). Heliports were identified by VH, the corps number, and numbered 500–700-plus.

VD Venereal disease. Principally gonorrhea (aka "the clap"), syphilis ("the syph"), "the drip," or "Vietnam Rose." (The term "sexually transmitted diseases" [STD] did not come into use until the 1990s.)

veteran Hollywood actors The list of movie and TV actors serving in Vietnam is minuscule. There are a half dozen who were in the service during the Vietnam War, but were not deployed. The years are their total service. (Any omissions are the author's error.)

> Dye, Dale. USMC, infantry and combat correspondent, 1964–84
> Ermey, Ronald Lee. USMC, aviation support, 1961–72
> Franz, Dennis. US Army, infantry, 1966–68
> Lauria, Dan. USMC, infantry, 1970–73
> Robertson, Silas. US Army, maintenance, 1968–93
> Sajak, Pat. US Army, clerk and newscaster, 1967–69
> Studi, Wesly "Wes." US Army, infantry, 1964–70*

* Service years in conflict in all sources.

Vietnamization The process of withdrawing US troops from Vietnam and turning over all fighting to the South Vietnamese to "expand, equip, and train South Vietnamese forces and assign to them an ever-increasing combat role." This was part of President Richard Nixon's plan to terminate US involvement. It involved turning over bases (closing some), equipment, and materiel as well as increased ARVN training and improved equipping. US troop withdrawals occurred from early 1970 to early 1972. The term "Vietnamization" originated accidentally at a 28 January 1969 National Security Council meeting, when it was said that the war should be "de-Americanized." Secretary of Defense Melvin Laird said, "What we need is a term like 'Vietnamizing'." It is not known who actually coined "Vietnamization."

Vietnam-oriented AIT   Of the six US Army infantry training centers—Ft Campbell, Ft Dix, Ft Gordon, Ft McClellan, Ft Ord, and Ft Polk—all were "Vietnam-oriented" with the exception of Ft Dix, New Jersey (nevertheless it possessed a simple mockup Vietnamese village.). Vietnam-oriented AIT brigades had mockup Vietnamese villages and emphasized close-range engagements, ambushes, and patrolling techniques.

Vietnam shots   Troops deploying to Vietnam were required to have smallpox, typhoid, and typhus inoculations within one year prior to arriving in-country, tetanus within six years, cholera within six months, plague within four months, oral polio on record, and current flu and yellow fever inoculations. Special Forces and others received a gamma globulin injection to temporarily boost immunity against disease, including hepatitis. "Square needle in the left nut," was an intimidating hoax perpetuated by medics describing the means of one of the many immunization inoculations one received in Basic.

Vietnam syndrome   A political phenomena of public aversion to American overseas military involvement. This was a result of the traumatic American withdrawal from Vietnam and the resulting fall of the Republic of Vietnam to the communist North Vietnam. This resulted in a new generation of isolationists and a policy of "retrenchment," a "Vietnam paralysis" in foreign, diplomatic, and military efforts. One result was the virtually complete absence of offensive military contingencies between 1975 and 9-11 in 2001. Rare exceptions were the 1984 Grenada and 1989–90 Panama interventions. Even through the 1990s many senior officers (junior and mid-rankers in Vietnam) strongly insisted the US Armed Forces would *never* again face guerrillas or insurgents. In spite of their skewed worldview, they were proved wrong, being colored by the defeat in Vietnam and a foolish assumption that a nation can pick and choose who its enemies will be and how and where they will fight.

Vietnam TV series   Only two post-war mainstream TV series depicted the Vietnam War, *Tour of Duty* (1987–90, 54 episodes) and *China Beach* (1988–91, 62 episodes). No wartime TV series were produced.

The Lieutenant

A TV series, *The Lieutenant*, staring Gary Lockwood (*2001: A Space Odyssey* [1968]), was aired in a single 29-episode season in 1963–64. It depicted the Stateside peacetime Marine Corps. The final episode, "To Kill a Man," was set in a fictitious Asian country paralleling events ongoing in Vietnam (the Marines were deploying helicopter units there since 1962) and 2ndLt William Tiberius Rice (Lockwood) was deployed as an advisor, leading to speculation that the second season would continue this storyline. Owing to events in Vietnam and the nation's political climate, the otherwise popular show was cancelled prior to its second season. The producer, Gene Roddenberry, went on to create *Star Trek* in 1966.

Viets   Vietnamese (VN). Not considered derogatory, but simply "verbal shorthand." "VICTOR-NOVEMBERS" was used over the radio. Aka "locals" or indig." See "gook."

vil *or* **ville**   Village. Common Vietnamese terms were: *làng* (town), *ấp* (village), and *xã* (hamlet), among other terms.

VNAF   Vietnamese Air Force, pronounced "vee-naff." The VNAF controlled all South Vietnamese fixed-wing and rotary-wing aircraft. No aircraft were assigned to the ARVN.

VOCO   Verbal Order of Commanding Officer. The authority to travel in-country without written orders. Pronounced "vo-co."

"Voice of Vietnam"   Actress/singer Chris Noel hosted the Armed Forces Radio and Television Service radio programs "Voice of Vietnam" and "A Date With Chris." They were recorded in California from 1966 to 1970. She made frequent visits to troops in the field and her helicopter was twice shot down. It was said the VC had a $10,000 price on her head.

voting age   Federal voting age was 21, but many state and local laws set the voting age at 18 or 20 within their jurisdictions—the age of half the KIAs in Vietnam. The Voting Rights Act of 1970 made 18 the universal voting age.

voting booths   Tongue-in-check statement referring to ARVN M113 APCs employed during military coups.

Vulcan   The 20mm XM168 rotary, electrically operated, six-barrel air defense gun mounted on an M113A1 APC and designated the XM163 Vulcan Air Defense System (VADS). Only six XM163s were deployed 1968–69. The similar M61A1 Vulcan was mounted in various fighters: F-104 Starfighter, F-105 Thunderchief, F-4 Phantom, A-7 Corsair, and F-111 Aardvark. Some sub-variants did not mount Vulcans.

W WHISKEY

wait-a-minute vines   Aka "wait-a-minute tree." Long vines growing from trees or prostrate (horizontal ground) plants. With or without thorns. The vines snagged arms, legs, heads, torsos, weapons, and equipment, slowing progress and causing noise because of "brush crunching." Machetes could not be used owing to their noise. The vines made night movement doubly difficult and noisy.

WAG   Wild Ass Guess. Pronounced "wag." You guessed it, an unsubstantiated "guestimate." Job description for meteorologists and intelligence analysts.

wagon wheel formation   A Remain Over Night position (RON—q.v.) formation for 4–8-man reconnaissance teams (RT) arrayed in a tight circle, either prone with their feet in the center ("axle"—to alert each other by foot tapping) or sitting with their backs resting on rucksacks in the center and feet outward. RTs strove to RON in the smallest clump of vegetation they could fit into to preclude attracting a search of their hide site.

Walker Bulldog   M41A3 light tank with a 76mm gun, used by the ARVN from 1965 when it replaced the M24 Chaffee light tank (q.v.). Named after GEN Walton "Bulldog" H. Walker (1889–1950) who died in a jeep accident in Korea. The original nickname was the "Little Bulldog." To honor GEN Walker after his death, "Little" was dropped and "Walker" prefixed "Bulldog."

Wannabes and Stolen Valor

Fakes, PX commandos, posers, impostures, medal cheat. During the war, even in Vietnam itself, there were those who claimed to be more than they were. After the war, increasing numbers of individuals made claims of Vietnam service, usually in combat units, and particularly with Special Operations Forces. Such claims have emerged during and after every war, but it skyrocketed after the Vietnam War, far exceeding earlier conflicts. It was encountered during the American Civil War, little in WWI (a relatively brief war for the US), and peaked in WWII, and less so in Korea. The nature of the Vietnam War boosted such claims, owing to the large numbers of small special operations units involved in countless small-scale missions and the supposed "glamour" of such units further enhanced by special headgear, uniforms, insignia, weapons, and equipment.

Such claims could range from modest to excessive, e.g., assignment to multiple special units, Medal of Honor winners, or POWs. The last two claims can be confirmed by checking online. Claims of decorations for valor, achievement, and service are also often boasted, along with Parachutist and Pathfinder Badges, Ranger tabs, Combat Infantryman Badges, and others. Some who served in Vietnam made such claims, but there are many who were never in Vietnam and claimed service there, along with others who had never left the States, or were not even in the armed forces. Such claims are also often accompanied by tales of derring-do, extreme valor, and declared self-importance or uniqueness.

The Stolen Valor Act of 2005 strove to criminalize such claims. It was ruled unconstitutional in 2012. The Stolen Valor Act of 2013 criminalized profiting from falsely claiming to have received a military decorations for serving in combat, e.g., charging for public speeches. There are other laws further restricting and punishing such false claims. The Department of Defense maintains a website, "valor.defense.gov", which provides public records of medal recipients. It is not uncommon for news media, veteran, civic, and political organizations to believe some wannabes and use them as speakers and commentators. No apparent veteran's claims should be taken at face value. It is easy to verify them through veterans organizations, the Freedom of Information Act (FOIA), and the appendices of the below *Stolen Valor* book.

The phrase "stolen valor" was not widely used until after the 1998 release of *Stolen Valor: How the Vietnam Generation Was Robbed of Its Heroes and Its History*, by B.G. Burkett and Glenna Whitley. "Poser" is an even later term. The charades used by "wannabes" can range from extremely amateurish to elaborate and believable, initially fooling even real veterans. Most simply make boastful claims and might possess bogus documentation, such as easily altered DD Form 214s (see "Spin Code"). Others wear uniforms with precisely correct insignia. More often "wannabes" wear uniforms that are outdated, incorrect, a mix of different periods' components, or display an overabundance of decorations, badges, and insignia, some invariably incorrect. They will also use incorrect unit designations and military terminology. It does not require very deep questioning for them to reveal their ignorance and falsehood. Common red flag words, phrases, and statements include:

- Claims of being in Special Forces, MIKE Force, MACV-SOG, Project Delta, LRRP/LRP, Rangers, SEALs, Marine Force Recon, sniper, etc.
- Claims of being an agent in the ASA (Army Security Agency), Counterintelligence (CI), Criminal Investigation Division (CID), or other investigative agencies.
- Claims to have been in multiple special units are especially specious ("I was a SEAL/Ranger").
- Claims of involvement/recruitment by the CIA. ("I was transferred directly from my supply unit to Special Forces because they needed me.")
- Claims the unit and/or operations are still classified and he cannot talk about it ("I shouldn't tell you this, but…" or "My records say I was in
- the States, but I was really in The Nam running black ops"). Reality: all wartime classifications have been dropped.
- Was the sole survivor of his unit/team.
- Was hand-picked by a specific officer.
- Conducted special missions into Laos, Cambodia, or North Vietnam.

- Static-line or freefall-parachuted or SCUBA-dived into a mission.
- Westmoreland himself decorated or promoted him.
- Was a POW, escaped or not.
- Was a sniper with an extraordinarily high body count.
- Describes graphically gross killings and atrocities.
- Confusion over courses and school titles, length, location, and duration.
- Cannot accurately describe the unit's internal organization.
- Claims to have forgotten particulars when questioned in detail.
- Evasive or cryptic of details, or changes the subject when questioned knowledgeably.
- "I worked with Special Forces"—he drove a truck delivering supplies to Special Forces camps.
- Underaged to have served in Vietnam. A 19-year-old in 1965 would be 73 in 2020. A 19-year-old in 1975 would be 65 in 2020. These are essentially the youngest possible ages. Most would be older.

war story   What's the difference between a fairy tale and a war story? One begins with, "Once upon a time," and the other with, "Hey, man, ya' ain't gonna believe this shit." "There I was, all alone and knee deep in grenade pins…." War stories tend to be more akin to "fish tales." In the Marines they are called "sea stories."

war taxes   The VC levied war taxes on villages to collect money, food, clothing, commodities, locally made goods, and labor. It was no more than banditry and extortion. The rice tax contributed 80–90 percent of the VC budget, taxing (or taking) 25–30 percent of farmers' crops.

War Zones C and D   Two operational areas established early in the war in III CTZ for operational planning by US forces. They included a number of VC/NVA major base areas. War Zone C encompassed northern Tay Ninh Province adjacent to Cambodia, 50mi northwest of Saigon, and the general location of the NVA's Central Office for South Vietnam (COSVN—pronounced "*CŎS vĭn*," q.v.). Some of the enemy base areas in War Zone C were known by their shape or the profile trace of the Cambodia/Vietnam border: Fishhook, Dog's Head, and further to the south, the Angel's Wing, Parrot's Beak, and Crow's Nest. War Zone D was 30mi northeast of Saigon, incorporating the northern one-third of Long Khanh and the southern one-fifth of Phuoc Long provinces. Its east end abutted II CTZ. Significant operations were undertaken in these areas. (War Zones A and B never existed. The NVA used the unrelated regional terms: War Zones A [North Vietnam], B [South Vietnam], and C [Laos].)

wash line   Set up of four or five 32gal garbage cans, three or four with immersion heaters boiling the water. Aka "wash can battery." Troops washed mess kits, canteen cups, and utensils passing through the wash line. 1st can: scrape waste into empty can. 2nd can: wash in hot soapy water with scrub brush. 3rd can: rinse in clear boiling water. 4th can: sanitize in clear boiling water. Sometimes a prewash dipping can with hot, clear water was placed after the 1st waste can. Lighting a gasoline immersion heater demanded caution, as the fuel vapor could ignite to flash-burn the operator. The requirements for safe operation, setup and breakdown times, and the amount of water and fuel, and cleanup time led to the use of paper plates and cups and plastic utensils. See "paper plates."

water buffalo   The 400gal 1½-ton M107 two-wheel water trailer. Usually towed by a 2½-ton truck.

water buffalos   Massive water buffalos (*con trâu*) were much more dangerous to American soldiers than the fabled tigers. They seemed to sense Americans and became aggressive. They can run 30mph, are the national animal of Vietnam, and make a quaking noise (there was also a deer that barked).

water can   The 5gal water can similar to the fuel can ("jerry can"—q.v.). Had a large latch-on cap as opposed to the fuel can's smaller screw-on cap. Often with WATER or "W" stenciled in black or white. Water cans were sometimes incorrectly referred to as "jerry" or "jeep" cans as well. (Plastic cans were not adopted until the late 1970s.)

watermelon truck   Stake bed semi-trailer with side panels used by training centers. Some 50 seated troops could be transported and only the tops of their green helmets* could be seen looking like a load of watermelons. Bench seats may or may not have been installed. If in an accident there was potential for large numbers of casualties. Aka "cattle car." See "S&P."

* Basic combat trainees did not wear camouflage helmet covers. Even with camo covers they appeared melon green.

water taxi   Small powered sampan (*xuồng nhỏ*) used to ferry persons and materials short distances on inland waterways in the Mekong Delta and between river communities. Smaller rowboats were also used.

weapon rewards   There were numerous efforts to encourage civilians and VC to turn in weapons for monetary rewards, what today would be called "guns for money" and "gun buyback" programs. It was part of the Chieu-Hoi Program. Numerous types of leaflets were distributed, typically with line drawings of various weapons and the reward paid for them in piastres ($ VN). Typical reward fees were:

Pistol 1,200$ VN	M16, AK-47, SKS 3,000$ VN
Light machine gun 10,000$ VN	Heavy machine gun 17,500$ VN
60mm mortar 20,000$ VN	81/82mm mortar 60,000$ VN
Landmine 500$ VN	Claymore mine 1,500$ VN

web gear   Belts, suspenders, ammunition pouches, carriers, canteens, misc. pouches, rucksacks, and other individual equipment carried by soldiers/Marines. Aka "load-bearing equipment" (LBE) or "load-carrying equipment" (LCE), "TA-50" (q.v.) gear (Army), "782 gear," q.v. (Marines).

Weekend Warriors   National Guardsmen and Reservists enlisted for six years. After their 4–6 months of active duty initial entry training, they returned home and trained with their unit one weekend a month and had two weeks' Annual Training ("summer camp"). Both could be mobilized for Federal or state (NG only) duty and some were for civil disturbances, natural disasters, or to replace active Stateside units deployed to Vietnam.

"We Gotta Get out of This Place"   A 1965 hit single recorded by The Animals to become popular in Vietnam. In the minds of the troops, "This Place" was obviously Vietnam, although the intended meaning was of working and slaving one's life away in the drudgery and boredom of a regular job and had nothing to do with Vietnam. There were several title variants in upper case letters and wordage. The above is the copyrighted title.

We have got all the _____ in the Free World. We have a lot of *whatever*.

West Point   US Military Academy, West Point, New York. "The Point" was a four-year military college from which graduates received Regular Army 2LT commissions* to serve at least five years' active duty. Graduates could be commissioned in other services. Cadets' four years in the Academy did not count toward their military time in service. (Future Marine officers could attend Annapolis [q.v.] or West Point.)

* Most ROTC and OCS graduating officers were commissioned in the Army Reserve rather than the Regular Army as were West Point cadets.

West Point Protection Society   Claimed to be nonexistent, the mythical alumni organization was comprised of West Point graduates—"West Pointers" or "ring-knockers"—who protected and aided the advancement of other "Pointers" by ensuring advancement and cherry assignments plus covering up or smoothing rough spots for Pointers experiencing difficulties and indiscretions. It may not exist as a "secret society," but the aid provided is real. Not to be confused with the West Point Association of Graduates, a legitimate alumni organization.

Westy   Nickname for GEN William C. Westmoreland (1914–2005), MACV Commanding General, January 1964–June 1968.

wet season   The June to October rainy or southwest monsoon season with frequent and prolonged rains. The daily rains often arrived at predictable times.

What are they going to do… bend my dog tags, send me to Vietnam? "So I did a no-no. What can they do about it?"

What, me Worry? Uttered when things were going badly. The *Mad* magazine (1952–2018) catchphrase of the fictional "cover boy," Alfred E. Neuman. He first appeared in *Mad* issue no. 21 (March 1955), but the character's image dates back to the 1930s, when the unknown person appeared in a number of publications. The phrase implied, "I've not a care in the world" or "It's not my problem."

What we've got here is failure to communicate. The oft-repeated iconic line from the movie *Cool Hand Luke* (1967). "You're not paying attention to me." "You don't understand me."

What's the difference between a helicopter and a Hoover vacuum cleaner? The Hoover has only one dirt bag inside. Some considered chopper pilots prima donnas. Most rightfully held roto-heads (q.v.) in high regard.

What's your bag? "Bag" represents one's problems or annoyances—a bag of troubles, a burden. "What's your problem?" "Where you comin' from?" It fell from use and is more or less replaced by "What's your issue?"

When I die bury me face down so the whole world can kiss my ass. A fatalistic and insolent slogan seen on cigarette lighters. To have the last laugh. Paratroopers sometimes engraved, "If I die on the old drop zone, just box me up and ship me home." Occasionally stamped on a third dog tag: "If you are recovering my body, fuck you."

When I die I'll go to heaven because I've spent my time in hell. No explanation necessary.

When the shit [stuff] hits the fan. When the higher ups hear about a problem, implying that someone's foul-up is going to affect everyone involved with collateral splatter (blame). It also means an action, like an enemy attack.

Where napalm goes, nothin' grows. Gasoline-based napalm bombs severely burned off vegetation. The heat of the ignition caused much of the gasoline fireball to rise quickly and vaporize. While terribly destructive, incineration was not always complete. Vegetation would eventually regrow after cleansing rains. See "nap."

Where the rubber meets the road. Proving that an event, plan, or action will work as expected. Implying that it is where a tire comes in contact with the road surface to positively work—gain traction. From a c.1963 Firestone Tire TV commercial jingle: "Wherever wheels are turning, no matter what the load, the name that's known is Firestone, where the rubber meets the road."

WHISKEY-TANGO-FOXTROT What the fuck (WTF)? Expressing disbelief or asking, "What is this? What the hell!"

Whispering Death   The Army's Grumman Mohawk OV-1 surveillance airplane fitted with infrared surveillance and MG pods. "Whispering Death" was purportedly bestowed by the enemy, but in all probability Americans coined the nickname. (Some six aircraft types have supposedly been called "Whispering Death" from WWII on to include the General Dynamics F-111 Aardvark attack aircraft used over Vietnam.)

white boot laces   White laces—manufactured laces or white training and reserve parachute suspension lines ("550 cord," q.v.)—sometimes worn on black combat or jump boots by honor and color guards (q.v.), bands, and MPs (formal occasions or high-profile guard posts). They could be cross-laced (normal lacing) or "ladder laced" (q.v.).

White Mice   Vietnamese National Police (*Canh Sat*). Specifically, the traffic police owing to their white shirts, caps, and gloves. Sometimes referred to the Vietnamese police in general.

white out   Ambient lighting conditions that exceeded the capabilities of "star-lightscope" (q.v.) night vision telescopes when suddenly overpowered by external light sources, e.g., flares, explosions, extensive muzzle flashes, full moonlight, etc. The starlightscope had to be refocused, aiming away from the light source. It might cause it to "cut off" all together.

Who lost the war?   "North Vietnam cannot defeat or humiliate the United States. Only Americans can do that," said President Richard Nixon (1913–94) in a 3 November 1969 speech, in conjunction with commencing the troop withdrawal. 82 percent of veterans who saw combat believe the war was lost because of lack of political will. 75 percent of the public agreed. Also responsible was the Democratic Congress, which in 1973 voted to not allow any US air support to RVN and severely cut RVN funding, especially in all munitions. The question of who won is riddled with controversy to this day.

WILCO   Radio procedure proword for "Will Comply"—will do or can do.

Willie Peter   White phosphorous (WP) screening smoke. It was additionally a casualty-producing agent in that it showered burning 5,000 degrees F (2,760 degrees C) WP particles on the enemy and ignited fires. "Willie Peter or Pete" was derived from the World War II phonetic alphabet for "WP," which was then WILLIAM-PETER, as opposed to the Vietnam-era WHISKEY-PAPA, which was seldom used. WP has a putrid odor, which is seldom mentioned in accounts.

WP Ammunition

landmine (test—not adopted)	hand grenade
40mm grenade launcher (test—not adopted)	100lb aerial bomb
57mm recoilless rifle	2.75in aerial rocket
	60mm mortar

75mm pack howitzer	75mm recoilless rifle
76mm tank gun (Walker Bulldog)	81mm mortar
3.5in bazooka rocket	90mm tank gun (Patton)
105mm howitzer	106mm recoilless rifle
4.2in mortar/howtar	155mm howitzer

Winter Ranger   Graduates of the Ranger Course conducted in the winter months (November to February), a practically difficult period with a propensity for frostbite, immersion foot, hypothermia, and upper respiratory illness. Some winter graduates unofficially sewed the gold-yellow-bordered Ranger Tab to their uniform with white thread.

wire, the   The barbed wire barrier surrounding a base or installation. Outside the wire was enemy territory at night and occasionally during the day. Even if only one belt of wire was emplaced it should have been outside of hand grenade range from the perimeter fighting positions. It was never clear on what that distance was—at least 30 meters.

wire on the windows   Arguably one of the most unforgettable first impressions when arriving in Vietnam was the bus ride from the airbase to the processing center. It was quickly realized the steel mesh on bus windows was to keep out grenades.

Wish I had two…   I'd shit on one and cover it up with the other. Something unimportant or disliked.

With negative results.   Final comment on an after action report (AAR) begrudgingly indicating no known losses were inflicted on the enemy during an engagement. Served as a response when a man reported he'd failed to accomplish his job or what he set out to do.

wiz-wheel   The CIRCE wheel (KAC-800) was a simple and quick pocket-sized device for transmitting grid coordinates, radio frequencies, and other numerical information by radio. It replaced earlier KAC (pronounced "cack") codebooks and simple unauthorized codes like the Shackle Code (q.v.).

Woke up on the wrong side of the bush.   The start of a bad day. Derived from the civilian, "Woke up on the wrong side of the bed."

work chopper   Regularly scheduled helicopter courier flights serving specified bases. Aka "ash and trash missions." They delivered replacements, picked up and returned men on R&R, ferried staff to meetings at higher HQs, delivered spare parts, mail, and movies, etc. They were usually scheduled once or twice a week. At major headquarters the flights could be twice daily.

Would you believe... From the TV series *Get Smart* (1965–70); a trope that signals an inverted de-escalation of pending threats when Agent 86 (Maxwell Smart) attempts to threaten villains. For example:

86: "Seven Coast Guard cutters are converging on us. Would you believe it?"

Villain: "I find that hard to believe."

86: "Would you believe six."

Villain: "I don't think so."

86: "How about two cops in a rowboat?"

X XRAY

Xenon searchlights AN/VSS-3 xenon arc searchlight (50 million candlepower) mounted atop the main gun on M48-series and M551 tanks. Another version was the larger AN/MSS-3 searchlight (100 million candlepower) mounted on M151A1 utility trucks for use on firebases. Pronounced "zee-non." VSS = Vehicle-Special-Detecting. MSS = Mobile-Special-Detecting.

XO Executive officer. A unit's second-in-command who generally oversaw administrative and support functions. One grade below the CO. Found in brigades, groups, battalions, squadrons, companies, batteries, and troops. Most service support company-sized units did not have an XO, but a lieutenant performing other duties was detailed second-in-command or "XO" as an additional duty.

Y YANKEE

Yard Mon-Khmer Montagnard Highlands tribesmen. *Montagnard* is French for "mountaineer." It is commonly misspelled "Montagyard," hence "Yards." Their own collective name is *Degar.* The Vietnamese referred to them as *người Thượng* (Highlanders) or more commonly, *Moi* (savages). They were not recognized as citizens of Vietnam, even though born there. There were 18 Montagnard tribal groups (depending on sources), but they identify only with their tribe. They were widely employed by the Special Forces in the CIDG.

Yea, though I walk through the valley of the shadow of death… I will fear no evil: for I am the meanest bad ass in the valley. A boisterous paraphrase of Psalm 23.

yes man Just as in the corporate and political worlds there are "yes men" in the military, but there they could cost lives. Bureaucrats in uniform akin to "brown-nosers."

You ask, we blast. Unofficial motto of artillerymen and mortarmen.

You better be smiling… when you call me boy.   Had nothing to do with race. One simply did not call anyone "boy."

You bragging or complaining?   Snappy comeback when someone expressed their woes.

You're shittin' me.   Incredulity. Are you kidding me? The usual response being, "I shit you not."

your shit   Your stuff, everything you own. "Pick a bunk and throw your shit under it." "Pack your shit, we're movin' out."

Your soul may belong to the Lord, but your ass belongs to me.   A subtle reminder of the authority of a drill instructor/sergeant.

You shine your boots with a Hershey bar?   Indicating a less than adequate job of boot polishing.

Z ZULU

Zap List   Informal name for the weekly casualty listing in *Army Times*, *Navy Times*, and *Air Forces Times*.

Zippo   Referring to flamethrowers, the term dates from WWII with the name taken from the Zippo cigarette lighter.

1) Army M134A1 mechanized flamethrower—modified M113A1 APC mounting an M10-8 flame gun turret and internal flame fuel tanks. Aka "flame track."
2) Marines used the M67A2 Patton flamethrower tank, a version of the M48A3 Patton with the 90mm gun replaced by an M7-6 flame gun and internal flame fuel tanks. Aka "flame tank."
3) M2A1-7 and slightly lighter M9A1-7 man-portable flamethrowers saw limited use owing to their excessive weight and the equipment necessary to refill them.

Zippo boat   Modified riverine monitor gunboat based on the LCM(6) landing craft, mounting two M10-8 flame gun turrets on the bow instead of a 105mm howitzer turret. Aka "Z-boat" based on the letter "Z" prefixing their hull numbers. See "Tango boat."

Zippo lighter   Zippo (American Zippo Manufacturing Company) and similar brand cigarette lighters, including Ronson lighters (Art Metal Works, Inc.) were popular among troops.* They were often inscribed with names, slogans, accolades, tour dates, outline of Vietnam, and unit insignia engraved on the side as mementoes, gifts, and appreciatives, a practice begun in WWII. Unit crests were sometimes soldered or glued to the lighter. Vietnamese vendors today sell "found" G.I. cigarette lighters with inscriptions and insignia, along with other paraphernalia claimed to be original. The lighters are fakes.

* Gasoline was sometimes used as lighter fuel, which was unsafe. Today's butane lighters were not yet available.

Zippo mission   Element of search and destroy (q.v.) missions in which villages and anything of use to the enemy were destroyed, mainly by burning. Sometimes riot control agents (CS powder) were sprayed over the area to deny the enemy passage and hamper the recovery of materials.

ZULU Report   A report conveyed ASAP after an engagement. Aka "Contact Report"—formats varied. Such a report might require time of engagement, friendly and enemy grid coordinates (in the clear), who initiated contact, enemy strength, friendly and enemy casualties, captured weapons and materiel, and direction of enemy withdrawal.

ZULU Time   Military or Greenwich Mean Time (GMT). Vietnam was in time zone GOLF. Vietnam Standard Time is seven hours ahead of Greenwich Mean Time (GMT+8). Daylight saving time was not observed in Vietnam. North Vietnam's official time was GMT+7 from 1 January 1968—GMT+8 prior to that. See "Date/Time Group."

Appendix A: Unit Nicknames

Many units bore official, "semi-official," and informal nicknames. A "special designation" is an "official nickname granted to a military organization," as authorized by the Center of Military History and recognized through a certificate. "Semi-official" nicknames were used within the unit—"self-named." Many of the informal nicknames were derogatory or sarcastic in nature. Others referred to the design of the unit shoulder patch, often derogatorily. *Italicized* nicknames are official. Unit mottos (not listed) are different from nicknames and were inscribed on the unit colors and distinctive unit insignia ("crests").

Unit	Nickname	Unofficial Nicknames
1st Infantry Division	*The Big Red One*	The Big Dead One, The Fighting First, The B-R-O
1st Cavalry Division (Airmobile)	*The First Team*	The Cav, 1st Air Cav, Jackasses
1st Marine Division	*The Old Breed*	Blue Diamond
3d Marine Division	*Fighting Third*	Caltrop*
4th Infantry Division	*The Ivy Division*	Poison Ivy Division
9th Infantry Division	*Old Reliables*	Psychedelic Cookie, Flaming Asshole
23d Infantry Division	*Americal Division*	AMCAL, It's a Miracle Division
25th Infantry Division	*Tropic Lightning*	Electric Strawberry
101st Airborne Division (Airmobile)	*The Screaming Eagles*	Puking Buzzards, Puking Pigeons, One-Oh-First, One-Oh-Worst
1st Brigade, 5th Infantry Division	*Red Diamonds*†	Red Devils
3d Brigade, 82d Airborne Division	Golden Brigade,	Almost Airborne Division,

	All-Americans†	African-American Division, 82d
		Airplane Division, African
		Airborne, Animal Farm
173d Airborne Brigade (Separate)	*Sky Soldiers*	The Herd, *Tien Bien* (Chinese),
		White Wing Warriors
11th Infantry Brigade (Light) (Sep)‡	*Jungle Warriors*	
196th Infantry Brigade (Light) (Sep)‡	*Chargers*	
198th Infantry Brigade (Light) (Sep)‡	*Brave and Bold*	
199th Infantry Brigade (Light) (Sep)	*The Redcatchers*	
11th Armored Cavalry Regiment	*Black Horse Regiment*	11th Cav, 11th ACR

* A caltrop was an ancient four-pronged device spread in front of horsemen and foot soldiers. One prong always pointed up.

† Parent division's nickname.

‡ Absorbed into the Americal (23d Infantry) Division.

Appendix B: Pidgin Vietnamese-English

What is variously known as "Pidgin Vietnamese-English" also includes a smattering of French. Many of these words and phrases are merely Americanizations of Vietnamese language (*Việt ngữ*) terms. It was also known as "Saigon Pidgin," spoken with little variance in other cities. It is sometimes called *tiếng Tây bồi*, but this actually means Pidgin French.

As with American slang, there is no "correct" spelling of Pidgin English or Pidgin French, of which remnants were still in use. Most of the terms were derived from Vietnamese, but pronunciation was distinctly Americanized. Variations of pronunciation were common. The formal meaning of the Vietnamese terms was sometimes altered to more closely match American contexts and catchphrases; e.g., *Á-mỹ-lợi-gia* (America).

The average G.I. simply picked up a few terms and phrases by listening to his buddies and through his limited interaction with Vietnamese. Most experienced only an extremely limited contact.

ao dai   The *áo dài* is the Vietnamese woman's traditional slit-sided tunic dress. Pronounced "ow die" in English, "ow yaee" in South Vietnam. Considered highly sensual. Literally translates as "long dress."

baby san   Pidgin English for a baby or young child.

bac si   *Bác sĩ* is Vietnamese for doctor, but also referred to a medic/corpsman. In Special Forces A-teams both the team members and CIDG strikers referred to medics as "Bac Si."

banh mi   Vietnamese *bánh mì*, a light French-style bread loaf derived from the baguette. Pronounced "ban my." American mess halls would purchase them and split them open to be served with canned chipped or ground beef and catsup or barbeque sauce for field-expedient sloppy joes.

beaucoup   French for many, a lot, much. Pronounced "boo-coo." "I see beaucoup VC."

beaucoup dau   Pidgin French-Vietnamese for "it hurts a lot," referring to a wound, injury, or illness. "Dau" from *đau* = in pain. "No dau" means "it does not hurt."

biet   Vietnamese verb for "to know" (*biết*). It became part of Pidgin English. Biet (I understand), Biet? (Do you understand?), and *không biết* (unknowing—I don't know). Also spoken, "no biet."

bo doi   *Bộ đội* is an NVA infantryman or soldier. Pronounced "boe-doy."

boi   *Bồi* is both French and Vietnamese phonetic spelling for "boy" or man-servant.

boom-boom   Sex. "Balling." "You make boom-boom G.I.?" A "boom-boom girl's" offer—prostitute. A "short time boom-boom" might be 500 Pees and a "long time"—all-nighter "two-thou" (2,000 Pees).

butterfly girl   Bar girls drifted from one table to another, working two or more customers as a butterfly flitting from one flower to another. In Vietnamese culture a "butterfly girl" was one loose and free. See "Saigon tea."

cam oun   *Cảm ơn.* Vietnamese for "thank you."

Cheap Charlie   Bar girls' and hookers' accusations of G.I.s ("flower seekers")* who would not buy further Saigon tea drinks or tried to get off cheap on the tab. "You cheap Charlie G.I.!" (The use of "Charlie" was not an accusation of being VC.)

* "Flower seekers" (*người tìm hoa*) was the Vietnamese newspapers name given to G.I.s on the prowl for girls.

choi oi   *Trời ơi.* Explanation of surprise. "Oh my gosh!" "Oh crap!" Pronounced "choy oy!"

chop-chop   Pidgin English general term for food. "Numbau one chop-chop," good chow. Possibly derived from chopping meat with a knife or cleaver or referring to chopsticks. Occasionally meant to hurry up, get it done fast—"Chop-chop, do it now." That is actually its origin in Pidgin Chinese-English in the 1800s—to hurry. Its meaning as food originated during the KW.

chow   *Chào.* Vietnamese for "hello."

co   Pidgin English for "girl," from *cô gái.* "Co Cong" is a female VC.

coka   Pidgin English for Coca-Cola or any soft drink.

con biet *or* **bit**   *Con biết.* Literally Vietnamese for "I know," but in Pidgin English, "I understand."

covan   *Co van* (advisor). *Co van My* (American advisor). US advisors assigned to ARVN units. (The correct spelling is "advisor," not "adviser" as frequently seen.)

dạ or co   Vietnamese for "yes."

dai uy Vietnamese for captain (*Đại Úy*). Special Forces A-team COs were captains and both the team members and CIDG strikers addressed them as Dai Uy. Pronounced "die we."

di-di *Đi đi*. Vietnamese for go away, leave. "Di di mau" is "go away fast!"

dinky dau Pidgin English for crazy, nuts, silly—*dien cai dau*. Also Pidgin French "Beaucoup dinky dau"—very crazy. "You beaucoup dinky dau G.I.!" ("Dau" pronounced "dow.")

Du dit *Đụ đít*. Vietnamese for "fuck you."

du ma may *or* **doe me my** There are multiple spellings for this Pidgin English term and even the Vietnamese interruption is questioned, *Đụ mẹ mày*. It may or may not mean "fuck your mother" or some variation thereof, but that is typically what it approximately meant, at least to G.I.s.

fini *Fini*. French for "the end," "finished." Sometimes spoken "fini het-roi" (q.v.), although a double-negative.

het-roi *Hết rồi*. Pidgin English for "done."

khum *Không*. Vietnamese for "no."

khum xau *Không xấu*. Literally means "not bad," but came to mean to Americans, "Don't worry about it."

mama san Pidgin English for a Vietnamese woman. Tended to identify an older woman. The term originated in Japan after WWII and referred to a woman with authority running a bar or restaurant.

mama san shop A small tailor, uniform, or souvenir shop typically run by a Vietnamese woman.

non la *Nón lá*. Vietnamese palm leaf or bamboo strip conical hat. They essentially replace umbrellas. Aka "gook hat" or "peasant hat." Some were actually made of corrugated cardboard from the outer sleeve of C-ration cases.

Number 1 Pidgin English for the very best, good, superior. "Number 1" pronounced "numbah one."

Number 10 The worst, bad. "Numbah 10." A degree worse was "Numbah <u>Focking</u> 10." Another degree worse was, "You numbah twell (twelve)."

Number 10-thou The very worst, horrible, very bad.

okay Universally understood for all is well, good, yes.

pac pac Pidgin English for "bang-bang" meaning to shoot, open fire. Not to be confused with "boom-boom" (q.v.).

papa san A Pidgin English term for an older Vietnamese man. From Japanese.

quân Any Vietnamese phrase containing *quân* is military related.

Sahlem Salem was a generic Vietnamese term for cigarettes.

Sat Cong Kill Viet Cong (*Sát Công*).

sin loy Xin lỗi. Vietnamese idiom for "Sorry about that"—to apologize, to say excuse me. Some Americans took it to mean "tough luck" or "too bad."

sucky-sucky Oral sex.

tee-tee *or* **ti-ti** Pidgin French for tiny, little, small. Derived from the French *petite*.

trung si Vietnamese for sergeant. CIDG strikers addressed US Special Forces advisors, mostly NCOs, as *Trung Sĩ*.

Úc Đại Lợi Vietnamese for an Australian.

You souvenir me. Pidgin English for "You give to me." "I souvenir you" = "I give to you."

Appendix C: US Rank Titles

Note that each armed service may have used different abbreviations for the same rank titles.

Army rank abbreviations are always in all upper case and three characters.

The Army ranks of Specialist 8 and 9 are not listed, having been discontinued in May 1968 (some sources incorrectly say 1965) and no one ever held the ranks.

Army chaplains (CHAP) are shown as, e.g., Chaplain (CPT) David Skypilot.

No hyphens in any spelled-out rank titles or abbreviations.

Note that specific rank structure, titles, and abbreviations may be somewhat different today.

Ranks are listed from lowest to highest.

The rank of chief warrant officer 5 (CW5) was not implemented until 1991.

These rank titles are as of 1968.

The term for each service's enlisted personnel was:

US Army	soldier(s)
US Marine Corps	Marine(s)
US Air Force	airman (airmen)
US Navy	sailor(s)
US Coast Guard	coast guardsman (guardsmen)

US Army Rank

Rank	Abbrev	Pay Grade
Private 1	PV1	E-1

Private 2	PV2	E-2
Private First Class	PFC	E-3
Specialist 4	SP4	E-4
Corporal	CPL	E-4
Specialist 5	SP5	E-5
Sergeant	SGT	E-5
Specialist 6	SP6	E-6
Staff Sergeant	SSG	E-6
Specialist 7	SP7	E-7
Sergeant First Class	SFC	E-7
Platoon Sergeant*	PSG	E-7
Master Sergeant	MSG	E-8
First Sergeant	1SG	E-8
Sergeant Major	SGM	E-9
Command Sergeant Major†	CSM	E-9
Sergeant Major of the Army‡	SMA	E-9
Warrant Officer 1	WO1	W-1
Chief Warrant Officer 2	CW2	W-2
Chief Warrant Officer 3	CW3	W-3
Chief Warrant Officer 4	CW4	W-4
Second Lieutenant	2LT	O-1
First Lieutenant	1LT	O-2
Captain	CPT	O-3
Major	MAJ	O-4
Lieutenant Colonel	LTC	O-5
Colonel	COL	O-6
Brigadier General	BG	O-7
Major General	MG	O-8

| Lieutenant General | LTG | O-9 |
| General | GEN | O-10 |

Note: SP8 and SP9 were abolished in 1968. SP7 was eliminated in 1978. SP5 and SP6 were eliminated in 1985 and SP4 abbreviation changed to SPC.

* From 1955 to 1988 E-7s in platoon sergeant positions held the rank of Platoon Sergeant. Few PSGs were actually referred to as such and many soldiers were unaware of the PSG rank as SFCs and PSGs wore the same rank insignia.

†CSM introduced on 28 May 1968.

‡ SMA introduced on 4 July 1966.

US Marine Corps Rank

Note there are no spaces within Marine rank abbreviations.

Rank	Abbrev	Pay Grade
Private	Pvt	E-1
Private First Class	PFC	E-2
Lance Corporal	LCpl	E-3
Corporal	Cpl	E-4
Sergeant	Sgt	E-5
Staff Sergeant	SSgt	E-6
Gunnery Sergeant	GySgt	E-7
Master Sergeant	MSgt	E-8
First Sergeant	1stSgt	E-8
Master Gunnery Sergeant	MGySgt	E-9
Sergeant Major	SgtMaj	E-9
Sergeant Major of the Marine Corps* (SMMC informal)	SgtMajMarCor	E-9
Warrant Officer 1	WO-1	W-1
Chief Warrant Officer 2	CWO-2	W-2
Chief Warrant Officer 3	CWO-3	W-3
Chief Warrant Officer 4	CWO-4	W-4

Second Lieutenant	2ndLt	O-1
First Lieutenant	1stLt	O-2
Captain	Capt	O-3
Major	Maj	O-4
Lieutenant Colonel	LtCol	O-5
Colonel	Col	O-6
Brigadier General	BGen	O-7
Major General	MajGen	O-8
Lieutenant General	LtGen	O-9
General	Gen	O-10

* SgtMajMarCor rank established 23 May 1957.

US Air Force Rank

Rank	Abbrev	Pay Grade
Airman Basic	AB	E-1
Airman*	Amn	E-2
Airman First Class*	A1C	E-3
Sergeant*	Sgt	E-4
Staff Sergeant	SSgt	E-5
Technical Sergeant	TSgt	E-6
Master Sergeant	MSgt	E-7
Senior Master Sergeant	SMSgt	E-8
Chief Master Sergeant	CMSgt	E-9
Chief Master Sergeant of the Air Force†	CMSAF	E-9
First sergeant‡	1st Sgt	E-7, E-8, or E-9

* On 1 August 1967 existing Airman Third Class (A3C), Airman Second Class (A2C), and Airman First Class (A1C) were renamed the above Airman, Airman First Class, and Sergeant.

† CMSAF introduced 3 April 1967.

‡ First Sergeant was a special duty appointment and was not a rank as such. It could be held by any of the top NCO grades (E-7, E-8, E-9), the 1st Sergeant's grade depending on the unit's size/echelon.

Warrant Officer 1	WO-1	W-1
Chief Warrant Officer 2	CWO-2	W-2
Chief Warrant Officer 3	CWO-3	W-3
Chief Warrant Officer 4	CWO-4	W-4

Note: The USAF ceased appointing warrant officers in 1958. Many existing CWOs were given commissions, but a small number remained through the Vietnam War.

Second Lieutenant	2Lt	O-1
First Lieutenant	1Lt	O-2
Captain	Capt	O-3
Major	Maj	O-4
Lieutenant Colonel	Lt Col	O-5
Colonel	Col	O-6
Brigadier General	Brig Gen	O-7
Major General	Maj Gen	O-8
Lieutenant General	Lt Gen	O-9
General	Gen	O-10

US Navy Rank

US Coast Guard ranks were the same with one exception noted.

Rank	Abbrev	Pay Grade
Seaman Recruit	SR	E-1
Seaman Apprentice	SA	E-2
Seaman	SN	E-3
Petty Officer, 3d Class	PO3	E-4
Petty Officer, 2d Class	PO2	E-5
Petty Officer, 1st Class	PO1	E-6

Chief Petty Officer	CPO	E-7
Senior Chief Petty Officer	SRCPO	E-8
Master Chief Petty Officer	MCPO	E-9
Master Chief Petty Officer of the Navy*	MCPON	E-9
* Coast Guard equivalent is:		
Master Chief Petty Officer of the Coast Guard	MCPOCG	E-9
Warrant Officer 1	WO1	W-1
Chief Warrant Officer 2	CWO2	W-2
Chief Warrant Officer 3	CWO3	W-3
Chief Warrant Officer 4	CWO4	W-4
Ensign	ENS	O-1
Lieutenant (Junior Grade)	LTJG	O-2
Lieutenant	LT	O-3
Lieutenant Commander	LCDR	O-4
Commander	CDR	O-5
Captain	CAPT	O-6
Rear Admiral (Lower Half)	RDML	O-7
Rear Admiral (Upper Half)	RADM	O-8
Vice Admiral	VADM	O-9
Admiral	ADM	O-10

US Army and Marine Corps Unit Commanders (according to T/O&E)

There are exceptions in the assignment of rank as commanders. They could be a rank below and occasionally a rank above the norm.

| Unit | Rank |
| Fire team | Sergeant (USMC, corporal) |

Squad	Staff Sergeant (USMC, sergeant)
Section	Staff Sergeant, Sergeant 1st Class, Lieutenant (depending on type)
Platoon	Lieutenant
Detachment	Lieutenant or Captain (Could be higher for special detachments.)
Company	Captain
Battery	Captain
Troop	Captain (Troop not used by USMC)
Battalion	Lieutenant Colonel
Squadron	Lieutenant Colonel (USMC squadrons are only in Aviation.)
Regiment	Colonel
Group	Colonel
Brigade	Colonel (divisional), Brigadier General (separate combined arms)
Division	Major General
Corps	Lieutenant General
Field Force	Lieutenant General
MACV	General

Note: Army aviation unit commanders were:

Section	Lieutenant
Platoon	Captain
Company/Troop	Major
Battalion/Squadron	Lieutenant Colonel

Appendix D: US Aircraft Designations and Nicknames

Only US and VNAF aircraft are addressed here. On 18 September 1962 the Department of Defense adopted the Tri-Service Aircraft Designation System based on the USAF's expanded 1948–62 system. All armed services adopted this new system. The earlier designations flown in Vietnam prior to the designation change are not provided here. Most Army aircraft were named after Indian tribes, but there were exceptions, with some bearing manufacturers' nicknames, e.g., the Canadian-made De Havillands.

Information listed for each aircraft includes: manufacturer, designation, and function followed by the official nickname, any slang nicknames, and using service(s): A—US Army, F—USAF, N—US Navy, M—US Marine Corps, and V—Vietnamese Air Force.

Aircraft designations include the basic aircraft type and if modified from a basic mission is preceded by a modification letter. The letter(s) are followed by a design number (within the basic mission series), and the series letter indicates modifications of the basic model. There were numerous specialized variants of many of the aircraft that are not listed as well as a few obsolescent aircraft seeing limited use in-country. Equally there were sometimes small numbers of such variants operated by services other than those listed. This listing includes aircraft based in Vietnam, operating off-shore from aboard ships, and those flying missions over Vietnam from Guam, Okinawa, and Thailand as well as from the States.

Aircraft	Official Nickname	Slang Nickname(s)	Service(s)
Cessna O-1A/E/F/G observation	Bird Dog	Cessna	A F M V
Grumman OV-1A/B/C observation	Mohawk	Whispering Death	A
Cessna O-2A/B observation	Skymaster	Oscar-Deuce	F

Lockheed YO-3A silent observation	Quiet Star		A
North American Rockwell OV-10A/D observation	Bronco		F N M
Ryan AQM-34A reconnaissance drone	Firebee		F
Gyrodyne QH-50DM arty spotter/recon drone	DASH		N
De Havilland U-1A utility	Otter		A
De Havilland U-6A utility	Beaver		A
Beechcraft U-8D/F utility	Seminole		A
Helio U-10B psyops/utility	Super Courier	Helio Courier	A F CIA
Cessna U-17A/B utility	Skywagon		V
Beechcraft U-21A utility	Ute	King Air	A
De Havilland CV-2A/B transport*	Caribou	Wallaby (Australia)	A F V
Douglas C-47D/EC-47N/P transport	Skytrain	Gooney, Electric Gooney (EC-47)	F V
Douglas C-118A/B transport	Liftmaster		F N
Fairchild C-119G transport	Flying Boxcar		F V
Fairchild C-123K/UC-123B/K transport	Provider		F V
Douglas C-124A transport	Globemaster II	Old Shaky, Aluminum Overcast	F
Lockheed C-130A/B/E/F/EC-130E transport	Hercules	Herc or Herk, Hercy Bird, Herkybird	F V
Lockheed KC-130R tanker	Hercules		M
Lockheed MC-130E special ops transport	Combat Talon	Blackbird	F
Convair C-131A transport	Samaritan		F
Boeing C-135A/E transport	Stratolifter	Silver Sow	F
Boeing KC-135A tanker	Stratotanker	Stratobladder, Flying Gas Station	F
Lockheed C-141A transport	Starlifter	Fat Albert	F

Lockheed C-5A transport	Galaxy	FRED	F
Bell OH-13G/H/S observation helicopter	Sioux		A
Hiller OH-23G observation helicopter	Raven		A
Hughes OH-6A observation helicopter	Cayuse	Loach, LOH	A
Bell OH-58A observation helicopter	Kiowa		A
Bell UH-1B/C/F/P utility helicopter	Iroquois	Huey short-body	A F V
Bell UH-1D/H utility helicopter	Iroquois	Huey long-body	A F V
Bell UH-1E utility helicopter	Iroquois	Huey	A M F
Bell UH-1N utility helicopter	Iroquois	Twin Huey	F
Bell AH-1G attack helicopter	HueyCobra	Cobra, Snake	A
Bell AH-1J attack helicopter	SeaCobra	Cobra	M
Sikorsky UH-19B/D/E utility helicopter†	Chickasaw	Horse (Navy only)	F V
Boeing Vertol CH-21B/C cargo helicopter	Shawnee	Flying Banana, Hog Two-One	A
Sikorsky UH-34D utility helicopter†	Seahorse	Dog, Huss	M V
Sikorsky CH-37B/C cargo helicopter	Mojave	Deuce	A M
Kaman UH/SH-2F multi-purpose helicopter	Seasprite	LAMPS	N
Sikorsky HH-3E rescue helicopter	Sea King	Jolly Green Giant	F
Kaman HH-43F rescue helicopter	Huskie	Pedro, Flying Shithouse	F

Boeing Vertol CH-46A cargo helicopter	Sea Knight	Phrog, Forty-Six	M
Boeing Vertol CH-47A/B/C cargo helicopter	Chinook	Hook, Shithook, Forty-Seven	A V
Boeing Vertol ACH-47A attack helicopter	Chinook	Go-Go Bird	A
Sikorsky CH-53A cargo helicopter	Sea Stallion	Buff	M
Sikorsky HH-53C/H rescue helicopter	Sea Stallion	Super Jolly Green Giant	F
Sikorsky CH-54A/B cargo helicopter	Tarhe	Flying Crane, Skycrane	A
Grumman A/EA/KA/RA-3B multi-role	Skywarrior	The Whale, All Three Dead (A3D)	N
Grumman F8F fighter	Bearcat	Bear	V
Douglas A-1E attack	Skyraider	Spad, Sandy	A N V
Lockheed P-2/AP-2E/OP-2E reconnaissance	Neptune	Snake	A N
Lockheed P-3B reconnaissance	Orion		N
McDonnell-Douglas A-4C/E/F attack	Skyhawk	Scooter, Kiddiecar, Bantam Bomber	M N
North American RA-5C recon-attack	Vigilante		N
Grumman A-6A/B/C/E attack/KA-6D tanker	Intruder	Dogship, Tadpole	M N
Ling-Temco-Vought A-7A/D/E attack	Corsair II	Man-Eater	N M F
Cessna A-37A/B attack	Dragonfly	Super Tweet (A-37B)	F
Cessna T-37B trainer	Tweet		V
Cessna T-41D trainer	Mescalero		V
North American AT-28D attack	Nomad		A V
North American T-28A trainer	Trojan		V

Douglas A-26B/C/K bomber‡	Invader		F CIA
Douglas A-3B bomber/EA-3B electronic	Skywarrior		N
McDonnell-Douglas F-4B/J fighter/recon	Phantom II	Fox-Four, Double Ugly, Lead Sled	F N M
Northrop F-5A/C/E fighter	Freedom Fighter (F-5A/C), Tiger II (F-5E)		F V
Vought F-8A/C/K/RF-8G fighter	Crusader		M N
North American F-100D fighter	Super Sabre	Hun	F
McDonnell RF-101C reconnaissance	Voodoo	Long Bird	F
Convair F-102A fighter	Delta Dagger	Deuce	F
Lockheed F-104C fighter	Starfighter	Widowmaker, Flying Coffin	F
Republic F-105D fighter	Thunderchief	Thud, Wild Wessel (EF-105F)	F
General Dynamics F-111A fighter/attack	Aardvark	Whispering Death	F
Lockheed U-2 strategic reconnaissance	Dragon Lady		F
Lockheed SR-71A strategic reconnaissance	Oxcart/Black-bird	Habu	CIA F
Douglas AC-47D gunship§	Spooky	Puff the Magic Dragon, Puff	F V
Fairchild AC-119G/K gunship	Shadow/ Stinger		F V
Lockheed AC-130A/H gunship	Gunship II, Spectre		F
Boeing B-52D/F bomber	Stratofortress	BUF, BUFF, bomb truck	F

Martin B-57B/RB-57F recon-bomber	Canberra	Cranberry, Patricia Lynn	F V
Douglas EB-66B/C/E electronic warfare	Destroyer		F
Lockheed EC-121D/R/S/J electronic warfare	Constellation	Connie, Blue Eagle (EC-121J)	F

* CV-2A/B redesignated C-7A/B Caribou transport 1 January 1967 when transferred to USAF.

† Sikorsky CH-19B/C/D Chickasaw and CH-34C Choctaw cargo helicopter equivalents were used by Army, but not deployed to Vietnam.

‡ Originally designated A-26, it was redesignated B-26 in 1947 as the original Martin B-26 Marauder bomber was retired. In 1966 it was again redesignated A-26 owing to Thailand's restriction on operating bombers in the country where some were based. Bomber basing was granted in April 1967, but the A-26 designation was retained.

§ Designated FC-47D in 1964, but changed to AC-47D in 1965 as fighter pilots complained of the "F" designation.

Royal Australian Air Force (RAAF) aircraft

De Havilland DHC-4 Caribou transport
English Electric B.20 Canberra bomber (USAF called them the "B-57")
Bell UH-1B/D Iroquois utility helicopter (Australians called them Iroquois rather than Hueys)
Commonwealth Aircraft Corporation Mk 30 and Mk 32 Sabre fighter*

* Licensed Australian copy of North American F-86F fighter (aka "Sabrejet")

Royal Thai Air Force (RTAF) aircraft

Douglas C-47A Skytrain transport
Fairchild C-123K Provider transport

Selected Bibliography

Brohaugh, William. *English Through the Ages*. OH: Writer's Digest Books, 1998.

Burkett, B. G. and Whitley, Glenna. *Stolen Valor: How the Vietnam Generation Was Robbed of Its Heroes and Its History*. TX: Verity Press, 1998.

Clark, Gregory R. *Words of the Vietnam War: The Slang, Jargon, Abbreviations, Acronyms, Nomenclature, Nicknames, Pseudonyms, Slogans, Specs, Euphemisms, Double-Talk*. NC: McFarland Publishing, 1990.

Dalzell, Tom. *Vietnam War Slang: A Dictionary on Historical Principles*. UK: Routledge, 2014.

Dawson, Alan. *The Official Lite History and Cookbook of the Vietnam War*. TX: Electric Strawberry Enterprises, 1992. (vvfh.org/book-offer)

Dickson, Paul. *War Slang: American Fighting Words and Phrases from the Civil War to the Gulf War*. NY: Atria Publishing Group, 1994.

Dunnigan, James F. and Nofi, Albert A. *Dirty Little Secrets of the Vietnam War: Military Information You're Not Supposed to Know*. NY: Thomas Dunne Books, 2014.

Ebert, James R. *A Life in a Year: The American Infantryman in Vietnam*. CA: Presidio Press, 1993.

Kelly, Michael. *Where We Were in Vietnam: A Comprehensive Guide to the Firebases, Military Installations and Naval Vessels of the Vietnam War 1945–75*. OR: Hellgate Press, 2011.

Kutler, Stanley I. *Encyclopedia of the Vietnam War*. NY: Scribner, 1997.

Olson, James S. *Dictionary of the Vietnam War*. CA: Greenwood Publishing, 1988.

Rawson, Andrew. *Vietnam War Handbook: US Armed Forces in Vietnam*. UK: Sutton, 2008.

Reinberg, Linda. *In the Field: The Language of the Vietnam War*. NY: Facts on File, 1991.

Rottman, Gordon L. *The Big Book of Gun Trivia: Everything you want to know, don't want to know, and don't know you need to know*. UK: Osprey Publishing, 2013. (e-book)

Rottman, Gordon L. *The Book of Gun Trivia: Essential Firepower Facts.* UK: Osprey Publishing, 2013.

Rottman, Gordon L. *FUBAR: Soldier Slang of World War II.* UK: Osprey Publishing, 2007.

Rottman, Gordon L. *SNAFU: Sailor, Airman, and Soldier Slang of World War II.* UK: Osprey Publishing, 2013.

Stanton, Shelby L. *The Rise and Fall of an American Army: U.S. Ground Forces in Vietnam, 1965–1973.* CA: Presidio Press, 1985.

Stanton, Shelby L. *Vietnam Order of Battle: A Complete Illustrated Reference to U.S. Army Combat and Support Forces in Vietnam 1961–73.* PA: Stackpole Books, 2003.

Stanton, Shelby L. *Uniforms of the Vietnam War.* PA: Stackpole Books, 2013.

Summers, Harry G. *The Vietnam War Almanac.* Novato, CA: Presidio Press, 1999.

Command Historian, U.S. Army Pacific, U.S. Army Vietnam. *Glossary of Terms in Vietnam.* Draft. Department of Defense, 1967.